The Financial Inclusion Imperative and Sustainable Approaches

Deepali Pant Joshi

FOUNDATION®
BOOKS
Delhi • Bengaluru • Mumbai • Kolkata • Chennai • Hyderabad • Pune

Published by
Cambridge University Press India Pvt. Ltd.
under the imprint of Foundation Books
Cambridge House, 4381/4 Ansari Road, Daryaganj, **New Delhi** 110 002

Cambridge University Press India Pvt. Ltd.
C-22, C-Block, Brigade M.M., K.R. Road, Jayanagar, **Bengaluru** 560 070
Plot No. 80, Service Industries, Shirvane, Sector-1, Nerul, **Navi Mumbai** 400 706
10 Raja Subodh Mullick Square, 2nd Floor, **Kolkata** 700 013
21/1 (New No. 49), 1st Floor, Model School Road, Thousand Lights, **Chennai** 600 006
House No. 3-5-874/6/4, (Near Apollo Hospital), Hyderguda, **Hyderabad** 500 029
Agarwal Pride, 'A' Wing, 1308 Kasba Peth, Near Surya Hospital, **Pune** 411 011

First Published 2011
Reprinted 2012

ISBN: 978-81-7596-800-4

Published by Manas Saikia for Cambridge University Press India Pvt. Ltd. and printed at Sanat Printers, Kundli.

For my father

Shri Jagdish Mohan Pant

(former Administrator General and Official Trustee of the state of Uttar Pradesh)

whose blessings make all things possible

Contents

Foreword

This book is concerned with the increasingly important and problematic area of financial inclusion. Financial inclusion is defined as the process of ensuring access to financial services and timely and adequate credit where needed by vulnerable groups such as weaker sections and low income groups at affordable cost. There is a growing concern even in the developed economies that while liberalisation improves financial products and services for the few, it simultaneously accentuates denial of services for others. There is a huge unmet demand for financial services. The poor are left with no alternative but to rely on informal credit providers and access finance at higher rates. Even when banking services are available, the high cost of accessing these services makes them prohibitive for the poor. Also, non-price barriers such as proof of identity are very difficult to surmount for shifting or migratory population.

This book shows how financial inclusion is viewed as a policy priority even in developed countries. The author provides interesting illustrations of international experience among others about the Financial Inclusion Task Force of the United Kingdom and the Community Reinvestment Act of the United States. In France, there is a law on exclusion of 1998 which emphasises the mandatory right to a bank account. In South Africa a low cost bank account "Msanzi" has been launched for the financially excluded. In India, initiatives for financial inclusion have come from the government and the RBI at the level of macro policy and have been translated into initiatives by banks.

The author suggests the need for banks to change their mindset in favour of social inclusion and shows how the RBI-advised banks introduced a 'No Frills' account, General Purpose Credit Card with a revolving facility of 25000. To leverage technology, the use of IT allows the use of smart cards for opening bank accounts with biometric information, linked to mobile or handheld connectivity devices ensures that the transactions are recorded in banks' books on a real time basis. State governments like Andhra Pradesh have pioneered the use of these accounts for routing payments under the National Rural Employment Guarantee Scheme (NREGS). Information Technology (IT) enables banks to economically handle large volume transactions.

This book discusses the important role played by banks and their linkages with Microfinance institutions and Self-Help Groups (SHGs) which make penetration to the poorest of the poor possible and provide them with hope and succour.

Apart from various supply side measures enumerated above, the author strongly argues for measures to raise the demand for productive credit from the hitherto neglected sections for sustaining financial inclusion in the long run. For achieving this the author suggests a strategy for broad-based development by giving adequate priority to agriculture, poverty alleviation, infrastructure development and human resource development. The author believes that the poor are bankable: even when margins are low, high volumes can make the business profitable.

There are a number of positive externalities of financial inclusion. One of the significant effects, according to the author, is the ability to reap the advantages of network externality of financial inclusion as the value of the entire financial system increases. The resulting fuller participation by all in the financial system makes financial inclusion a public good. In developing countries access to financial services is typically limited and ensuring wider access to such services provides a necessary impetus to financial and economic development.

The author combines academic rigour and objectivity with lucid presentation by asking searching questions and offering carefully thoughtout responses. This compelling book presents a blueprint for effective inclusive growth with a human face. The writer, being a Development Economist and senior Central Banker, is uniquely placed to study and analyze diverse questions of financial inclusion which beset India's economy, polity and society from the perspectives of both policy formulation and scholarly evaluation. I am sure, the book will fruitfully contribute to the debates on public policy and enable better understanding of underlying issues for effective decision making.

C. H. Hanumantha Rao
Centre for Economic and Social Studies,
Hyderabad

Acknowledgment

This book has been possible due to the blessings of my late father, my elders and the beneficence and grace of the good Lord Hanuman who showers his blessings upon me.

As far as this work goes, I humbly acknowledge my indebtedness to my mother, Professor Dr Chandra Pant, and to Dr C Hanumanth Rao who has been a great source of inspiration and has also very kindly written the foreword to the book. I also acknowledge Dr C Rangarajan and countless others who have been a source of inspiration through the years.

I could not have devoted time to this work but for the guidance and constant support of my husband Shri Rajeev Joshi and my affectionate encouraging sons, Paritosh and Kunal.

The views expressed are personal and do not reflect the views of the institution with which I am associated. I also thank Cambridge University Press India Pvt. Ltd., and convey anticipatory thanks to the prospective readers.

Deepali Pant Joshi
Reserve Bank of India

Chapter 1

An Overview on Development

Development is a value-laden issue demanding explicit ethical analysis. Debates on development have for long been viewed in reductionist economic terms. From a policy perspective, economic development can be defined as efforts that seek to improve the economic well-being and quality of life for a community. This is achieved by creating and retaining jobs and supporting or growing incomes and the tax base. There are significant differences between 'economic growth' and 'economic development'. The term 'economic growth' refers to the increase (or growth) of a specific measure such as real national income, gross domestic product, or per capita income. National income or product is commonly expressed in terms of a measure of the aggregate value-added output of the domestic economy termed gross domestic product (GDP). When the GDP of a nation rises, economists refer to it as 'economic growth'.

The term 'economic development' on the other hand, implies much more. It typically refers to improvements in a variety of indicators such as literacy rates, life expectancy and poverty rates. GDP is a specific measure of economic welfare that does not take into account important aspects such as leisure time, environmental quality, freedom, or social justice. Economic growth of any particular measure is not a sufficient indicator of economic development.

The contemporary social scientific study of economic development encompasses, inter alia, broad theories of the causes of industrial economic modernisation plus organisational and related aspects of enterprise development in modern societies. Economic development can be seen as a complex multi-dimensional concept involving improvements in human well-being, howsoever defined.

Professor Dudley Seers argues that development is about outcomes, that is, development occurs with the reduction and elimination of poverty, inequality, and unemployment within a growing economy. Professor Michael Todaro sees three objectives of development:

- generating more 'life sustaining' necessities such as food, shelter, and health care and broadening their distribution

- raising standards of living and individual self-esteem
- expanding economic and social choice and reducing fear.

The UN has developed a widely accepted set of indices to measure development against a backdrop of composite indicators. UN's Human Development Index (HDI) measures a country's average achievements in three basic dimensions of human development: life expectancy, educational attainment, and adjusted real income (PPP–Purchasing Power Parity in US$ per capita). UN's Human Poverty Index (HPI) measures deprivation using the percentage of people expected to die before the age of 40, the percentage of illiterate adults, the percentage of people without access to health services and safe water and the percentage of underweight children under five.

Development economics emerged as a self-evident 'branch' of economics because economists after the Second World War became concerned about the low standard of living in many countries of Africa, Asia and Latin America.

Grappling with the Problem of Inequality

The question of how inequality is generated and how it multiplies over time has been a major concern for social scientists for more than a century. Economists have focused more on efficiency and less on equity. This paradigm is now changing as the need for inclusion is engaging increased attention. A new concept has emerged in the process of facilitating rapid economic growth: that of financial inclusion. Today we are painfully aware that there are a vast number of people unreached and excluded from the financial system. The impoverished, potential entrepreneurs, small enterprises and others fail to grow and prosper due to a denial of opportunities. Financial inclusion is essential due to its implications for the welfare of citizens. It has to be stressed that it needs to be pursued as an explicit strategy for fostering faster economic growth in a much more inclusive fashion.

Development Thought Post-World War II

In the post war period, planned industrialisation became a major doctrine for tackling economic backwardness in developing countries. Though the development theories did not lay any emphasis on the role of Banks at this stage, they did lay down the framework for policies pursued by developing countries during the fifties and sixties as Meir and Rauch (2000) have expressed. Though some economists like Gurley and Shaw (1955) pointed out the significance of financial intermediation in the processes of economic development, they argued that the increased role of financial intermediaries increases the debt–income and the debt–wealth ratio.

It also focuses on the need for developing economies to allow real interest rates (along with other financial indicators) to be determined by market forces. Though originally focusing on interest rates, the financial repression approach also incorporated the adverse affects of high reserve ratios and government directed credit programmes, which together contributed to low savings, credit rationing and low investment.

The hypothesis led the two economists to focus on the effects of the so called financial repression, low or negative real interest rates on savings, and investment levels in developing countries. More recently, the debate has been extended to consider other affects of financial repression on economic growth, financial crisis and poverty; for example, the effects of an overvalued exchange rate. 'The fact that growth is a tremendous force in eliminating poverty… is really essential… .

Indian Planners in the 1950s viewed growth 'as the natural strategy, as a pull-up strategy, not as a trickle-down strategy, not as a conservative option but as a radical option.' Rapid accumulation would 'pull people on board' from under-employment. Creating jobs was seen not only as a spillover effect of growth that just happens inadvertently, but the central goal of development. However, Bhagwati fears that many people still think that anyone concerned with growth or efficiency is incapable of understanding poverty. In Bhagwati's view, growth and the reduction of poverty are not at all incompatible, and one is the instrument of the other. Without growth, in the long run there is no way of generating the resources to uplift the standard of living of the poor.

Financial Market Imperfections

Writing in 1993, when most of the developing countries transformed to mature economies, in the setting of the nineties, Galor and Zeire disputed upon Kuznet's theory. They attributed the persistence of inequality squarely to financial market imperfections. These Financial Market Imperfections (FMI) inhibit the poor from taking full advantage of opportunities for growth and education. Banerji and Neumann (1993) asserted that individual's occupational choices are a function of their initial endowments which limit and constrain these choices. Thus, they favour affirmative action such as land redistribution policies to address the initial endowment gap. In practice, most redistributive policies, no matter how well designed, degenerate to easy sops which entrench perverse incentives. However, Aghion and Bolton writing in the late nineties (1997) assert correctly that 'A key challenge in the transition to a market economy is to expand the depth and breadth of financial activity.'

Demigur, Kurc and Levine (2007) hold the firm position that reducing financial market imperfection leads to an expansion of individual opportunities and choices and thereby creates positive and not perverse incentives. A large body of empirical research supports the view that development of the financial system contributes to economic growth. Thus, functioning of financial systems equalises opportunities. Hence, in this perspective, the processes of financial inclusion assume an even greater urgency. This again brings us to the question whether banking has a key role to play.

A distinction has been made between the demand-following and supply-leading approach to financial development. Demand-following approach arises when the demand for financial services creates financial institutions and instruments. In the case of supply-leading approach, the financial development precedes and stimulates the process of economic growth. In developing countries supply-leading theories have been dominant for the following reasons:

- to keep pace with developed countries
- the large size of projects necessitating large financial outlays
- the lumpiness of investments
- the scarcity of capital.

With the supply-leading approach to financial institutions in many developing countries, a belief developed that the government could intervene to kick-start financial and economic development. Social banking was a manifestation in India of the supply-leading approach. A counterfactual argument is, whether development outcomes would be similar, had a demand-following approach been adopted in India, whether trade and increased economic activity bring forth private banks and whether the inequities in regional development issues would be addressed by them, whether the development of backward states and of backward people would receive equal attention. The rationale advanced for the nationalisation of banks was prompted by the need to ensure growth with equity. The Narasimham Committee has expressed it as 'Nationalisation was recognition of the potential of the Banking System to promote broader economic objectives such as growth, better regional balance of economic activity and the diffusion of economic power.' It was designed to make the system reach out to the small man and the rural semi-urban areas and to extend credit coverage to sectors hitherto neglected by the banking system and through affirmative action provide for such expansion of credit to agriculture and small industry in place of what was regarded as a sort of oligopolistic situation where the system served mainly the urban and industrial sectors and where the grant of credit was seen to be an act of patronage and receiving it an act of privilege. Government ownership of banks was also an instrument to address the issue of asymmetric information by providing bank credit to the neglected and weaker sectors and sections of the economy.

Liberalisation as a Catalyst for Higher Savings

McKinnon (1973) and Shaw (1973) analysed the benefits of eliminating financial repression. Their analysis referred to in economic literature as the 'complementarities hypothesis' concluded that financial restrictions where artificially imposed from outside as an intervention by the state as interest rate ceilings, seriously inhibit the free operation of market forces. If such restrictions are removed, the market is free to determine the rates of interest which based on the laws of market, will settle at realistic rates. The market will reach an equilibrium. The basic idea of the Complementaries Hypothesis is that mutual dependence between money, demand and investment implies that financial development complements economic growth. To stimulate economic growth, measures promoting financial development must be emphasised. According to this tradition, artificial ceilings on interest rates reduce savings, capital accumulation, and discourage the efficient allocation of resources. Additionally, McKinnons' view is that this process can foster dualism whereby firms that have access to subsidised funding will tend to choose technologies that are relatively capital intensive; whereas those not so favoured by policy will only be able to implement high-yield projects with short maturity. Liberalisation which is associated with higher growth rates owing to the flexibility of interest rates would stimulate savings. The underlying assumption is that savings are responsive to higher interest rates. The higher savings rate would finance a higher level of investment, leading to higher growth. Thus liberalisation will lead to higher levels of savings investment and growth. The literature of financial repression questioned the distortion role played by banks in developing countries and argued in favour of financial repression. This included deregulating interest rates and removing quantitative ceilings and rate-price restrictions. According to McKinnon and Shaw, loan rate ceilings distort the economy in four ways.

There are:

(i) reduced savings
(ii) low yielding projects
(iii) lead to capital intensive projects
(iv) poor quality projects.

Not only does it imply that the quantity of savings and investments are low, or perhaps irregular, but it also means that the level of activity which does occur is of poor quality. If the real interest rate is not allowed to clear the money and credit markets, both the overall level as well as the quality of savings and investments will be repressed. The quantity and quality effects compound each other. The processes of financial repression encourage a 'feast and famine' approach whereby the typical borrower may borrow too much (or too little) and this tendency will reinforce the feast and famine problem. Therefore, we should expect to see higher savings rates as well as higher levels of investment and growth following financial liberalisation.

Liquidity Constraints Credit Channels and Financial Liberalisation (Campbell–Mankiw)

Campbell Mankiw concluded that it is reasonable to assume that not all households have access to credit markets and hence some households have no ability to smoothen consumption over time. Thus, for such liquidity the consumption decisions of households financially constrained and those that are excluded are entirely determined by current income.

Financial Depth and Economic Growth

Government intervention through banks in the allocation of credit was one of the direct outcomes of nationalisation of banks in India. Extensive empirical evidence suggests that there is a significant and robust relationship between financial depth and growth. Financial deepening serves to reduce income inequality and is consequently beneficial to the poor. A significant outcome of the nationalisation of banks in India, consequent to the increase of bank branches, was the increase in deposits. The rapid spread of bank branches led to the development of the banking habit, performing banking transactions preceded or even promoted the growth of the economy. Economists have always held widely divergent views on the importance of financial development for economic growth. Walter Bagehot (1873) and John Hicks (1969) argued that it facilitated the mobilisation of capital in England for immense works. Scumpeter shows that bank credit acts as 'money-capital' and therefore constitutes the necessary premise for the realisation of innovative processes planned by entrepreneurs. In contrast, Joan Robinson held the view, 'where enterprise leads, finance follows' funding innovative products. However, a well functioning financial system creates necessary conditions for more rapid economic growth so that there is a positive correlation between economic growth and the financial system. Porter in 1966 had argued that the development of the habit of banking would lead to an increase in savings and investment, improve the efficiency of allocation of capital and increase the ability of monetary authorities to stabilise the economy. Lewis (1955) had held that experience shows that the amount of savings depends partly on how widespread these facilities, i.e. savings institutions, are. If they are pushed right under the individual's nose, people save more than if the nearest saving institution is some distance away. Financial deepening results in improvement in the quality, depth and range of financial products and services from which the poor also benefit. Till the fifties, 'development' implied the development of underdeveloped areas. In the fifties, it was associated with economic growth wherein growth in the per capita income was the objective of development. This led to the emphasis on industrialisation. Amartya Sen lays stress on the need for inclusive growth. Reducing the imperfections of the financial market to expand individual's opportunities and choices, creates positive incentives. This book argues that financial exclusion means lost or neglected business opportunities as it limits growth and effectiveness. Excluding the people at the bottom of the pyramid has economic consequences.

Sustainable High Economic Growth with Stability

Financial exclusion is a barrier to achieving a high growth rate with sustainability. It should be the endeavour of the banking system to provide the basic banking facilities of savings bank accounts to those without it. A developed financial system broadens access to funds; conversely, in an underdeveloped financial system, access to funds is limited and people have to resort to high cost informal sources as moneylenders. Lower the availability of funds and higher their cost, fewer would be the economic activities that can be financed and hence lower the resulting economic growth. Financial deepening is a necessary condition for economic growth though it is not a sufficient condition and other inputs have also to be given due importance. According to Prime Minister Manmohan Singh, 'The goal of the development process must be to include every last member of our society, particularly those who are at the margins. This not only broadens the support base for development, it also strengthens the government's ability to perform its core developmental role.'

The Human Development Index

Mahbub ul haq and Amartya Sen defined human development as the process of enlarging peoples' choices. Economic growth is thus only a means to capability expansion and not an end in itself. The HDI used in the UNDP Human Development Reports to compare countries in the world, is designed as an alternative to per capita income, the single-most commonly used measure till the 1990s to evaluate development outcomes. The index incorporates three important choices, namely to lead a long and healthy life, to acquire knowledge and to have a decent standard of living. Significantly, while developed as an alternative to the use of per capita income for evaluating development outcomes, it also gives due acknowledgement to the income dimension. It went beyond the PQLI–the Physical Quality of Life Index devised by Dave Morriss in 1979.

Capabilities and Entitlements in Determining the Nature of Poverty

Poverty is not related to income poverty but to an inhibition in reaching the full flowering of personality. Poverty is not just a matter of being relatively poorer than others in the society, but of not having some basic opportunities of material well-being – the failure of certain minimum capabilities. The criteria of minimum capabilities are absolute not in the sense that they must vary from society to society, or over time, but peoples' deprivations are judged in absolute terms and not simply in comparison to the deprivations of others in society. If a person is considered poor because he is unable to satisfy his hunger then that diagnosis of poverty cannot be altered merely by equating the extent of hunger in others in order to prove that this person may not be relatively worse off than most others. A person's advantage is judged in this approach by his capabilities vis-a-vis what he can or cannot do, can or cannot be. The relevant capabilities are of many kinds. The ranking of 'capability vectors' can be used to rank people's advantage vis-a-vis others. However, in the context of poverty analysis it is a question of setting certain absolute standards of minimum material capabilities relevant to that society. Anyone failing to reach the absolute level would be classified as poor no matter what his position is vis-a-vis others. Poverty, in this view, is not a matter of incomes at all; it implies failure to achieve certain minimum capabilities.

The distinction is important since the conversion of real incomes into actual capabilities varies with social circumstances and personal traits. Amartya Sen maintained that the most important thematic deficiency of traditional development economics is its concentration on National Product, Aggregate Income and Total Supply of Particular Goods rather than on the 'entitlements' of people and the 'capabilities' and that these entitlements enable them to enjoy what is being offered as opportunities.

The Millennium Development Goals

The Millennium Development Goals are agreements among nations to eradicate poverty. It is widely acknowledged that the range of human development in the world is vast and uneven with astounding progress in some areas and stagnation and dismal decline in others. Balance and stability in the world will require the commitment of all nations, and global development agreements to extend the wealth of possibilities to all people.

The Millennium Development Goals (MDGs) are eight goals to be achieved by 2015 that respond to the world's main development challenges. The MDGs are drawn from the actions and targets contained in the Millennium Declaration that was adopted by 189 nations and signed by 147 heads of state and governments during the United Nations Millennium Summit in September 2000. The eight MDGs break down into 21 quantifiable targets that are measured by 60 indicators.

Goal One: The Eradication of Extreme Poverty and Hunger
Goal Two: To Achieve Universal Primary Education
Goal Three: To Promote Gender Equality and Empower Women
Goal Four: To Reduce Child Mortality
Goal Five: To Improve Maternal Health
Goal Six: To Combat HIV/AIDS, malaria and Other Diseases
Goal Seven: To Ensure Environmental Sustainability
Goal Eight: To Develop a Global Partnership for Development

The Millennium Development Goals (MDGs), thus:

- synthesise, in a single package, many of the most important commitments made separately at the international conferences and summits of the 1990s
- recognise explicitly the interdependence between growth, poverty reduction and sustainable development
- acknowledge that development rests on the foundations of democratic governance, the rule of law, respect for human rights and peace and security are based on time-bound and measurable targets accompanied by indicators for monitoring progress, and

- bring together, in the eighth Goal, the responsibilities of developing countries with those of developed countries, founded on a global partnership endorsed at the International Conference on Financing for Development in Monterrey, Mexico, in March 2002, and again at the Johannesburg World Summit on Sustainable Development in August 2002.

Since its adoption, the Monterrey Consensus has become the major reference point for International Development cooperation. The document embraces six areas of Financing for Development:

(i) mobilising domestic financial resources for development
(ii) mobilising international resources for development: foreign direct investment and other private flows
(iii) international trade as an engine for development
(iv) increasing international financial and technical cooperation for development
(v) external debt
(vi) addressing systemic issues: enhancing the coherence and consistency of the international monetary, financial and trading systems in support of development.

Some critics suggest that the US has ignored the consensus because the total amount of US official development assistance, while very large, is still a small percentage of the US Gross Domestic Product. One of the great achievements of the Millennium Declaration was its success in focusing the world's attention on precise targets, which, if achieved by 2015, would mark a real turn of the tide in our struggle against life-destroying poverty.

As Kofi Annan expressed it: 'Households that operate solely on a cash budget, are unable to make savings via direct debits on utility bills, are more vulnerable to loss or theft and they are far more likely to use the alternative credit market and pay interest many times that of a standard personal loan, often contributing to spiraling debt. In addition, for those who do get into debt or who struggle to make payments, the supply of free face-to-face money advice falls far short of demand.' Two groups of countries require urgent changes. First are the countries that combine low human development and poor performance towards the goals – the top priority and high priority countries. Second are countries progressing well towards these goals but with deep pockets of poor people being left behind. These are less often in the public eye, but their problems nevertheless remain grave. All countries should address significant disparities between men and women, ethnic groups, races and urban and rural areas. Economic growth has two faces: growth can be ruthless or it can be poverty-reducing depending on its pattern, structural aspect of the economy and public policies. Poverty has increased even in some countries that have achieved overall economic growth. Over the past two decades, as per available data, income inequality has worsened in 33 of the 66 developing countries. Countries need to implement policies that strengthen the links between economic growth and poverty reduction.

Financial Exclusion

There is a crucial need to map the supply of other financial services against indices of financial exclusion. Financial exclusion can be both Involuntary and Voluntary: People that are at the bottom of the pyramid or Below the Poverty Line (BPL), groups of households are often considered unbankable by banks, financial institutions and markets as they may have Price and Non-Price barriers inhibiting their access to financial systems and services.

Price Barriers

Price barrier is the perception that services offered are too expensive and unaffordable. The poor sometimes suffer from the following disadvantages:

- may not have steady income streams
- may not have any collateral security to offer against which loan can be extended to them
- contractual and informational networks often inhibit outreach as the transaction costs are too high to be commercially viable.

Classens (2006) and Kempson (2000) have distinguished between Voluntary and Involuntary Exclusion. According to them:

Voluntary Exclusion arises when the target population chooses voluntarily to stay away from banks and financial institutions for the following reasons:

(i) The fee charged for financial services are perceived to be too high; the minimum requirements may be prohibitively expensive for those below poverty line and bottom of the pyramid borrowers.
(ii) Product design features may be unsuitable (like the fixed cost static amount of Rs10,000/- two buffalo/IRDP Loan Model) loans admissible only for milch animals and not for consumption, for milch animals but with no forward or backward linkages, no fodder for the animal, no milk routes and no collection centres.

Such loans become impossible to service and only serve to increase the borrower's debt, which is why borrowers choose to opt out of the clutches of banks. The poor have to spend time and money for multiple visits to avail banking services, be it opening a savings bank account or availing a loan. These families find it more difficult to save a plan financially for the future. Thus, the population without bank accounts is largely cut-off from banking products and services.

(iii) They do not consider banks to be trustworthy and safe. For poor and illiterate borrowers, document-related work is repulsive.

(iv) They have no collateral to pledge: this is the case with indigent, landless and poor borrowers. In case of tribes, land is often owned by the tribe and hence cannot be pledged as acceptable collateral for individual loans.

(v) The lack of financial literacy: lack of information and knowledge of the various products and services leads to an ignorance of economic opportunities.

(vi) There are also Non-Price barriers to access; there may be no bank branch located in the area.

(vii) As borrowers lack a permanent address or formal sector employment, they are unable to fulfil the document-related formalities of Banks.

(viii) The physical infrastructure may be underdeveloped and serve as a barrier to access.

The India Scenario

Since deregulation of the global economy from 2004–2008, India's economic growth has continued to exceed expectations, surging ahead at an annual rate of more than 8 per cent. Strong growth ensures reduction of poverty further and improving living standards. Yet, there are concerns that India may be overheating with consumer prices, asset prices, and wages all rising, capacity utilisation at high levels, and skill shortages developing. What are the real prospects for India's economy and can growth continue in a balanced and sustainable way? Much of the answer lies in how quickly the bulk of the growing population can be mainstreamed and basic banking facilities can be extended to the unorganised sectors. In India, 31 per cent population has a bank account while 51 per cent is indebted. Of the 51 per cent, only 27 per cent have access to institutional finance. Moving from a mechanical approach of directed credit to a Fluid Financial Systems Approach is necessary, where financial inclusion becomes the cornerstone of the entire financial architecture. There are very few studies on the impact of bank branches and development of the states. In 2003, Burgess and Pande examined the branch expansion policy of commercial banks implemented post-nationalisation. From 1990 till 1997 the RBI branch authorisation policies specified that banks could establish a new bank branch in a location with one or more bank branches, only if they set up four branches in a location with no bank branches. This rule encouraged banks to open rural branches in states where financial development was lower to address the regional inequities in development. Their results to evaluate the impact of a new rural branch on poverty and output suggested that a one per cent increase in the number of banks in rural locations reduced rural poverty by 0.36 per cent and increased total output by 0.55 per cent. Rural branch expansion also increased non-primary sector output, and non-agricultural employment. Between 1977 and 1990, banks disbursed a greater share of credit to the less developed states, though the trend reversed after 1990. These favourable effects show the positive influence of bank branches on economic development.

The growth story in India has been steadily coming of age and the performance of the Indian economy has attracted worldwide attention. It is now mentioned in the same breath as that of China. It would be appropriate to place financial inclusion within the broad context of economic growth. India is on a high economic growth path accompanied by financial strengthening.

Broadbasing Growth

Broadbased and inclusive financial systems significantly raise growth, alleviate poverty, and expand economic opportunity. Households, enterprises, and the rural poor often have difficulty obtaining such services, because of transaction costs, risk perceptions, inadequate infrastructure, information barriers, and other factors. Yet many financial institutions are making profitable inroads into these hitherto unsought markets, through formal banking, equities, venture capital, postal banks, and microfinance. Can these be emulated? Can technologies and government policies support the expansion of financial access to enable financial inclusion?

In most developing countries, financial services are only available to a minority of the population. Most people in these countries do not have savings accounts, do not receive credit from formal financial institutions, and do not have any type of insurance. They seldom make or receive payments through formal financial institutions. The limited use of financial services in developing countries has become an international policy concern. As the Secretary General of the United Nations, Kofi Annan, has stated: 'The stark reality is that most poor people in the world still lack access to sustainable financial services, whether it is savings, credit or insurance. The great challenge before us is to address the constraints that exclude people from full participation in the financial sector.... Together, we can and must build inclusive financial sectors that help people improve their lives.'

The reason for this global concern about widespread financial 'exclusion' in developing countries is straightforward: access to a well-functioning financial system can economically and socially empower poor and low income people and micro and small enterprises and can help them to better integrate into the economy of their countries. Access to financial services also, actively contributes to their human and economic development, to the economic growth of the countries where they live, and to the social safety net that can help protect them against economic shocks. Despite the broad consensus of the importance of 'microfinance' as a poverty alleviation tool, CGAP (Consultative Group to Assist the Poor) estimates that between two and three billion people around the world are still excluded from access to financial services. The situation is particularly dire in the Least Developed Countries where often more than 90 per cent of the population is excluded from the formal financial system. The Least Developed Countries are those where the average income is generally less than $1 per day, and most of the Least Developed Countries are in Africa.

Inclusive Development

Textbooks on economic growth, while detailing the causes of poverty or explaining poverty in terms of deprivation of capabilities, provide little or no discussion of how changes in financial sector policies and regulations affect resource allocation, poverty and income distribution. A general consensus has emerged that economic growth with equity has great potential for ensuring distributive justice and helps to raise incomes. Economic conditions, technological change, and financial sector policies and innovation can all affect the level and evolution of financial market frictions. The degree of adverse selection, moral hazard, and resultant credit constraints are not immutable. Policies that augment the economic prospects of the poor could have enormous ramifications for current and future generations. Furthermore, expanding the economic liberties of the poor can boost aggregate economic growth. Not doing so can slow down the rate of economic growth. For example, when parental poverty and financial sector policies combine to deter the poor from obtaining training and capital, this can lower the efficiency of aggregate resource allocation and hence slow down the rate of economic growth. Under these conditions down therefore, financial market reforms can increase the size of the economic pie, while disproportionately helping the poor.

Role of Financial Sector Policies

Emphasis on the role of the financial sector policies in shaping economic opportunity cuts across political boundaries. A variety of theories and empirical work suggest that financial development influences the economic efficiency of resource allocation and the comparative economic opportunities of individuals. Inflation affects the poor the most as they spend a majority of their incomes on food. In the hierarchy of needs, the most basic need to be satisfied is hunger. In most developing countries, formal financial services such as savings accounts, credit from formal financial institutions and insurance, is restricted from a large part of the population. Prime Minister Dr Manmohan Singh has time and again stressed upon the need to make inclusive development as an integral element in overall policy formulation. We can and must build inclusive financial sectors that help to improve the lives of the poor. Greater access to financial services actively contributes to human and economic development, to economic growth and to the social safety net. CGAP estimates that between 2–3 billion people are still excluded from access to financial services, with often the proportion of exclusion being more than 90 per cent in the Least Developed Countries. Global experience underlines the need to reduce the adverse consequences of the exclusion of vulnerable sections from the financial system. Today, the majority of people in developing countries are excluded from access to basic financial services.

Policy Agenda and Development Thrust of Economic Policies

The objective of promoting financial inclusion has moved higher up in the policy agenda in many countries, supported by new evidence that increased access to financial services can promote faster economic growth and also reduce poverty and income inequality. The challenge was spelt out by the then Indian Finance Minister, Mr P. Chidambaram who maintained:

> I believe that reforms in India since 1991 have changed the face of the Indian Economy. India is slowly but surely being recognised as

> an economic superpower of the future. Sustainability of the reform process demands that all sections of the society stand to gain from it. Only if the poorer sections of the society also perceive a visible change in quality of their life will the reforms process continue in our vibrant democracy. It is a well-accepted fact that economic reforms in India have resulted in a sharp decline in the people below the poverty line. What is needed is not less, but more reforms. The successful evolution of India as a major economic power now rests on the deepening of reforms on the institutional and governance fronts. It is only with fundamental reforms that we can attain our cherished goal of balancing economic reforms with equity. Economic reforms are necessary to sustain economic growth at 8–10 per cent for at least two decades to provide a durable solution to the problems of poverty, unemployment, poor health and education for the entire population.

Conclusion

Welfare and optimum utilisation of human resources are central to development planning. Welfare Economics focuses on issues of distributional justice and lays due emphasis on equity concerns in the development process. Sustained high rates of economic growth and equitable distribution of resultant economic gains are preconditions and drivers of human development. If individuals are healthy, educated and adequately skilled, they can contribute a great deal more to the processes of economic development. Welfare Economics as opposed to Growth economics, concerns itself with the welfare of individuals and deals with techniques that simultaneously determine both the allocative efficiency of the macroeconomy and the income distribution consequences associated with it, conventionally. It concerns itself both with Economic Efficiency and Income Distribution. The former relates to the size of the pie and the latter relates to dividing the pie. Welfare economics provides the basis for judging the achievement of markets and policy makers in allocating resources. Inclusive growth is an essential aspect of welfare economics. Overlapping inequality has to be altered through affirmative action by the state to a virtuous cycle of perpetual equity and growth. The role of the financial system in the process of mainstreaming is critical. Even after decades of emphasis there are large segments of society that are outside the financial system. It is important to recognise that in the policy framework for development of the formal financial system in India, the need for financial inclusion and covering more and more of the excluded population by the formal financial system has always been consciously emphasised.

References

Fukuda-Parr, Sakiko (2003). Rescuing the Human Development Concept from the HDI Reflections on a new agenda in Sakiko Fukuda-Parr and A. K. Shiva Kumar (eds). *Readings in Human Development*, New Delhi, Oxford University Press.

Chidambaram, P. 'India's Growth Performance and Prospects' statement delivered at the Economic Editors' Conference, November 7, 2006, New Delhi.

Banerjee, A. (2001). 'Contracting Constraints, Credit Markets and Economic Development', MIT Working Paper Series 02–17.

Demirguc-Kunt, Asli. (2006) 'Finance and Economic Development: Policy Choices for Developing Countries', World Bank Policy Research Working Paper No. 3955.

Chapter 2

Financial Inclusion: The Nature and Extent of the Challenge

Financial inclusion is one of the biggest challenges in the world of economics. It is enabling the delivery of banking services at an affordable cost to the vast sections of disadvantaged and low income groups. Unrestrained access to public goods and services is the *sin qua non* of an open and efficient society. Banking services are essentially for welfare of the public. It is imperative that the availability of banking and payment services to the entire populace without discrimination should be the prime objective of public policy. Thus, banking is perceived as a public good. Financial inclusion has positive externalities: it leads to increase in savings, investment and thereby spurs the processes of economic growth. When 69 per cent of the people are beyond the pale of the formal financial system, their savings remain untapped and their credit needs remain unfulfilled. In the specific Indian context, financial savings of the household sector have been declining from 48.2 per cent in 2000–01 to 46.7 per cent in 2004–05 commensurably. There has been an increase in physical savings from 51.2 per cent to 53.3 per cent during the same period. One plausible reason could be the lack of banking/financial services which would encourage savings in many places. The extent of bank branch expansion reflects the extent of availability of financial services through mainstream providers. Interestingly, there has been a decline in the number of rural branches of banks; as per available data, there were 32,562 branches in rural areas during 2001, i.e. 49.4 per cent. These came down to 30,750, i.e. 44.5 per cent in 2006. In semi-urban areas the branch expansion has remained consistent. In metropolitan cities, it has increased from 8767 branches, i.e. 12.9 per cent to 11,173 branches i.e. 16.2 per cent in 2006. The branch authorisation policy of the RBI tries to address these anomalies. As per the 2001 census figures, 72 per cent of our population lives in the rural areas. 60.4 per cent or 89.35 million of 147.9 million rural households are farming households.

The dimensions of financial exclusion background, types of indicators and the implications of exclusion reveal that there are several features of poverty which can lead to exclusion such as:

(i) Rural and urban poverty
(ii) Agricultural poverty
(iii) Gender and poverty
(iv) Economic reforms and poverty.

These contribute to capability deprivation and inhibit financial inclusion necessary for mainstreaming the poor. Poverty anywhere can threaten prosperity. There are several dimensions of exclusion. Amartya Sen contends that in a world of unprecedented increase in overall wealth, millions of people living in rich and poor countries are still unfree. They are denied elementary freedom and remain imprisoned in some way or the other by economic poverty, social deprivation, political tyranny or cultural authoritarianism. The main purpose of development is to spread freedom to the unfree. If freedom is considered synonymous with inclusion, then we can say with full justification that inclusion is the ultimate goal of development.

Financial Development and Economic Growth

Financial development is correlated with economic growth and provision of services. Banks provide finance to entrepreneurs and enterprises for investments. They seek deposits from the public to mop up liquidity and lend to the government. As an economy grows, it generates additional and new demands for these services, while bringing about a supply-response in the growth of the financial system. In this view, the lack of financial institutions in underdeveloped countries is merely indicative of a lack of demand and consequent need of such financial services. The corollary of a 'demand-following approach' is one where the setting up of financial institutions, their financial assets and liabilities as well as related financial services is in response to a demand for these financial services by investors in the real economy. The evolutionary development of the financial system is in response to the processes of economic development.

Demand-Following Approach

The nature of the demand for financial services depends upon the growth of real output and the commercialisation and monetisation of agriculture and other traditional subsistence sectors, as Arthur Lewis explained it. As a consequence of real economic growth, financial markets develop, widen and become more perfect, thus increasing the opportunities for acquiring liquidity and for reducing risk, which in turn feeds back as a stimulant to real growth. The demand-following approach implies that finance is essentially passive and permissive in the growth process. The examples cited are of late eighteenth and early nineteenth century England. In fact the increased supply of financial services in response to demand may not at all be automatic, flexible or inexpensive in the underdeveloped countries. The oft-cited examples are of restrictive banking legislation in early nineteenth century France; religious barriers against loans and interest charges and Gerschenkrons analysis of the abortive upswing of Italian industrial development in the 1880s: 'Mainly it is believed because the modern investment bank had not been established in Italy.' In underdeveloped countries today, similar obstacles including inaccurate information leading to imperfections in the operation of the market mechanisms dictate an inadequate demand-following response by the financial system. The lack of financial services thus, in one way or another, restricts or inhibits effective growth patterns and processes. A major deficiency in praxis and policy discourse has been the lack of attention to the 'Supply-leading' responses which are at the base of financial inclusion.

Supply-Leading Approach

The supply-leading phenomenon rests on the base of the supply of financial assets, liabilities, and related financial services in advance of demand for them, especially the demand of the entrepreneurs in the modern growth-inducing sectors. 'Supply-leading' has two functions: to transfer resources from traditional (non-growth) sectors to modern sectors, and to promote and stimulate an entrepreneurial response in these modern sectors. Financial intermediation which transfers resources from traditional sectors whether by collecting wealth and saving from these sectors in exchange for its deposits and other financial liabilities or by credit creation and forced saving, is akin to the Schumpeterian concept of innovative financing. This enables entrepreneurs to think big as per the proponents of the theory. Gerschenkron sounds a note of caution: 'By its very nature a supply-leading financial system may not be able to operate profitably by lending to the nascent modern sectors.' There are, however, several ways in which new financial institutions can be made viable. First, they may be government institutions using government capital and perhaps receiving government subsidies. The neutral view is that it cannot be said that the supply-leading finance is a necessary condition or precondition for inaugurating sustained economic performance and development. Rather, it presents an opportunity to induce real growth by financial means. In actual practice there is likely to be an interaction of supply-leading and demand-following approaches in the processes of economic growth. Financial inclusion forms an integral part of both approaches and growth is widely acknowledged to be the best anti-poverty programme.

Financial Exclusion

Many people, particularly those living on low incomes, cannot access mainstream financial products such as bank accounts and low-cost loans. This financial exclusion imposes real costs on individuals and their families. Households with low income are most likely to lack access to a bank account and have to spend time and money for multiple visits to avail banking services, whether it is opening a savings bank account or availing a loan. These families find it more difficult to save and to plan financially for the future. Thus, the unbanked are largely cut off from banking products and services due to price (cost of the services) and non-price barriers which are: unsuitability of the products offered, distance from the bank branch, required paperwork and documentation, restrictions on access as lack of formal address or fixed occupation resulting in steady streams of income. 'Bank the unbanked' is the slogan of financial inclusion. It should be the endeavour of the banking system to provide basic banking facilities of savings bank accounts to the unbanked. As banking services are in the nature of public good, it is essential that availability of banking and payment services to the entire population without discrimination be treated as the prime objective of the public policy. Unrestrained access to public goods and services is the *sine qua non* of an open and efficient society.

In India, the government and the banks cooperate to promote financial inclusion. This process has been termed 'Social Banking'. The theoretical case in development economics for bank nationalisation rested on the belief first articulated by K.N. Raj at a public lecture in 1965: 'There are important reasons why banking enterprises seeking to maximise their profits would not venture out into areas and sectors of activity to which high priority needs to be attached from a larger social and economic point of view.' Thus rural credit was not a commodity that needed to reach the poor to free them from usurious moneylenders but a public good critical to the development of a backward agrarian economy like India, especially as Indian agriculture moved decisively into the green revolution phase, where private investments by richer farmers needed massive credit support. Private banks operating in an imperfect credit market would only exacerbate existing imperfections. Keynes and Kalecki had already provided the theoretical foundation of this view in the 1930s. 'The most important prerequisite for becoming an entrepreneur is the ownership of capital…firms below a certain size have no access whatsoever to the capital market…a state of business democracy where anybody endowed with entrepreneurial ability can obtain capital for starting a business venture is, to put it mildly, unrealistic.' In general theory, Keynes distinguished 'two types of risk that affect the volume of transactions'. The borrower's risk arises because he is unsure whether the business venture will provide the expected yield. One wants a low rate of interest especially if the venture is a risky one; the same situation creates the 'lender's risk' of default by the borrower on voluntary basis, which Keynes terms as *'moral hazard'* where the borrower has, prima facie, the intention to default or involuntary, due to poor returns on investment. This necessitates that the lender charges a rate of interest high enough to induce him to lend. Keynes inimitably expresses the result 'the hope of a very favourable outcome which may balance the risk in the mind of the borrower is not available to solace the lender'. Applying the insights of Keynes and Kalecki, Raj argued that in a deeply unequal agrarian economy like ours, 'The very basis of profit-making in Banking activity sets limits in underdeveloped economies to the enterprise it can display.' There are high information and transaction costs of dealing with many small borrowers that act as a major disincentive also because profitability of banks is greater. The higher the proportion of their earning assets to the idle cash reserves they have to hold, servicing illiterate customers, who insist on payments in cash on the spot, means higher idle cash reserves of banks and lower profitability. Mere legislation and control, he stated, has not led to an 'optimal allocation of investible resources', as a result of which nationalisation of large banks was the way forward. The bureaucratic element in decision-making may introduce considerable rigidity in large private banks too, the element of impersonality with all the rigidity it introduces is almost as great as in the case of state-owned banks, except in case of favoured customers known to the bank. The larger private banks are no less impervious to the needs of small customers who have no security to offer. Fourteen of India's largest scheduled commercial banks were nationalised in 1969 and in 1980. Since nationalisation of banks, the effort at mainstreaming has been a work in progress but if we look at the number of transaction accounts the challenge of reaching out to the population still remains largely unfulfilled. Affordable credit is the next big step which goes beyond the possession of a savings bank account.

Affordable Financial Services Delivery

Today a chance to increase business opportunities by widening access to affordable financial services to those at the bottom of the pyramid presents itself before banks. People with low incomes typically require loans with short settlement cycles. These are hard to find and those offered by moneylenders are prohibitively expensive. Thus, the first step is to offer affordable financial services to the poor. For banks this will be a niche clientele and for borrowers a unique opportunity for engagement with financial services, to become part of the India Growth story. For borrowers from banks this will also represent an affordable legal option and a first step to avoiding a cycle of perennial debt and perpetual poverty. The banking industry has shown tremendous growth in volume and complexity during the last few decades. Despite making significant improvements in all the areas relating to financial viability, profitability and competitiveness, there are concerns that banks have not been able to include vast segments of the population, especially the underprivileged sections of the society, into the fold of basic banking services. Internationally too efforts are being made to study the causes of financial exclusion and design of appropriate strategies to ensure financial inclusion of the poor and disadvantaged. The reasons for exclusion vary from country to country leading to a variation in strategy, but all efforts are being made as financial inclusion can truly lift the financial condition and standards of life of the poor and the disadvantaged. Meagre assets, inaccessible markets and scarce job opportunities lock people in material poverty which is why promoting opportunity by stimulating economic growth, ensuring financial inclusion, making financial systems and financial markets work better for poor people and building up their assets is the key to reducing poverty.

The Voices of the Poor Study

The Voices of the Poor Study, based on realities of more than 60,000 poor men and women in 60 countries was conducted as the background for the World Development Report 2000/2001. It consisted of two parts: a review of recent participatory poverty studies in 50 countries involving about

40,000 poor people, and a new comparative study in 1999 in 23 countries also engaging about 20,000 poor people. The study showed that poor people are active agents in their lives but often powerless to influence the social and economic factors that determine their well-being. That is why financial inclusion facilitates the empowerment of poor people by making state and social institutions more responsive to them. It is a key to reducing poverty. As the World Development Report had expressed it, 'Actions will generally be necessary in all three clusters–opportunity, empowerment and security, because of the complementarities among the three'. The World Bank Report accepts the traditional view of poverty reflected in World Development Report of 1990 that poverty encompasses not only material deprivation measured by an appropriate concept of income or consumption, but also low achievements in education and health. The notion of poverty also includes vulnerability and exposure to risk and voicelessness.

All these substantively restrict what Amartya Sen terms as the 'Capabilities that a person has, that is the substantive freedom he or she enjoys to lead the kind of life he or she values and enjoys the freedom of choice and action and the power to control ones' life.' Voices of the Poor identified five types of well being – material, physical security, freedom of choice and action, and social. Of course, poverty has not always been the prime concern of the 'development community'. In the 1950s and 1960s, the main objective was economic growth. Recognising that growth alone had not eliminated poverty, a series of poverty-reducing strategies were adopted in the 1970s including Basic Needs Strategies. But these concerns were again forgotten in the 1980s when stabilisation and adjustment policies and the advancement of the market dominated official discourse and policies. The poor economic performance and sharp rise in poverty in many countries in the 1980s led to renewed interest in poverty alleviation. Following UNICEF's Adjustment with a Human Face in 1987 and UNDP's first Human Development Report in 1990 and the World Bank's 1990 World Development Report on poverty, poverty reduction once more became central to the development agenda. In the early 1990s, the World Bank President, Lewis Preston declared that 'Poverty is the benchmark against which we must be judged.'

The Four Approaches to Defining and Measuring Poverty

The elimination of poverty is a key concern to all those interested in development and economic growth. The halving of poverty by 2015 is also the central objective of the Millennium Development Goals agreed to by 149 countries at the UN Millennium Summit in New York. While the objective of poverty reduction currently has overwhelming support, there is a lack of clarity as to what the objective implies. If we have to work towards inclusive growth it becomes necessary to clarify how poverty is defined. The elimination of poverty is one of the major goals of inclusive development. If we remove poverty we foster inclusive development. Through inclusive growth we create enabling conditions for the removal of poverty. There is acknowledgement of the multi-dimensionality of poverty while at the same time the monetary approach to the determination of poverty has always held sway. Clarification of how poverty is defined is extremely important as different definitions of poverty imply use of different criteria for its measurement and entail the adoption of different policy solutions to address the issues raised. There are differences in the approaches to poverty, both conceptually and empirically. Broadly the four approaches have been categorised as:

(i) The Monetary Approach
(ii) The Capability Approach
(iii) Social Exclusion
(iv) The Participatory Model.

(i) The Monetary Approach

The Monetary Approach to the identification and measurement of poverty is the most commonly used. It identifies poverty with a shortfall in consumption (or income) from some poverty line. The valuation of the different components of income is done at market prices which need identification of the relevant market and the imputation of monetary values for those items which are not valued through the market, such as subsistence production and in principle public goods. The assumption related to this is that with appropriately devised tools, uniform monetary metrics can take into account all the relevant heterogeneity across individuals and their situations. For economists the appeal of the monetary approach lies in its compatibility with utility maximising behaviour which underpins microeconomics, i.e. the objective to maximise utility for consumers and that expenditure or consumption is at market prices which reflect the marginal value or utility people place on commodities. Welfare can then be measured as the total consumption enjoyed, proxied by either expenditure or income data and poverty is defined as a shortfall below some minimum level of resources which is termed the poverty line. The validity of the approach then depends in part on:

- whether utility is an adequate definition of well being
- whether monetary expenditure is a satisfactory measure of utility
- whether a shortfall in utility encompasses all we mean by poverty.

The justification of adopting a particular poverty line is as necessary as the determination of the extent to which poverty is defined relative to a given context or whether it is intended to reflect some absolute standards of deprivation. For the most part, nutritional requirements form the fundamental justification and practical basis of defining poverty and the poverty line in the monetary approach. The monetary approach to poverty measurement was pioneered in the seminal work of Booth and Rowntree who studied poverty in London and York respectively in the nineteenth and early twentieth centuries. The issue of how to translate the identification of poverty at an individual level into an aggregate value is closely linked to the literature on social valuation. Following Sen's pioneering contribution in 1976 which applied a similar approach to that used in the measurement of inequality to poverty measurement, the literature generally adopts an axiomatic approach in setting the desirable properties of a poverty index. Foster Greer and Thornbecke (FGT) in 1984 has made a fundamental contribution offering a general formulation including 'alpha' a valuation parameter of choice, which incorporates some of the most widely used indexes. It has become the standard practice to compute FGT indexes for values of alpha ranging from 0 to 2 in order to test the sensitivity of the poverty assessment to the distribution of resources among the poor.

(ii) The Capability Approach

The Capability Approach was pioneered by Amartya Sen. He expressed powerfully that development ought to be viewed as the expansion of human capabilities (CA) and not as the maximisation of utility or its proxy – money income. The Capability Approach rejects monetary income as its measure of well-being and instead focuses on indicators of the freedom to live a valued life. In this framework, poverty is defined as deprivation in the space of capabilities, or failure to achieve certain minimal basic capabilities where basic capabilities are the ability to satisfy certain crucially important functionings up to certain minimally adequate levels. The capability approach constitutes an alternative way of conceptualising human behaviour, assessing well being and identifying policy objectives, based on the rejection of utilitarianism as the measure of welfare and of utility maximisation as a behavioural assumption. In the Capability Approach, well-being is seen as the freedom of individuals to live lives that are valued – termed as the capabilities of individuals, i.e. the realisation of human potential. The emphasis laid on the outcomes characterising the lives of individuals is a clear shift from monetary indicators which represent an indirect measure of those outcomes and a focus on non-monetary indicators for evaluating well-being or deprivation. In this context, monetary resources are considered a means of enhancing well-being only rather than the actual outcomes of interest. The UNDP Poverty Index (Human Poverty Index or HPI) has deprivation in three essential elements of life – longevity, knowledge and decent standard of living. The indicators adopted in the Human Development Reports are: 40 years' life expectancy at birth, adult illiteracy and under-five mortality. Both choices of dimensions and cut-off standards are somewhat arbitrary and are likely to be revised according to the general standards attained in the world, the region or the country where poverty assessments are being made. For instance, the UNDP adopted a different HPI for developed countries where life expectancy is below 60, lack of functional literacy among adults, the long-term unemployment rate and the population below an income overt line of below 50 per cent of median disposable household income in the country are being assessed. Whether a universal conception of poverty from a Capability Approach can be reconciled with such changing measures has not often been discussed. The multi-dimensional emphasis of the capability framework makes the issue of aggregation particularly pertinent as each capability is deemed to be intrinsically valuable and no tradeoffs between achievements in one or the other dimensions can be introduced. This severely limits the type of aggregate strategies that can be adopted. The Capability Approach represents a major contribution to poverty analysis as it provides a coherent framework for defining poverty in the context of the lives people live and the freedoms they enjoy. This approach draws attention to a much wider range of causes of exclusion and poverty as compared to the Monetary Approach. The shift from the private resources to which individuals have access to the type of life they lead addresses the neglect of social goods in the Monetary Approach and its tunnel vision of human well-being. However, there are also congruities between the two approaches. In principle, both take an individualistic perspective since both utility deprivation and capability failure are characteristics of individuals, though, in both cases, community and households are determinants of achievement.

(iii) Social Exclusion

The concept of social exclusion was developed in industrialised countries to describe the processes of marginalisation and deprivation that can arise even within rich countries with comprehensive welfare provisions. Social exclusion contrasts with the two previous approaches in making a social perspective central. That is to say, social exclusion takes place when an individual does not participate in key activities of the society in which one lives. It is also often the characteristic of discrimination against groups, either in an overt manner or otherwise. Racial, religious, gender, sexual preferences, ethnicity, etc., relational or group approaches as exemplified in the wider social exclusion approach, open up a different policy agenda as opposed to individualistic approaches or policies addressed to groups relate to the elimination of discrimination and various forms of affirmative action. Social Exclusion is perhaps the least well defined and most difficult to interpret concepts of deprivation. Multi-dimensionality is an intrinsic feature of social exclusion. Indeed, in general, being deprived in more than one and perhaps many dimensions is a key feature of the social exclusion approach which raises aggregation issues similar to the Capability Approach. Furthermore, there can be causal connections between different dimensions of exclusion, e.g. between employment and income, housing and employment, formal sector employment and insurance. Social exclusion has a strong connection with monetary poverty; for instance, lack of monetary income is both an outcome of social exclusion arising from lack of employment and a cause of social isolation and low wealth.

(iv) Participatory Model

Conventional poverty estimates including both monetary and capability issues have been criticised for being externally imposed and not taking into account the views of poor people themselves. The Participatory Approach pioneered by Chambers, aims to change this and get people themselves to participate in decisions about what it means to be poor, and the magnitude of poverty. The practice of Participatory Poverty Assessments (PPA) evolved from Participatory Rural Appraisal (PRA) is defined as 'a growing family of approaches and methods to enable local people to share, enhance and analyse their knowledge of life and conditions, to plan and to act.' Initially intended for small projects, PPAs were scaled up by the World Bank as a complement to their poverty assessments. By 1998, half the completed World Bank poverty assessments included a participatory element. An extensive multi-country exercise covering 23 countries was carried out as a background to the World

Development Report published as the Voices of the Poor Study. Poverty Reduction Strategy Papers (PRSPs) of the World Bank and IMF which form an important element in International Financial Institution (IFI) lending to poor countries may have further institutionalised the use of participatory methods. Cornwall (2000) differentiates three types of PPA:

- Exercises intended to promote self-determination and empowerment
- Those primarily intended to increase the efficiency of programs and
- Those emphasising mutual learning.

There has been a criticism levied against the World Bank. Critics have held that while the use of participatory learning by the World Bank, especially in their poverty assessments, has tended to be instrumental, i.e., adopting PPA primarily so that the poor would cooperate with the programs rather than to change the nature of the programs themselves increase efficiency of programs. While Voices of the Poor emphasises mutual learning which also enables changes in progressions.

There is not much self-determination and empowerment in most of the work. The major advantage of this approach is that PPAs go some way to getting away from externally imposed standards. They also provide a way of solving some of the problems encountered with the other methods, for example, helping to define an appropriate minimum basket of commodities for the Monetary Approach, a list of basic capabilities in the Capability Approach, and whether the concept of social exclusion can be applied in a particular society and what its main elements might be. There are two major differences from the other approaches. The significant difference being that the perspective is that of the poor, who, at least in theory, make the judgments which in other approaches are imposed from outside. The other is in the small samples – even in the scaled-up version – relative to other methods. Each of the different approaches to poverty and to inclusion by extension derives from a different perspective on what constitutes a good life and a just society. With respect to the question of policy consequences of different approaches, the definition and measurement of poverty will influence the emphasis given to different types of policy. Thus, if poverty is defined as lack of household income, then policies towards it are likely to be primarily directed towards controlling this – for example, by income generation programs or money transfers. In contrast, if a Capability Approach is adopted, policies would tend to focus more on provision of public services, while a Social Exclusion Approach leads to anti-discrimination and redistributive policies and more generally, policies to promote the inclusion of marginalised groups through affirmative action.

The Indian Scenario

The Nationalisation of Banks

The nationalisation of banks is considered as a watershed in inclusion of the financially excluded in the banking system even though through the 1950s and 1960s the role of private commercial banks in rural credit remained minimal and indirect. The All India Rural Credit Survey itself had wanted the involvement of these banks in agricultural marketing and processing but not directly in farm output. Rural branches at the time were few and far between despite a 1954 RBI directive for them to open at least one branch in unbanked rural and semi-urban areas, for every branch opened in previously banked areas. The Imperial Bank of India, as the SBI was known then, was nationalised in 1955 and asked to establish 400 branches in semi-urban areas and commence agricultural bank lending even if at a loss. Till 1971, the share of banks in rural credit was no more than 2.4 per cent with most loans being extended to plantations. Their main activity was to finance agro-processing firms and purchase bonds floated by land development banks. The industry enjoyed the overwhelming share of bank credit at 62 per cent till the 1960s while trade and commerce constituted the remaining 26 per cent. Within the industry, the distribution of credit was skewed in favour of large borrowers. An allegation was also levied that 'advances by private banks were diverted to sister companies of banks or to companies in which their directors had an interest. Twenty years after independence, cooperatives were dominated by the rural elite and commercial banks had an urban bias. The 1961 census showed that nearly 50 per cent of India's towns and none of its villages had bank branches. In 1969 the National Credit Council was set up to guide the branch expansion program. At the time not even 1 per cent of India's villages were served by bank branches. Agricultural credit was negligible despite the contribution of agriculture to GDP of 50 per cent while the industry cornered 67 per cent of bank credit. Hence, nationalisation was instituted to redress these inequities in 1969.

In India, the focus of financial inclusion at present is to ensure a bare minimum access to a savings bank account, without frills, to all. Internationally, financial exclusion has been viewed in a much wider perspective. Having a current account or a savings account on its own is not regarded as an accurate indicator of financial inclusion. There could be multiple levels of financial inclusion and exclusion. At one extreme, it is possible to identify the 'super-included', i.e. those customers who are actively and persistently courted by the financial services industry, and who have, at their disposal, a wide range of financial services and products.

At the other extreme, we may have the financially excluded, who are denied access to even the most basic financial products. Lying midway are those who use banking services only for deposits and withdrawals of money. But these people may have only restricted access to the financial system, and may not enjoy the flexibility of access offered to more affluent customers.

Gender and Poverty

Women are victims of poverty and marginalization to a greater extent compared to men, since the condition of being a woman results in the phenomenon of exclusion.

Role of Banks in Including Women in the Development Paradigm

The social and political exclusion is a corollary of economic deprivation and economic poverty. It is necessary to encourage an agenda which places social and gender equity at the centre of the development paradigm. The equity issue *has* to be addressed as there is either growth with equity or there is no growth. Banks, as they channel credit to entrepreneurs and the poorer sections of the society must play a critical role in this process.

Growth with Equity

'Long years ago we made a tryst with destiny, and now the time has come when we shall redeem our pledge. ...The achievement we celebrate today is but a step, an opening of opportunity to the great triumphs and achievements that await us. ...It means the ending of poverty and ignorance, disease and inequity of opportunity.' Jawaharlal Nehru's visionary statement on the elimination of deprivation was identifying inequality of opportunity as one of the principle deficiencies that needed to be addressed. Economic developments, as Amartya Sen says, can in fact, be seen in terms of 'expansion of opportunities' that the individual in the society enjoy. Much of economic developments consist in bringing capability and achievements within the realm of possibility for all. Poverty is ultimately a matter of 'capability deprivation'. Hence, the basic objective of development is expansion of human capability. There is a need for inclusive development which addresses these issues. Banks can and do facilitate economic growth by ensuring removal of liquidity constraints in production by providing capital to start new ventures or adapting new technology and help producers assume production risk. In recent years, finance is increasingly being used as an anti-poverty tool. Finance helps the unemployed to gain employment thereby increasing income and consumption and reducing poverty.

The requirement and the benefits of inclusive development of putting women at the centre of the development paradigm to address the issues of poverty and economic deprivation through greater investment in women mainstreaming hardly needs to be stressed. Gender concerns are a pivotal element of the microfinance poverty alleviation strategy. Across microfinance assisted projects, women have proved to be a driving force in achieving project success and reducing poverty. In south Asia, across the board, the Gender Development Index and the Gender Empowerment Index do not favour women. Poverty concentrated among women is intractable. Microfinance ensures that in projects and activities, gender specificities at the household and community levels are taken into account. These projects also enable them to address the household food security and nutrition goals. The feminisation of credit is a process which has demonstrably established that a loan extended to a poor woman is a loan which helps to uplift the entire family, as women prioritize family. Thus, increasing the economic resilience of the poor is largely about enabling women to realise their socio-economic potential and improve the quality of their lives. Improvement in the socio-economic status, health and education of women has an immediate and lasting impact on the well-being of the entire family. Development initiatives can have adverse consequences for women if gender specificities are not taken into account. For e.g., women play a major role in agricultural and livestock development. In order to succeed, projects intending to increase agricultural productivity must ensure that the distinct needs, labour constraints, knowledge and decision-making roles of women are analysed with a view to being addressed. A sector specific approach is necessary. Women invest a large part of their time, labour and expertise in agricultural and livestock production. They have significant responsibilities in the care and management of the animals and the processing of livestock products. Extension workers are generally male; fewer women extension staff members are there, which is a barrier to earnings. Similarly, in several development projects, women are asked to find additional time to devote to investment in income generating projects as *papad* and pickle-making for which there are often far and fewer marketing opportunities. Similarly, though a loan for buffaloes is extended, forward and backward linkages are not provided. In the absence of grass to feed the animals, a milk route, milk collection centres, and chilling plants, to collect and sell milk enterprise inevitably collapses.

Rural enterprise requires marketing support. The promotion of micro enterprises is an important component of several microfinance projects. However, the issue of marketing outlets for women's enterprises is often ignored leading to the failure of the enterprises. Promoting women-based micro enterprises is an important first step, allowing women to build confidence in dealing with markets, credit repayment and cash flow. The role of women in markets is widely recognised. Microfinance projects strengthen women's ability to take advantage of market opportunities particularly as the modern economy expands by providing training in market skills and in building relationships with suppliers and buyers. Microfinance is increasingly pertaining to women. Projects with a financial services component give priority to women because they are good savers, prudent investors and conscientious borrowers. Credit related activity serves as a medium for organising women and empowering them on a broader scale of parameters. Empowering women economically first makes it easier to empower them socially. These efforts are even more effective when they are combined with skills, management, leadership and literacy training. Strengthening women's involvements in projects which benefit them leads to greater participation in decision-making and thereby to social empowerment, further leading to an overall improvement in the quality of women's lives through improved health and sanitation. An attempt is made to build women's assets through microfinance income generating projects affecting credit, income and livestock. Developing and disseminating technologies appropriate for and most needed by women is important. This process ultimately leads to the transformation of gender relations to emphasise women's control over resources and involvement in household and community decision-making. This contributes to improved rural infrastructure, local institutions and capacity building. Hence, investing in women's development fetches reliable, secure and ongoing returns. It alleviates the burden of poverty and is a successful development initiative in improving the social indicators that affect women.

Gender Focus Initiatives

Within the framework of a democratic polity, our laws, development policies, plans and programmes have aimed at women's advancement in different spheres. From the Fifth Five Year Plan (1974–78) there has been a marked shift in the approach to women's issues from welfare to development. In recent years, the empowerment of women has been recognised as the central issue in determining the status of women. The National Commission for Women was set up by an Act of Parliament in 1990 to safeguard the rights and legal entitlements of women. The 73rd and 74th Amendments (1993) to the Constitution of India have provided for reservation of seats in the local bodies of Panchayats and Municipalities for women, laying a strong foundation for their participation in decision-making at the local levels. The national policy for women will be a step forward in building up a strong women's movement. The goal of this policy is to bring about the advancement, development and empowerment of women.

The Approach paper of the 11th Five Year Plan is committed to women's empowerment. The principle of gender equality is enshrined in the Indian Constitution in its Preamble, Fundamental Rights, Fundamental Duties and Directive Principles. The Constitution grants not only equality to women, but also empowers the State to institute implement remedial measures in favour of women.

Women constitute half the world's population and make up for one-third of its labour force. In India, although literacy levels have registered an increase, majority of women are still illiterate, without access to property and credit. Banks should devise ways making it easier for women who are largely financially excluded and therefore vulnerable to access credit from banks.

Facilitating Women to Use the Services

Women require credit to enable them to set up income-generating projects which allow them to generate sufficient income to establish a livelihood on a sustainable basis. The Banking Division of the Ministry of Finance in consultation with the Reserve Bank of India (RBI) and other institutions, ascertained the problems faced by women entrepreneurs in order to overcome the hurdles being faced by them in accessing bank credit and credit plus services. Some of the problems which were identified are:

- Difficulty in identification of women borrowers and establishing direct dialogue with prospective women borrowers, who normally do not come to banks.
- Cumbersome and time-consuming documentation and procedures of the banks and funding agencies in processing of loans.
- Urban bias of branch managers and officials of banks coupled with lack of region/area based approach for development of women.
- Absence of credit at doorsteps unequal inheritance laws and practices and control over property and income by men.

- Women entrepreneurs are by and large engaged in a few selected activities and operate at small scale. Their lack of wide market exposure restricts the level of operation to suit the limited local demand.

On the basis of these findings, a 14-point action plan was drawn for implementation by public sector banks, which includes redefining of banks' policies/long term plans, setting up of women's cells and designating an officer in each branch exclusively to handle flow of credit to women, simplification of existing procedural formalities, sensitisation of bank officers/staff on gender concerns, publicity campaign for creating awareness about credit facilities, entrepreneurship development programmes for women, motivational strategies to enthuse bank staff to achieve targets for women, and a proper data collection and monitoring system, involving NGOs and Self Help Groups (SHG).

Critical Role of Banks in Furthering the Process

The Bank–SHG linkage approach is a process-oriented project which lays great emphasis on the qualitative and socio-economic aspects of development of women rather than setting mere statistical targets. NGOs and commercial banks come together to work to achieve common objectives related to socioeconomic development of women leading to their empowerment. SHG approach is a participatory, people-centred and process oriented approach. The 'SHG revolution' has been instrumental in increasing participation of women in decision-making in households, community and in the local democratic set up, besides helping to prepare them to take up leadership responsibilities. Facilitating empowerment of the poor is a challenging task. Economic Empowerment is Promoted through:

- Greater access to financial resources outside the household
- Reduced vulnerability of poor women to crisis situations like famine, flood, riots, death/accidents in the family, etc.
- Significant increase in women's own income and the power to retain/save such income and use it at her discretion
- Equal access and control over various resources at the household level
- Financial self-reliance of women, both in the household and in the external environment

The concept of empowerment has its roots in Paulo Friere's idea of conscientisation – a process that enables those discriminated to challenge the entrenched power structures and gain control of their lives. Empowerment of poor and disadvantaged women through capacity-building through better awareness, improved functional literacy and better communication skills, better leadership skills, self help and mutual help leads to overall improvement and accrue directly to the individual woman and women's groups. Through a ripple-effect this also benefits other poor families in the neighbourhood, the community and the village as a whole in the long run. Under Swarn Jayanti Gram Swarozgar Yojana (SGSY) which is one of the major poverty alleviation programmes of the government, there is an emphasis on formation of SHG groups. SGSY particularly focuses on the vulnerable groups among the rural poor. Accordingly, specific targets have been earmarked for fulfillment in the interests of vulnerable groups; the SC/STs account for at lease 50 per cent of the Swarozgaris, while women account for 40 per cent, and the disabled for 3 per cent. Fifty per cent of the groups formed in each block should be exclusively for women. In the case of disabled persons, the groups formed should ideally be disability specific wherever possible. However, in case sufficient number of people for formation of disability specific groups are not available, a group may comprise of persons with diverse disabilities. Mahilar Thittam is a significant example under which several Self Help Groups have been formed in Tamil Nadu. District Kanchipuram has made much progress in establishing SHG. The SHG under Mahilar Thittam is inclusive of a compulsory savings component.

Building Partnerships

The SHG approach believes in establishing long-term partnerships in the interest of poor women. The project has four main actors – Government, NGOs, banks and the poor women themselves. It recognises that building satisfactory working relationships is a very important step in building the capacities of the poor. Training inputs are provided on team-building, communication skills, time management, etc. NGOs are carrying out exhaustive fieldwork in the remote villages of India. Community mobilisation through village level meetings and interaction has been their forte. The staff of the SHGs are benefited through interaction with NGOs leading to adoption of participatory practices, besides leading to change in attitudes as NGOs offer role models. Banks are also one of the important partners. Participation of women in the process of development has significantly moved forward. Formation of SHGs is a critical process with conscientisation and voluntarism as a necessary basis for formation. Identification of families is done with the help of the Below Poverty Line (BPL) lists prepared by DRDAs in each district. Steps are being taken to cover each and every habitation while forming groups and giving preference to SC/ST coverage.

SHG Facilitation: Best Practice

Weekly meetings and optional savings are encouraged so that poor women are able to capture most of their surplus savings. A larger percentage of SHGs have switched over to weekly meetings (to a lesser extent weekly savings). Efforts are made to further strengthen groups through adoption of both weekly meetings and compulsory savings. Groups are trained in a phased manner to maintain accounts and registers. Discipline, shared vision, a common identity and sense of unity have been remarkably created through these groups with the practice of joint taking of the Mahilar Thittam pledge. This has clearly given the SHGs a sense of identity and a common mission. Group meetings are convened by SHGs in their respective villages at convenient locations and at convenient times. Each SHG visits the bank to which it is linked on rotational basis. Deposit savings are introduced so that SHGs become familiar with the various bank practices. After completion of one year, it is necessary for SHGs to have their account audited by an external agency and also carry out internal audit by the field staff.

Training for Transformation

The purpose of training under the project is to develop a shared vision and to bring about transformation in perception through exposure. A strong and cohesive SHG can be formed only by providing systematic training and adopting participatory methods. Impact of training can be easily seen in better communication skills, greater confidence, higher unity and wider mobility of SHG women. However, it is felt that training in the interactive and participatory methodologies needs to be strengthened. The use of pictorials and charts is not widespread. As a consequence, efforts should be made at the district level to organise trainers' camps where charts and visuals may be prepared and wide use of these thereafter should be ensured. Under SGSY, bankers' orientation was organised in several districts and bank managers were sensitised to scheme concerns. It is important that larger numbers of branch managers are sensitised. The foremost impact of such orientation has been the ease with which SHGs are able to open accounts. Increased interest shown by bankers in credit linkage to eligible SHGs is also a matter of great significance. Bankers now look at lending to women SHGs as a promising business segment, with 100 per cent repayment rates. Banks have been closely associated with SGSYs throughout the country.

Economic empowerment of women starts with savings and internal lending. However, this does not take the rate of growth to sustainable levels to raise family income above poverty line. External credit linkage with banks is therefore, a necessary event in the accelerated path to financial sustainability of each SHG and thereby of each household. After successful completion of six months of effective performance, credit rating of such SHGs is undertaken to assess credit -worthiness of such groups. Group standards set by SHG credit guidelines (satisfying the credit rating parameters) are recommended for linkage under SGSY scheme, National Bank for Agriculture and Rural Development (NABARD) has also evolved rating mechanisms. Rating mechanisms inculcate commercial/business skills among SHG members for undertaking economic activities. There is a growing need to orient and build capacity of NGO staff in micro-enterprise facilitation. Business orientation for SHG members is necessary to cultivate entrepreneurship skills. District level and block level workshops should be held with banks, DRDA, NGOs, and SHGs to identify business opportunities. There is also a need to facilitate linkages between SHGs, local industries and business networks for marketing and skill upgradation. Banks have to identify and build credit linkages with SHGs, taking up income generating project activities. Subsidy support should be extended for training and capacity- building which banks should help to initiate and take up in a big way. Marketing skills of SHGs, need to be substantially improved by promoting SHG products first locally (among SHGs themselves) and then upgrading to district/state levels. Flexible savings by group members should be allowed so that savings do not become an unnecessary imposition on groups. They should not be compelled to set aside a fixed amount towards savings but should be allowed to save whatever they can as a flexible saving option, i.e. to save as and when able. Groups should declare dividends to members out of accumulated interest on savings on an annual basis. However, this cannot be imposed and will be as per the bylaws of the group. Also, SHGs may consider and develop need-based 'financial products' as the group matures and is trained to fulfill financial functions beyond its regular savings and small loan operations. Banks have managerial and financial expertise which they can impart to the SHGs. Following a period of sound credit activities at the group level, linkages between SHG members and commercial banks are to be institutionalised. Women's groups should, after having undergone training, be formed into cluster level federations. Eventually, the women's groups can be federated at block, district and even State levels. This will contribute to the self-reliance and sustainability of the women's groups. Federation can also contribute to strengthening savings and loan activities. Financial intermediation by banks in the non-formal sector has gained increasing importance and recognising the financial services to assetless, poor and disadvantaged, particularly to women, holds the key to mainstreaming them with the development of the country. We have laid increasing emphasis on micro credit interventions which have been accepted internationally as an effective tool for poverty alleviation as it contributes to individual and household security and change social relations for the better. RBI has issued exhaustive guidelines to banks in February 2000 for mainstreaming micro credit and enhancing the outreach of micro credit providers. These guidelines afford banks considerable operational freedom for their effective implementations.

Globalisation is beneficial once the fruits are shared more equitably within society. India is growing at a steady rate. Led by strong performance of the industry and services sectors, the Indian economy has built upon its recent phase of high growth in 2005–06. Growth in real GDP accelerated from 7.5 per cent in 2004–05 to 8.4 per cent in 2005–06. The Indian economy has thus recorded an average growth of over 8 per cent from 2004–07. There is a large body of literature examining the building of women's social assets or capital and their empowerment through microfinance and poverty programmes... Gender discrimination, unequal access to resources and opportunities, women's paltry representation at Board level in organisations, in politics, as corporate head honchos in business, and the power imbalances that characterise personal relationships between men and women hamper the progress of not just women but of society at large. Gender mainstreaming means being explicit about the differing needs and experiences of men and women, making space for all stakeholders, giving voice and visibility to women's as well as men's perspectives, and ensuring that the design is informed by gender-disaggregated data. It means asking both women and men what they themselves see as the most pressing issues. In the implementation stage, it means making sure that both men and women are participating equally in the decision-making process and are treated with equal respect. In monitoring, it means tracking indicators that measure the differential impact of interventions by gender group. In evaluation, it means making sure that both women and men take part in determining the evaluation criteria, that gender equality is explicitly assessed, that the evaluation team is gender balanced and gender sensitive. Thus, mainstreaming becomes a major issue and includes recognition of the work of women in the unorganised sector. Policies and programmes that ignore differential impact on gender groups are often gender-blind; potentially harmful for human development. Gender mainstreaming requires a focus on results to improve the well-being of poor women. Whilst microfinance has been treated as synonymous with women, the motivation for many

MFIs to target women is often instrumental based on women being more compliant, reliable and easier to reach. There are also important motivations based on the need to impact on poverty. This, however, distinctly impacts poverty and leads to the feminisation of credit. Economic well-being changes the impact on social relations and sense of well-being and confidence of women. The international community made strong commitments for women's equality and empowerment at the world summits and global conferences of the 1990s. UNDP must help countries to translate these commitments into practical realities. It must contribute in expressing the noble goals set forth in the Convention on the Elimination of All Forms of Discrimination against Women (CEDAW) and the Millennium Development Goals (MDGs) into specific policy reforms and operational programmes that make a difference for women, especially women victims of poverty.

With a view to ensuring adequate credit flow to women, the public sector banks had been advised to lend at least 5 per cent of their net bank credit to women. The credit extended to women by all public sector banks stood at 4.98 per cent of overall net bank credit at the end of December 2006. Eleven public sector banks have opened 18 specialised women branches. 18 public sector banks have achieved the target. This process has led to an increase in the flow of credit to women and to some extent women entrepreneurs have been direct beneficiaries of this process.

Problems Faced by Women to Avail Bank Services

Problems faced in access to credit

- restricted mobility
- illiteracy and low social status
- lack of security/collateral
- micro loans and savings
- traditional perception of banks about lending to women entrepreneurs.

Problems in accessing bank credit

- illiteracy and lack of skill training
- difficulty in identification of women borrowers and establishing direct dialogue with prospective women borrowers who normally do not visit banks
- cumbersome and time-consuming documentation and procedures of banks in processing of loans
- urban bias of bank managers
- absence of credit at doorsteps and on time

- absence of credit and credit plus services through a single window
- gender discrimination
- women engaged in few selected activities and operating at a small scale
- time constraints to look after the enterprise
- women rarely come forward to take up income generating activities and most are first generation entrepreneurs
- limitations in working hours
- decision of choice of activity influenced by other family members
- unequal inheritence laws/control over property and incomes of women by men – difficulty in offering security/collateral.

Measures for improving women's access to credit

- identification of appropriate economic activity to be assisted
- financial sustainability of activities identified
- promoting entrepreneurship and managerial skills
- ensuring an effective credit delivery system
- monitoring and follow-up on utilisation of assistance given
- extending non-financial support
- inculcating savings and thrift habits and credit management
- long-term plans/area plans for women
- banks to play proactive role in reaching out to women
- publicity campaign/awareness programmes
- entrepreneurship development programmes and trainings
- common marketing facilities through federations/cooperatives
- data collection about entrepreneurs.

Action plan for implementation by banks

- redefining of bank's policies/long term plans
- setting up of women cells
- simplification of procedural formalities
- orientation of bank officers/staff on gender concerns/credit requirements of women
- publicity campaign for creating awareness about credit facilities
- entrepreneurship development programmes/training facilities for women
- specialised branches for women
- motivational strategies to enthuse staff
- monitoring system
- data collection
- involving NGOs.

Consequences of Financial Exclusion

There is a general consensus among economists that financial development spurs economic growth. A large body of empirical research supports the view that development of the financial system contributes to economic growth. In their work *Saving Capitalism from the Capitalists: Unleashing the Power of Financial Markets to Create Wealth and Opportunity* Raghuram Rajan and Zingales (2003) have shown that empirical evidence consistently emphasises the nexus between finance and growth, though the issue of direction of causality is more difficult to determine. At the cross-country level, evidence indicates that various measures of financial development (including assets of the financial intermediaries, liquid liabilities of financial institutions, domestic credit to private sector, stock and bond market capitalisation) are robustly and positively related to economic growth. King and Levine (1993) first established the correlation between financial development and economic growth establishing a causal relationship between finance and growth. Levine and Zervos (1998) presented cross-country econometric evidence showing that, in a sample of 47 countries, stock market liquidity contributed a significant positive influence on GDP growth between 1976–93. Other studies establish a positive relationship between financial development and growth at the industry level (Rajan, Raghuram G. and Zingales). One recurring question with regard to economic development is the importance of the financial sector for the growth of the overall economy. The financial sector is important for development. It has been demonstrated that financial development has occurred pari passu with economic development. Even the recent endogenous growth literature, building on 'learning by doing' processes, assigns a special role to finance (Aghion and Howitt, 1998 and 2005).

Characteristics of Rural Financial Markets

Until recently, conventional wisdom held that imposing low ceilings on interest rates and allocating massive amounts of credit to rural financial markets would speed rural development and improve income distribution. But by and large policies directed along these lines have failed. Indeed, most often they have made matters worse. Low interest rate ceilings provide income transfers to loan recipients, distorting the real price ratio of investment opportunities by sectors. To the standard cost of distorted resource allocation, add the specific costs and consequences of implementing credit programmes in impact. The record overwhelmingly shows that the objectives of the credit programme have not been met.

These credit policy failures can be attributed to basic flaws intrinsic to formal rural credit markets out of which arose persistent problems as described below.

Basic Flaws

- Weakness of competitive forces
- Weak legal enforcement of contracts
- Computation and lack of accountability in institutions, patronage and income transfer practices, which are partly due to poorly designed or non-existent incentive mechanisms to induce accountability on both sides of the market
- Significant information problems and uncertainty regarding the ability of borrowers to meet future loan obligations
- Inability to monitor the use of funds
- Lack of collateral security often due to land tenure arrangements or ill-defined property rights (e.g. parts of Africa)
- Lack of coherent financial savings mobilisation programme
- Higher opportunity cost of capital in other sectors because of interest rate ceilings

Persistent Problems

- Credit loans to wealthy farmers, small farmers being rationed out of the credit market
- Loans for agricultural programmes diverted to non-agricultural users
- Credit policies that encourage consumption and discourage savings
- The term structure of agricultural loans contracts or fails to expand
- Low adoption rates of cost-saving technologies in agriculture and in financial services
- Low recovery rate
- Significant distortions in the optional allocation of resources across markets
- Extensive use of interlinking credit contracts with labour and contracts

Informal lending was once the only form of credit in rural settings. Evidence suggests that as farm size increases, private credit sources, village moneylenders and pawnbrokers, chit funds with an array of implicit interest rates, and friends or relatives grow less important than banks. With the implementation of development plans, official lending complements but clearly does not supersede informal sources.

Sample surveys supply the information on the extent of informal lending practices. They indicate that its volume is far greater than that of organised institutions. It is characterised by a much shorter processing time, better screening techniques or enforcement devise (noted in the lower default rate), and higher interest rates, with a median around 50 per cent and a variance much higher than institutionalised credit rate. The lower delinquency rates reported in informal credit sources are, to a large extent, due to better assessment of creditworthiness, ability to exert social pressure for repayment, and the frequent practice of tying (interlinking) credit contracts with other input or output contract. Documentation of the use and characteristics of the latter practice is quite extensive. Sharecropping contracts are quite often interlinked with credit contracts. Credit contracts between landlords and tenants are often in the form of production loans and tied to the purchase of fertiliser, seeds and other forms of capital with different tenants paying different interest rates on their loans. These interlinkage practices have been viewed as a way to address the adverse selection problem and the moral hazard problem indigenous to these markets.

Characteristics of Rural Financial Markets

Rural finance markets lead to processes of exclusion from the formal financial system of banks by their very nature. To understand this phenomenon, it is necessary to understand the characteristics of rural finance markets. The modern theory of contractual equilibrium under imperfect information focuses on the moral hazard and adverse selection features commonly found in rural developing economies. Listed below are some 'moral hazard' features pertaining to the interlinking credit with labour and land contracts.

- Individuals are not paid on the basis of observable work that is done by them, and they often do not rent land for a fixed sum since that imposes too much risk on them. Hence, the contractual arrangements involve at least some form of sharecropping; as a result, tenants do not obtain the full marginal product of their efforts.
- In particular, the landlord has an incentive to induce tenants to behave as he wishes. This is attempted through influencing the amount and terms of credit the tenant borrows and by the goods he can purchase.
- Another rationale for interlinking is the 'adverse selection' effect, where interlinking credit and tenancy contracts may screen the high-ability from the low-ability types.

Braverman and Stiglitz have shown that there is no presumption that innovation results either in a reduction or in an increase in tenants' demand for credit. Whether the demand for credit itself is increased or decreased depends critically on both how the technical change affects the probability distribution of yields and on the tenants' utility functions. The presence of interlinkage between credit and land markets does not preclude either resistance to or encouragement of the adoption of technological innovations. Either is possible. In some cases, it might actually encourage the adoption of technologies which otherwise would not be adopted, even though the innovation itself reduces tenants' demand for credit. So it becomes clear that the impact of an innovation on a landlord-cum-lender may be quite different from the impact of the same innovation on a landlord who does not control the borrowing activities of his tenants. It is important to understand these features of rural financial markets while designing financial systems for the poor clients who have hitherto operated only in these financial markets.

Developed vs Underdeveloped Financial System

A developed financial system broadens access to funds; conversely, in an underdeveloped financial system, access to funds is limited and people are constrained by the availability of their own funds and have to resort to high cost informal sources such as moneylenders. Lower the availability of funds and higher their cost, fewer would be the economic activities that can be financed and hence lower the resulting economic growth on financial inclusion have emanated from the results of the All-India Debt and Investment Survey (AIDIS) 2002. Over a period of 40 years, the share of non-institutional sources of credit for cultivator households had declined sharply from about 93 per cent in 1951 to about 30 per cent in 1991, with the share of moneylenders having declined from 69.7 per cent to 17.5 per cent. In 2002, the AIDIS revealed, however, that the share of moneylenders had again increased to 27 per cent, while the overall rose to 39 per cent in the non-institutional sources. In other words, notwithstanding the outreach of banking, the formal credit system has not been able to adequately penetrate the informal financial markets; rather it seems to have shrunk in some respects in recent years. Consequences of financial exclusion are always dire but will vary depending on the nature and extent of services denied. It may lead to increased travel requirements, higher incidence of crime, general decline in investment, difficulties in gaining access to credit or getting credit from informal sources at exorbitant rates, and increased unemployment, etc. The small businesses may suffer due to loss of access to middle class and higher income consumers, higher cash handling costs, delays in remittances of money. According to certain researches, financial exclusion often leads to social exclusion.

Conclusion

Hence, the biggest challenge facing the world is ensuring financial services reach the unreached sections to provide an impetus to the processes of inclusive economic growth. Amartya Sen speaks of the need for the expansion of the capabilities of persons to lead the kind of lives they value and have reason to value. These capabilities can not only be enhanced by public policy, but also can be influenced by the effective use of participatory capabilities by the public. The bi-directional relationship is central and there are two distinct reasons for the crucial importance of individual freedom in the concept of development related respectively to evaluation and effectiveness. In the normative approach used here substantive individual freedoms are taken to be critical. The success of a society is to be evaluated, in this view, primarily by the substantive freedoms that the members of that society enjoy. This evaluation position differs from the informational focus of more traditional normative approaches which focus on other variables such as utility or procedural liberty or real income. Having greater freedom to do the things one has reason to value is:

- Significant in itself for the person's overall freedom and
- Important in fostering the person's opportunity to have valuable outcomes and result in the society's inclusive development.

It is increasingly being realised that maximisation of income and wealth cannot simply be the basic objective of life; as Aristotle stated wealth and income were 'merely useful and for the sake of something else.' For the same reason, economic growth cannot sensibly be treated as an end in itself. Development has to be more concerned with enhancing the lives we lead and the freedoms we enjoy. Expanding the freedoms that we have reason to value not only makes our lives richer and more unfettered, but also allows us to be fuller social persons, exercising our own volitions and interacting with and influencing the world in which we live. In the book *Hunger and Public Action*, Jean Dreze and Amartya Sen distinguish between two types of successes which are called respectively 'growth-mediated' and 'support led' processes. The former works through fast economic growth, and its success depends on the growth process being wide-based and economically broad (strong employment orientation plays a major role in this process) as also on the utilisation of the enhanced economic prosperity to expand the relevant social services including health care, education and social security. In contrast with the growth-mediated mechanism the support led process does not operate through fast economic growth, but works through a programme of skilled social support of health care, education and other relevant social arrangements. This process is well exemplified by the experience of economies such as Sri Lanka, pre-reform China, Costa Rica or Kerala which have experienced rapid reductions in mortality rates and enhancement of living conditions without much economic growth. The synapses between poverty, employment and growth have been the subject matter of great debate. Two strands of thought have clearly emerged. Firstly, there is a school of thought led by the economists of the World Bank-IMF who lay emphasis on economic reforms along with their natural concomitants – liberalisation, privatisation and globalisation which are expected to raise GDP growth and bring down poverty and unemployment which are natural corollaries of the growth process. Ahluwalia (2001), Jagdish Bhagwati (1993) and T.N. Srinivasan (2000) are all proponents of this view. The second strand of thought propounded by Etienne Gilbert (1992), Martin Ravaillon (1997), (1999 and 2002), Mahendra Dev (1997), Gaurav Datt (1997), Pranab Bardhan (1987) holds that growth per se may not result in pro-poor growth. The content of growth must lay emphasis on policies which promote and help to mainstream the poor and enable them to participate in the development process rather than remain residuary beneficiaries of the growth process.

The National Sample Survey Organisation (NSSO) results on the basis of large sample survey data on household consumer expenditure (NSS 61st Round) for 2004–05 are the basis of poverty estimates. The data was collected on uniform recall period (URP) using 30 days for all items. The data was also available using 365 days for five frequently purchased non-food items, namely, clothing, footwear, durable goods, education and institutional medical expenses, and a 30-day recall period for the remaining items, known as mixed recall period (MRP). The Planning Commission, using the Expert Group methodology estimated poverty in 2004–05 using both the distributions and arrived at the following analysis.

- Poverty estimates based on URP indicate 28.3 per cent of rural population and 25.7 per cent of the urban population was below the poverty line. For the country as a whole, 27.5 per cent of total population was below the poverty line in 2004–05.
- The corresponding figures obtained from MRP indicate 21.8 per cent in rural areas, 21.7 per cent in urban areas and 21.8 per cent for the country as a whole was in poverty in 2004–05.

The Planning Commission in its approach to the 11th Five Year Plan (December 2006) states: 'Using the methodology of the Expert Group on Estimation of Proportion and Number of Poor in 1993, the percentage of population below the poverty line is provisionally estimated at 27.8 per cent in 2004–05. Thus the average decline in percentage of population below the poverty line over the period 1993 to 2004 is 0.74 percentage points per year, much less than implied by the official 1999–2000 data. Because of the slower pace of reduction in the percentage of the poor, the estimated number of poor is now estimated to be approximately 300 million in 2004–05, larger than the official estimate of 1999–2000.' It may be recalled that the official estimate for poverty in 1999–2000 was 26.1 per cent for the country as a whole and 260 million were estimated as being poor. Table 2.1 provides state level data on poverty ratios during 2004–05. The lowest poverty ratio was 5.4 per cent for Jammu and Kashmir and highest poverty ratio was for Orissa (46.4 per cent). States with poverty ratio of less than 15 per cent were Jammu and Kashmir, Punjab, Haryana, Himachal Pradesh, Delhi and Goa. As against them, States with poverty ratio above 30 per cent were Maharashtra, Uttar Pradesh, Bihar, Jharkhand, Madhya Pradesh, Chhattisgarh, Uttarakhand and Orissa.

Table 2.1 Number and Percentage of Population Below Poverty Line (2004–05) based on URP Consumption.

	Rural Percentage		Urban		Combined	
State	Percentage of Persons	No. of Persons (in lakhs)	Percentage of Persons	No. of Persons (in lakhs)	Percentage of Persons	No. of Persons (in lakhs)
Jammu & Kashmir	4.6	3.7	7.9	2.2	5.4	5.9
Punjab	9.1	15.1	7.1	6.5	8.4	21.6
Himachal Pradesh	10.7	6.1	3.4	0.2	10.0	6.4
Goa	5.4	0.4	21.3	1.6	13.8	2.0
Haryana	13.6	21.5	15.1	10.6	14.0	32.1
Delhi	6.9	0.6	15.2	22.3	14.7	22.9
Kerala	13.2	32.4	20.2	17.2	15.0	49.6
Andhra Pradesh	11.2	64.7	28.0	61.4	15.8	126.1
Gujarat	19.1	63.5	13.0	27.2	16.8	90.7
Assam	22.3	54.5	3.3	1.3	19.7	55.8
Rajasthan	18.7	87.4	32.9	47.5	22.1	134.9

(*Continued*)

Table 2.1 (*Continued*)

	Rural Percentage		Urban		Combined	
State	Percentage of Persons	No. of Persons (in lakhs)	Percentage of Persons	No. of Persons (in lakhs)	Percentage of Persons	No. of Persons (in lakhs)
Tamil Nadu	22.8	76.5	22.2	69.1	22.5	145.6
West Bengal	28.6	173.2	14.8	35.1	24.7	208.3
Karnataka	20.8	75.0	32.6	63.8	25.0	138.9
All-India	28.3	2209.2	25.7	808.0	27.5	3017.2
Maharashtra	29.6	171.1	32.2	146.3	30.7	317.4
Uttar Pradesh	33.4	473.0	30.6	117.0	32.8	590.0
Madhya Pradesh	36.9	175.7	42.1	74.0	38.3	249.7
Uttarakhand	40.8	27.1	36.5	8.9	39.6	36.0
Jharkhand	46.3	103.2	20.2	13.2	40.3	116.4
Chattisgarh	40.8	71.5	41.2	19.5	40.9	91.0
Bihar	42.1	336.7	34.6	32.4	41.4	369.2
Orissa	46.8	151.8	44.3	26.7	46.4	178.5

Note: States have been arranged in the ascending order on the basis of combined poverty ratio in 2004–05. Poverty line: Rs 356.0 in rural areas and Rs 538.6 in urban areas (Per capita monthly expenditure).

Source: Planning Commission, Press Release, March 2007.

Five states, namely, Uttar Pradesh, Maharashtra, Bihar, West Bengal and Orissa accounted for 166 million poor (about 55 per cent of the total poor estimated at 302 million). This shows the high concentration of poor in these five states.

S. Mahendra Dev and C. Ravi have also analysed in depth the data of the 61st round of NSS (2004–05) and compared it with the period 1983–1993. The major findings of the study are:

- The overall poverty in India in 2004–05 was 28.3 per cent, slightly higher than the estimate of the Planning Commission, although the study uses the official poverty lines as updated for 2004–05, that is, Rs 356 for rural areas and Rs 538.6 of per capita monthly expenditure for urban areas. Accordingly, rural poverty ratio was 29.2 per cent and for urban areas it was 26.0 per cent for 2004–05.
- The absolute number of poor declined to around 315.5 million from around 324 million in 1993–94, indicating a decline of nine million during the 11 year period.

- The 'very poor' are those who are below 75 per cent of the poverty line. There was a decline in the proportion of the 'very poor' from 15.5 per cent in 1993–94 to 10.3 per cent in 2004–05. This implies the very poor accounted for 115 million among the total poor reckoned at about 316 million. Obviously, the share of hard-core or chronic poor is quite high, around 37 per cent of the total poor.
- Decline in poverty from 44.9 per cent in 1983 to 36.0 per cent in 1993 and further to 28.3 per cent in 2004–05 as can be analysed from Tables 2.2 and 2.3. This phenomenon was also observed in both rural and urban areas. However, it was noted that total poverty declined at the rate of 0.85 percentage points in the pre-reform period (1983–93), while the corresponding figure for the post-reform period was 0.70 percentage points per annum. From this, it can be inferred that the rate of decline in total poverty was slower in the post-reform period than in the pre-reform period. The same pattern was observed in the rural as well as urban areas.

Table 2.2 Poverty Estimates based on URP.

	1993–94	2004–05
Rural	37.3	28.3
Urban	32.4	25.7
Total	36.0	27.5

Source: Planning Commission, Press Release, March 2007.

Table 2.3 Percentage of Poor and Very Poor in India (URP basis).

	Poverty Ratios (in per cent)			Change in Poverty (Percentage points per annum)	
	1983	1993–94	2004–05	1983–94	1994–05
Rural Poor	45.8	37.3	29.2	–0.81	–0.73
Very Poor	25.5	15.4	9.6	–0.97	–0.52
Urban Poor	42.3	32.3	26.0	–0.92	–0.59
Very Poor	22.5	16.0	12.0	–0.61	–0.36
All-India Poor	44.9	36.0	28.3	–0.85	–0.70
Very Poor	24.8	15.5	10.3	–0.88	–0.48

The normal method of measuring poverty in India is by the poverty or headcount ratio which is simply the number of people below the poverty line.

References

Sen, Amartya (1999). *Development as Freedom*, Oxford University Press.

Kalecki, M. (1954). *Theory of Economic Dynamics*.

Keynes, J. M. (1927). *A Treatise on Money*, Vol. I.

Keynes, J. M. (1936). *The General Theory of Employment, Interest & Money*. USA: Macmillan Cambridge University Press, for Royal Economic Society in 1936.

Keynes, J. M. (1971). *Indian Currency and Finance, Collected Writings*, Vol. I.

Raj, K. N. (1974). 'Monetary Management and Nationalisation of Banks in India' in A. Mitra (ed.) *Economic Theory and Planning Essays in honour of A.K. Dasgupta*, Oxford University Press.

World Development Report, 2000/2001, Attacking Poverty.

Rajan, Raghuram G. and Luigi Zingales (2003). *Saving Capitalism from the Capitalists: Unleashing the Power of Financial Markets to Create Wealth and Opportunity,* New York: Crown Business.

King, Robert G. and Ross Levine (1993). *Finance and Growth: Schumpeter Might be Right. The Quarterly Journal of Economics*, Vol. 108, No.3, pp. 717–737.

Levine Ross and Sara Zervos. (1998). 'Stock Markets Banks and Economic Growth' *The American Economic Review*, pp. 537–558.

Rajan, Raghuram G. and Luigi Zingales, (1998). 'Which Capitalism? Lessons from the East Asian Crisis' *Journal of Applied Corporate Finance*, Vol. 11, No. 3, Fall 1998.

Joshi, Rajeev (2006). 'Credit to women borrowers monograph'.

Chapter 3

Financial Inclusion: The Indian Perspective

Strategic Context Background and Types of Indicators

Poverty and exclusion continue to dominate socio-economic and political discourse in India as they have done since the last six post-independence decades. Poverty reduction has been an important goal of development policy since the inception of planning in India. Various anti-poverty, employment generation and basic services programmes have been in operation for decades in India. The ongoing reforms attach greater importance to removal of poverty and address the specifically wide variations across states and the rural–urban divide. The anti-poverty strategy has three broad components. These are:

- The promotion of economic growth
- The promotion of human development, and
- Targetted programmes to address the multidimensional nature of poverty. The multitude of programmes has, in recent years, been strengthened through the National Rural Employment Guarantee Scheme (NREGS).

In a country with sharp regional inequalities in development and levels of living, the centre has a role in redistribution of financial resources to enable the poorer states to provide basic public services at a reasonably comparable level. In this chapter we discuss the poverty estimates, turn our attention to the methods of poverty analysis and analyse the impact of programmes initiated to combat poverty and exclusion and suggest a broader framework required to reduce, if not eliminate, these two major scourges.

From Efficiency to Equity

The focus of development policy in India has undergone a paradigm shift from an exclusive focus on efficiency to one on equity from the rate and pattern of growth, and on inequalities, distribution of income and wealth to the extent to which people are deprived of the requirements for a fulfilling life and suffer 'capability deprivation', to use Amartya Sen's terminology. Banks always had a critical role to fulfill in this process. They act as mobilisers of savings and allocation of credit for production and investment. The other functions of banks are supplying transaction and portfolio management services and are a source of liquidity for firms. They monitor borrowers, match illiquid assets with liquid liabilities and integrate credit and liquidity provision functions. Banks boost economic growth by identifying the entrepreneurs with the best chances of successfully initiating new production processes.

Uneven Growth

Though the Indian economy continues to record impressive growth rates, the impact has not fully percolated to the lowest deciles. Despite being one of the ten fastest growing economies of the world, India is still home to one-third of the world's poor. Further analysis shows that poverty is getting concentrated continuosly in the poorer states. In terms of absolute numbers, Uttar Pradesh, Bihar and Jharkhand account for around 27 per cent of India's population. 30 per cent of India's poor lived there in 1974 which has increased to over 41 per cent by 1999–2000.

The growth in State Domestic Product is uneven. This influences the Human Development Indicators and this incongruity also impacts the banking penetration which is not uniform across the country. To address the issue of financial inclusion, we have to pay due regard to equal growth. The major area of concern in India is that growth has not been uniform across regions and a variety of sections of the population are not integrated into the wider society and large sections are not equipped to enjoy the opportunities offered by rapid economic growth. There is a sharp disjunction between the states in the Southern region and the BIMARU* states. A look at the Selected Indicators of Human Development for major states tells its own story. India is a union of 29 states and 6 union territories, half of which are larger than many countries in the world, with populations above 30 million. India's constitution grants considerable power to the states in terms of

* BIMARU is an acronym coined by taking the first letter of four northern Indian states – Bihar, Madhya Pradesh, Rajasthan and Uttar Pradesh. This term has definite derogatory undertones as it is a take on the Hindi term 'Bimar', which means sick. The acronym 'BIMARU' brings forth images of a collection of sick people.

regulatory oversight, tax and expenditure assignments, provision of infrastructure and provision of social services. Before the 1990s, the states' discretion in policy-making was limited. India also enjoyed several decades of uniparty rule. The rise to power of regional parties and coalition governments changed this paradigm. States now enjoy discretionary powers and greater autonomy. The quality of state's own economic and social management is a critical determinant of its growth. As per the 2001 census, 73 per cent of the country's rural population resided in rural areas. States of the Southern region are performing better than others. It is estimated that over 50 per cent of banking business in the country is concentrated in eight major cities: Mumbai, Delhi, Chennai, Kolkata, Bangalore, Hyderabad, Ahmedabad and Pune. In December 2003, 62 per cent of all rural households, 51 per cent of farming households and 78 per cent non-farming households did not have access to basic banking services. It has also been estimated that 12 per cent of urban households too lack access. Thus over 485 of all households in the country remain excluded from the benefits of banking. The extent of exclusion is skewed across states and regions. While financial exclusion is as low as 27 per cent in the southern region, Andhra Pradesh with less than 25 per cent has the lowest degree of exclusion among all the states. 60 per cent of the households in the eastern region are in the zone of exclusion with over 75 per cent of the households in the states in the North Eastern region with no access to banking services. The RBI committee's Financial Sector Plan for the North Eastern Region (NER) recommended that banks in the NER should draw up plans to provide at least 50 new households per branch each month for the next four years with a deposit account and taking into account the balances maintained in such accounts over a period, the bank may offer small overdrafts or general credit cards against such accounts and other products in terms of the RBI guidelines. The committee has also suggested that extensive recourse may be taken to the bank/Self Help Group linkage programme, business correspondent/ business facilitator model for this purpose. The committee also suggested recourse to IT based solutions including smart cards for carrying out banking transactions with a view to increase outreach. The report includes inter-alia suggestions for expanding the banking outreach, simplification of system and procedures for opening of bank accounts, land collateral substitutes, currency management, funds transfer and payment facilities. It thus addresses important issues to the provision of hassle-free credit. However, disparities in credit penetration

Table 3.1 State-wise Life Expectancy and Infant Mortality Rates.

Serial no.	State	Life Male	Expectancy Female	At birth (1998–2000) total	Infant Male	Mortality Female	Rate* total	Birth rate	Death rate
1	Andhra Pradesh	62.0	64.6	63.5	59	59	59	20.4	8.0
2	Assam	57.7	58.1	57.9	69	65	67	26.3	9.1
3	Bihar	61.4	59.5	60.8	59	61	60	24.6	7.6
4	Gujarat	62.4	64.4	63.4	54	61	57		
5	Haryana	64.7	65.4	65.2	54	65	59	26.3	7.1
6	Karnataka	62.8	66.2	64.5	51	52	52	21.8	7.2
7	Kerala	70.8	75.9	73.5	11	12	11	16.7	6.3
8	Madhya Pradesh	57.0	56.7	56.9	77	86	82	30.2	9.8
9	Maharashtra	65.0	67.4	66.2	32	54	42	19.9	7.2
10	Orissa	58.4	58.5	58.5	82	83	83	23.0	9.7
11	Punjab	67.4	69.5	68.5	46	52	49	20.6	7.0
12	Rajasthan	60.5	61.6	61.1	70	81	75	30.3	7.6
13	Tamil Nadu	64.2	66.3	65.2	44	41	43	18.3	7.6
14	Uttar Pradesh	59.4	58.5	59.1	69	84	76	31.3	9.5
15	West Bengal	63.3	64.8	63.9	45	46	46	20.3	6.6
	India	61.6	63.3	62.5	57	64	80	24.8	8.0

*(per 1000 live births 2003). Birth rate, death rate per 1000.

Source: Office of the Registrar General of India Ministry of Home Affairs as reported in the Economic Survey 2005–06.

and outreach due to the unequal growth of banking penetration in the states have considerably hampered the processes of financial inclusion.

These states have lagged behind in most parameters of economic progress, especially since independence. Social and economic indices are highlighted as ailments.

- Higher than average population growth rate
- Lower than average literacy rate
- No effort to involve the local population of these states in the planning process.

Analyses of indicators of banking penetration of scheduled commercial banks including regional rural banks show that the population per branch has decreased for urban areas and increased for rural areas which is indicative of the fact that branch expansion has not kept pace with the population increase in the rural areas. Burgess and Pande also found that

Table 3.2 Average Population per Branch Office (APPBO).

Year	1991	2001	2005
Population per branch	13711	15209	15680
Population per rural branch	13642	15667	16650
Population per urban branch	14484	14137	13619

since the inception of the economic reforms, several rural branches had been relinquished as unviable by banks.

It is seen that the deposits (current and savings) accounts per 1,000 people in the rural areas as a whole is about 60 per cent of the urban areas. North Eastern states, Orissa, Bihar and Chhattisgarh have particularly low ratio. Similar position is generally evident even in terms of credit accounts per 1,000 people. However, southern states are relatively better off in this aspect.

The number of deposit (current and savings) and credit accounts per thousand people is given below

The number of deposit and credit accounts per branch in the rural areas is generally lower than the position in urban areas as shown in table four:

Table 3.3 Number of Accounts per 1000 people.

	Deposit (C+S) Accounts per 1000 population		Credit Accounts per 1000 Population	
Region/State	Rural	Urban	Rural	Urban
Northern Region	338	652	55	71
North Eastern Region	186	281	35	41
Eastern Region	185	413	45	47
Central Region	242	375	45	49
Western Region	263	526	46	121
Southern Region	393	486	136	185
All India	270	483	64	104

Source: Computed from BSR 2005 and Census data 2001.

Table 3.4 Number of Accounts per Branch.

	Deposit (C+S) Accounts per Branch		Credit Accounts per Branch	
Region/State	Rural	Urban	Rural	Urban
Northern Region	4130	6677	675	771
North Eastern Region	3716	5340	702	781
Eastern Region	3676	6087	887	693
Central Region	4586	6075	859	797
Western Region	3826	6630	663	1530
Southern Region	4549	5571	1577	2121
All India.	4202	6155	1000	1321

Source: BSR 2005.

The deposits and credit outstanding per branch also reflect the rural urban divide.

Table 3.5 Outstanding Balances per Branch.

	Deposit (C+S) per Branch (Amt. Rs Crore)		Credit per Branch (Amt. in Rs Crore)	
Region/State	Rural	Urban	Rural	Urban
Northern Region	6.43	25.22	7.19	46.99
North Eastern Region	5.41	21.03	4.99	13.80
Eastern Region	4.99	18.80	3.99	23.62
Central Region	5.26	15.40	4.51	15.15
Western Region	4.67	26.51	7.72	63.77
Southern Region	4.01	14.41	8.73	32.68
All India	4.98	19.92	6.37	37.94

Source: BSR 2005.

It is seen that deposits per branch in the rural areas are far lower than that in the urban areas, notably in the North East, Northern and Western regions. In terms of credit per branch, the difference is more pronounced in Northern and Western regions.

The outstanding balance per account, both deposit as well as credit, reveals the much larger values in urban areas as evident from Table 3.6.

Table 3.6 Outstanding Balances per Account.

	Deposit (C+S) Bal per A/c (Rs 000)		Credit Bal per A/c (Rs 000)	
Region/State	Rural	Urban	Rural	Urban
Northern Region	15.56	37.78	106.46	609.72
North Eastern Region	14.56	39.38	70.59	176.85
Eastern Region	13.57	30.88	44.58	341.00
Central Region	11.46	25.35	52.49	190.06
Western Region	12.19	39.99	116.42	416.71
Southern Region	8.82	25.87	55.39	154.08
All India	11.84	32.36	63.74	287.91

The average size of a deposit account in the rural areas is about one-third the size in urban areas and ranges from about Rs 7,000 (Andhra Pradesh) to about Rs 17,000 (Punjab). The divide, as expected, is sharper in terms of credit per account. The average credit account in rural areas ranges from Rs 19,000 (Tripura) to Rs 1.31 lakh (Haryana). The share of different agencies in the total cash dues of rural and urban households reveals the extent of penetration of formal financial sources.* The category of moneylenders is the sum of agricultural moneylender and professional moneylender.

Table 3.7 Share of Different Credit Agencies in the Total Cash Dues of Households.

(Share in percentage)

	Rural Households			Urban Households		
Credit Agencies	1981	1991	2002	1981	1991	2002
Institutional	61.2	64.0	57.1	60.0	72.0	75.1
of which						
Co-operative Soc/Bank	–	21.6	27.3	–	17.2	20.5
Commercial Banks	–	33.7	24.5	–	21.6	29.7
Government	–	6.1	2.3	–	11.1	7.6
Non-Institutional	38.8	36.0	42.9	40.0	28.0	24.9
of which						
Moneylenders*	–	17.5	29.6	–	10.2	14.1
Total	100	100	100	100	100	100

*The category of moneylenders is the sum of agricultural moneylender and professional moneylender.
Source: Computed from All India Debt and Investment Surveys covering various decades.

This table clearly shows that the coverage of banks in the rural areas has fallen from 64 per cent to 57 per cent, while significantly, the share of money lenders has increased from 17.5 per cent to 29.6 per cent.

There is a pressing need for greater financial inclusion in the Rural Sector.

- The savings rate has increased to nearly 31 per cent in the recent period. Remittances from urban to rural areas are becoming more significant due to increase in migration. The need for banking facilities – savings, remittances and credit – has increased in rural areas.
- The share of agriculture in GDP has fallen from 43 per cent in 1970s to 20 per cent in 2005–06. The share of food grains and cereals has declined from 31.7 per cent to 24.1 per cent and increased of commercial crops. Within the agricultural sector, the share of fishing and livestock has gone up from 20.3 per cent to 29.3 per cent. Agriculture is getting increasingly diversified as floriculture, horticulture and other value added activities.
- The proportion of rural households, described as low income by National Council for Applied Economic Research (NCAER), has gone down from two-thirds in early 90s to 25 per cent in 2005–06 and those with middle income from one-third to 70 per cent. This represents increase of 50 million middle income households in rural areas.
- Retail credit has grown by nearly 50 per cent per annum from 2003–08 mostly at urban centres. As income increases, demand for retail credit in rural areas too increase, which is perhaps being met by the informal sector. Anecdotal evidence suggests that money lenders in rural areas face more competition from other moneylenders rather than from the banks.
- With the growing rural connectivity and tele-density, a host of non-farm activities are mushrooming in the rural sector. Currently, the rural market accounts for 53 per cent of the Fast Moving Consumption Goods (FMCG) and 59 per cent of the durable market in India. The rural consumers represent more than 50 per cent of the country's 'consuming classes'.

There is an untapped business potential for aggressive banking in the rural areas. The challenge lies in locating these areas and providing them with the financial services through appropriate delivery channels and

Table 3.8 Estimates of Incidence of Poverty in India.

Year	Poverty Ratio (Percentage)			Number of Poor (million)		
	Rural	Urban	Combined	Rural	Urban	Combined
1973–74	56.4	49.0	54.9	261.3	60.0	321.3
1977–78	53.1	45.2	51.3	264.3	64.6	328.9
1983	45.7	40.8	44.5	252.0	70.9	322.9
1987–88	39.1	38.2	38.9	231.9	75.2	307.1
1993–94	37.3	32.4	36.0	244.0	76.3	320.3
1999–00	27.1	23.6	26.1	193.2	67.1	260.3
2007	21.1	15.1	19.3	170.5	49.6	220.1

Source: Government of India, Ministry of Finance and Company Affairs Economic Survey, 2002–03, pp. 213.

products. The banks with their extensive network of branches in the rural areas will be able to leverage their presence and meet these challenges.

Poverty Projection

Table 3.8 above provides the estimates of the incidence of poverty in India. The latest available large sample survey data on consumer expenditure collected for the 55th round covered the period from July 1999 to June 2000. The poverty ratios above relate to the period from 1972–74 to 1999–2000. Poverty at the national level is estimated as the weighted average of state-wide poverty levels. Thus, the poverty ratio shows a decline from 54.9 per cent in 1973–74 to 36 per cent in 1993–94. The poverty ratio declined by nearly 10 percentage points in the six years period, from 36.0 per cent in 1993–94 to 26.1 per cent in 1999–2000 while the proportion of the poor declined from 320.3 million to 260.3 million during this period. The table shows that the proportion of the poor under reference in the rural areas declined from 37.3 per cent in 1993–94 to 27.1 per cent in 1999–2000. The percentage of urban poor declined from 49 per cent to 23.6 per cent during this period. In absolute terms, the number of poor declined to 260 million in 1999–2000, with about 75 per cent in the rural areas. The rural and urban poverty ratios are expected to decline to 21.1 per cent and 15.1 per cent.

The incidence of rural poverty has been below the national average in the case of states such as Gujarat, Haryana, Himachal Pradesh, Karnataka,

Table 3.9 Head Count Poverty Ratios – Rural India and Urban India in percentage terms.

State	55th round Rural India	55th round Urban India
Andhra Pradesh	11.1	26.6
Assam	40.0	7.5
Bihar	44.3	32.9
Gujarat	13.2	15.6
Haryana	8.3	10.0
Himachal Pradesh	7.9	4.6
Karnataka	17.4	25.3
Kerala	9.4	20.3
Madhya Pradesh	37.1	38.4
Orissa	48.0	42.8
Punjab	6.4	5.8
Rajasthan	13.7	19.9
Tamil Nadu	20.6	22.1
Uttar Pradesh	31.2	30.9
West Bengal	31.9	14.9
All India	27.1	23.6

Source: Planning Commission. See also Economic and Political Weekly Jan 25, 2003, pp. 323–324.

Maharashtra, Kerala, Punjab and Rajasthan. The incidence is higher in Assam, Bihar, Madhya Pradesh, Orissa, Uttar Pradesh and West Bengal. Conversely, the level of urban poverty is higher as compared to the national average in the case of Andhra Pradesh, Bihar, Kerala, Maharastra and Uttar Pradesh and lower than national average in Gujarat, Haryana, Himachal Pradesh, Kerala, Punjab, Rajasthan, Tamil Nadu, and Delhi. Though this has not been empirically verified, the incidence of exclusion, especially financial exclusion is greater in the poorer states as the levels of literacy and quality of life are commensurably lower.

Estimates of HCR PGI FGT and SI for 1983 are drawn from Tendulkar et al (1993). Parallel estimates for 1993–94 with uniform and mixed reference periods and with mixed reference period for 1999–2000 have been estimated from unit record data for the 50th rounds at consumer expenditure survey.

Table 3.10 clearly shows that in both rural and urban India, and also at the national level, there is a clear reduction in the Head Count Ratio

Table 3.10 Alternate Measures of Poverty in India Reflecting Poverty Trends in India between 1983 to 1999–2000.

Segment measure	Measures 1983	On Uniform Reference Period (URP) 1993–94	Measures on 1993–94	Mixed Reference period (MRP) 1999–2000
All-India (Rural)				
Head Count Ratio (per cent) (HCR)	49.02	39.66	37.85	28.93
Poverty-gap Index (PGI)	0.1386	0.0928	0.0825	0.0579
FGT	0.0545	0.0315	0.0267	0.0173
Sen Index (SI)	0.1882	0.1278	0.1145	0.0806
No of poor*	65.720	72.586	67.675	63.827
All India (all areas)				
Head Count Ratio (per cent)	46.47	37.35	35.47	27.32
Poverty-gap Index	0.1293	0.0881	0.0785	0.0558
FGT	0.0502	0.0302	0.0257	0.0170
Sen Index	0.1758	0.1214	0.1089	0.0775
Number of poor (2000)	333.782	333.955	317.116	274.325
Memorandum item				
Total (all areas) population (2000)	718.300	894.006	894.006	1004.086
Share of urban population	23.87	26.28	26.28	27.53

(HCR), Poverty Gap Index (PGI), Squared Poverty Gap (FGT) and Sen Index (SI). In rural India, the annual average decline in the Head Count Ratio over the ten and a half year period of July 1983 and January 1994 was 0.7 per cent points per year, for rural and urban areas taken together, the average decline in HCR was close to below 0.9 per cent per annum. While in rural India, the size of the poor population declined by a little under 6.9 million over the ten and a half year period, the number of poor people increased by 6.9 million in urban India during the same period, despite the corresponding reduction in the Head Count Ratio. However, there was a rapid growth of more than 3 per cent per annum in the urban population during the period. From 1 January 1994 to 1 January 2000, the Head Count Ratio declined by close to 9 percentage points translating to only an average decline of 1.5 percentage points. This was significantly higher than the average annual decline in the Head Count Ratio of 0.9 per cent points between 1983–1994. During the same period, a 5.7 per cent point decline in HCR corresponding to an annual average decline of 0.95 per cent translates into a decline in the number of urban poor by a little over 3.8 million between 9 January 1994 and 1 January 2000. The period 1988–89 witnessed an increase in the number of urban poor by around 7 million. The PGI, FGT as well as the Sen Index show that the performance has been better in 1990s urban India. At the national level, the overall performance in all dimensions of poverty was far better between 1994 and 2000 than in the preceding ten and a half years. Though an exact correlation has not been drawn up, it is still clear that greater poverty translates to greater social and financial exclusion. This is evident from the states which are not doing well. Consequently financial inclusion strategy which has been so successful in Puducherry remains a distant dream in Pratapgarh (Uttar Pradesh). In measuring poverty, the Head Count Ratio remains the most widely used but perhaps the crudest estimate. A standard is set and the number of persons who satisfy the standard in different regions of the country and at different points of time are estimated. A poverty norm of Rs 20 per capita per month in rural areas and Rs 25 per capita per month in urban areas at 1960–61 prices was suggested by a working group of eminent economists and social thinkers in 1962. Subsequently in 1993, the expert group set up by the Planning Commission under the chairmanship of late Professor Lakdawala recommended a poverty line anchored in a given calorie norm 2,400 calories per capita per day for rural areas and 2,100 calories per day for urban areas and expenditure required for the corresponding all India consumption basket for the year 1973–74 as the poverty line. It came to Rs 49.09 per capita per month in rural areas and Rs 56.64 for urban areas. The poverty line is updated by estimating what it would cost to obtain the base year consumption basket with prices prevailing in subsequent years. This process does not account for the substitution that consumers may make when the relative prices of some items of consumption change or their tastes change. The change in consumption pattern has been significant. A person in the poorest quartile in rural Uttar Pradesh spent 69 per cent of her total expenditure on cereals in 1972–73 but only 40 per cent in 1993–94. It can be shown that this would in general overestimate the poverty line.

Limited Reach of Banking System

Statistics from the results of the All India Debt and Investment Survey (AIDIS), 2002 on financial inclusion show that alarmingly 51.6 per cent of households suffer exclusion from the financial sector. Of these, rural households comprise 147.9 million farmers – of which farmer households are 89.35 and non-farming households are 58.55 million, small and marginal farmers are 74.97 million and of these 40.27 are financially excluded, and only 8.72 million are financially included. Over a period of 40 years, the share of non-institutional sources of credit for cultivator households had declined sharply from about 93 per cent in 1951 to about 30 per cent in 1991, with the share of moneylenders having declined from 69.7 per cent to 17.5 per cent. In 2002, the AIDIS revealed that the share of moneylenders had again increased to 27 per cent, while overall shares of non-institutional sources rose to 39 per cent (Table 3.11). In other words, notwithstanding the outreach of banking, the formal credit system has not been able to adequately penetrate the informal financial markets; rather it seems to have shrunk in some respects in recent years. Measuring Financial Exclusion presents its own set of difficulties.

A significant aspect of financial deepening is the expansion of access which enables the formal institutional sectors to develop sophisticated appraisal techniques, and information gathering and sharing mechanisms which then enable banks to finance those activities or firms which are at the margin, thereby extending the frontier of finance and allowing

Table 3.11 Relative Share of Borrowing of Cultivator Households (per cent).

Sources of Credit	1951	1961	1971	1981	1991	2002
Non-institutional	92.7	81.3	68.3	36.8	30.6	38.9
of which						
Moneylenders constitute	69.7	49.2	36.1	16.1	17.5	26.8
Institutionals constitute	7.3	18.7	31.7	63.2	66.3	61.1
of which:						
Cooperative societies, etc.	3.3	2.6	22.0	29.8	30.0	30.2
Commercial banks	0.9	0.6	2.4	28.8	35.2	26.3
Unspecified	–	–	–	–	3.1	–
Total	100.0	100.0	100.0	100.0	100.0	100.0

#: Borrowing refers to outstanding cash dues.
$: AIDIS, NSSO, 59th Round, 2003.
Source: All India Debt and Investment Surveys.

productivity to grow and new entrepreneurship to come up. It is difficult for the poor to access mainstream financial services in any part of India, rural or urban. This is a double-edged sword – the individual is deprived of services and the banking system of savings. Financial exclusion may sometimes be voluntary which may be dictated by a fear of bank's environment and staff, fear of indebtedness, lack of confidence that the venture set up with bank loan will be successful. Financial exclusion means no bank account, no assets or savings, or insurance, or access to money advice, or affordable credit. Clearly it is an unsustainable position. Bank nationalisation in India marked a paradigm shift in the focus of banking as it was intended to shift from the class banking to mass banking. The rationale for creating Regional Rural Banks was also to take banking services to the poorest of the poor. The branches of commercial banks and the RRBs have increased from 8,321 in the year 1969 to 14,750 branches as at the end of March 2005. The average population per branch office has decreased from 64,000 to 16,000 during the same period. However, there are certain under-banked states such as Bihar, Orissa, Rajasthan, Uttar Pradesh, Chattisgarh, Jharkhand, West Bengal and a large number of North Eastern states, where the average population per branch office continues to be quite high compared to the national average. The new branch authorisation policy of Reserve Bank encourages banks to open branches in these under-banked states and the under-banked areas in other states. The new policy also places a lot of emphasis on the efforts made by the Bank to achieve, inter alia, financial inclusion and other policy objectives. The credit from Scheduled banks comprises only 45 per cent of GDP in comparison with other South East Asian countries which is low. There are increasing concerns that banks have not been able to include vast sections of the population specially the vulnerable sections of the society into the fold of basic banking services. Banks have launched financial inclusion projects but are faced with multiple constraints. Their margins are getting narrower; there is greater competition especially in the retail segments.

- As corporates are demanding finer rates, there is a fear of the economy going into a slowdown, so financial inclusion has to be viewed as a business opportunity for it to become a success and not as a variant of government largesse or subsidised credit.
- Significant government subsidies channelized through the banks and cooperatives, as well as through related government programmes.

- A dominant perspective that finance for rural and poor people was a social obligation and not a potential business opportunity.
- Access to products which reduce vulnerability to economic shocks is critical. Access to finance is believed to have a positive impact on poverty alleviation (Burgess and Pande 2003, Honohan 2004), and that some definitions of poverty look at levels of economic vulnerability (Matin and Hulme 2003). Improving access to risk mitigating products has to be a key part of any policy that seeks to increase financial inclusion.
- There is evidence to show that low income communities value savings as much as debt, yet are denied access to safe and secure savings products. From a policy perspective, RBI has attempted to address the issue through the business facilitator – Banking Correspondent and Business Correspondent models which enables MFIs to collect savings and is an attempt at encouraging Branch banking.
- Greater infrastructure for data collection and sharing of historical data is required for developing index based products – particularly weather stations/gauges in underserved areas in the country.
- A micro-commodities/microderivatives platform within the National Commodities and Derivatives Exchange Limited (NCDEX) framework could be developed as this would definitely help to encourage smaller volumes of trade and also consider newer channels like MFIs, KIOSKS, etc. as a platform for disseminating future prices and for enabling trading.

One of the benchmarks employed to assess the degree of reach of financial services to the population of the country is the quantum of deposit accounts (current and savings) held as a ratio to the adult population. In the Indian context, taking into account the Census of 2001 (ignoring the incremental growth of population thereafter), the ratio of deposit accounts (data available as on 31 March 2004) to the total adult population was only 59 per cent (details furnished in Table 3.14). There is a wide variation of this ratio across states in India. For instance, the ratio for the state of Kerala is as high as 89 per cent while Bihar is marked by a low coverage of 33 per cent. In the North Eastern states like Nagaland and Manipur, the coverage was a meagre 21 per cent and 27 per cent, respectively. The Northern Region, comprising the states of Haryana, Chandigarh and Delhi, has a high coverage ratio of 84 per cent. Compared to the developed world, the coverage of our financial services is quite low. For instance, as per a recent survey commissioned by British Bankers' Association, 92 to 94 per cent of the population of UK has either current or savings bank account. Legislation of UK, enacted in June 2001, requires all banks to provide accounts without minimum opening balances to all Canadians, regardless of employment or credit history, with minimum identification requirements. A Financial Consumer Agency of Canada has been established to monitor whether financial institutions adhere to their public commitments.

Present Situation in India

The share of deposits and credit in rural and semi-urban areas is on the decline whereas the share in metropolitan areas is rising. The share of credit is lower than that of deposits in all regions except metropolitan areas, implying that resources get intermediated into metropolitan areas (Table 3.12). This in itself may not necessarily be undesirable or unexpected if resources are being intermediated to their best uses.

Table 3.12 Spatial Distribution of Banking Services (per cent).

	Offices			Deposits			Credit		
	1969	1996	2005	1969	1996	2005	1969	1996	2005
Rural	22.2	51.2	45.7	6.4	14.4	12.2	3.3	11.4	9.5
Semi-urban	40.4	21.3	22.3	21.8	19.5	16.9	13.1	13.1	11.3
Urban	19.2	15.2	17.6	26.5	22.4	21.5	21.8	17.7	16.4
Metropolitan	18.2	12.3	14.4	45.3	43.7	49.4	61.8	57.8	62.7
Total	100.0	100.0	100.0	100.0	100.0	100.0	100.0	100.0	100.0

Source: Reserve Bank of India.

However, they do provide some indication for concern and deserve further investigation.

The total number of saving accounts, considered to be a better indicator of banking penetration than other deposit accounts, as per cent of number of households, was 137 in rural areas and 244 in the urban areas on the eve of reforms in 1991. By 2005, despite the reforms, the differential continues to be similar. In the case of credit accounts, the situation has deteriorated for rural households while showing significant improvement in the urban areas (Table 3.13), corroborating the very significant increase in retail credit.

Table 3.13 Number of Deposit and Credit Accounts in Scheduled Commercial Banks (per cent of number of households).

Deposit Accounts		1981	1991	1996	2001	2004	2005
Current Accounts	Rural	3.6	5.5	4.7	4.9	4.4	4.6
	Urban	15.0	23.4	24.1	19.2	17.5	18.3
Savings Accounts	Rural	59.6	137.0	129.8	123.3	126.8	131.5
	Urban	135.5	243.7	249.7	197.4	206.5	213.1
Current and Saving Accounts	Rural	63.2	142.6	134.5	128.2	131.1	136.1
	Urban	150.5	267.2	273.7	216.6	224.0	231.4
Term Deposits Accounts	Rural	22.9	41.8	45.5	52.0	48.3	45.7
	Urban	74.6	96.9	105.0	105.6	113.4	104.0
Total Deposits Accounts	Rural	86.1	184.4	180.0	180.1	179.4	181.8
	Urban	225.1	364.1	378.7	322.2	337.4	335.4
Credit Accounts	Rural	18.0	44.3	36.0	26.5	28.7	32.2
	Urban	15.1	29.9	27.1	28.4	42.5	50.2

Notes:

1. The census population groups are 'rural' and 'urban', whereas the population groups used in BSR data are 'rural', 'semi-urban', 'urban' and 'metropolitan'. There is no unique relationship between the two. For comparison purpose and simplicity, 'Rural' and 'Semi-Urban' are taken as 'rural', and 'urban' and 'metropolitan' are combined as 'urban'.
2. For three new-formed states, number of households in 1991 has been estimated based on 2001 data. Population is as per 1981, 1991 and 2001 census. For 1996, 2004 and 2005 projected population has been used, and rural and urban proportion of past census is applied.

Sources: 1. Reserve Bank of India. 2. Census, 2001.

Total deposits, as per cent of GDP, increased from 32.2 in 1991 to 47.1 in 2005 in rural areas, and from 37.3 to 61.2 in urban areas. Similarly, credit extended, as per cent of GDP, increased from 17.3 to 22.3 in rural and from 24.8 to 45.0 in urban areas (Table 3.14). In terms of banking penetration, the number of deposit and credit accounts of scheduled commercial banks, as per cent of adult population, are significantly lower in the rural areas as compared with the urban areas (Table 3.15).

Table 3.14 Deposits and Credit Amounts in Scheduled Commercial Banks. (per cent of GDP).

Deposit Accounts		1981	1991	1996	2001	2005
Current Accounts	Rural	2.6	2.7	2.4	2.9	3.3
	Urban	5.5	7.1	7.0	7.0	8.7
Savings Accounts	Rural	9.8	11.2	10.5	13.6	18.6
	Urban	7.2	9.0	7.9	9.8	13.3
Current and Saving Accounts	Rural	12.4	13.9	12.8	16.4	21.9
(1 + 2)	Urban	12.7	16.1	14.9	16.8	22.0
Term Deposits Accounts	Rural	13.8	18.3	20.5	27.9	25.2
	Urban	16.6	21.2	22.4	29.2	39.1
Total Deposits Accounts	Rural	26.3	32.2	33.3	44.4	47.1
(3 + 4)	Urban	29.3	37.3	37.3	46.0	61.2
Credit Accounts	Rural	13.0	17.3	14.4	15.8	22.3
	Urban	20.0	24.8	25.5	31.1	45.0

Notes:
1. GDP at market prices (current prices) is used. The rural and urban figures of GDP are based on ratio of monthly per capita Total Consumer Expenditure, NSSO.
Source: Reserve Bank of India.

Table 3.15 Number of Deposit and Credit Accounts in Scheduled Commercial Banks. (per cent of Adult Population, Age above 15).

Deposit Accounts		1981	1991	1996	2001	2005
Current Accounts	Rural	1.0	1.6	1.4	1.4	1.4
	Urban	4.5	6.6	6.8	5.4	5.2
Savings Accounts	Rural	16.1	39.6	37.6	36.5	39.0
	Urban	40.3	69.2	70.9	55.8	60.2
Current and Saving Accounts	Rural	17.1	41.3	38.9	38.0	40.3
	Urban	44.8	75.8	77.7	61.2	65.4
Term Deposits Accounts	Rural	6.2	12.1	13.2	15.4	13.6
	Urban	22.2	27.5	29.8	29.8	29.4
Total Deposits Accounts	Rural	23.3	53.4	52.1	53.4	53.9
	Urban	67.0	103.4	107.5	91.0	94.7
Credit Accounts	Rural	4.9	7.7	8.0	7.9	9.5
	Urban	4.5	12.8	10.4	8.0	14.2

Note: Reserve Bank of India.
Source: Computed from BSR 2005 and Census data 2001.

Challenge of Rural Poverty and the Role of the Non-Farm Sector

The approach of tackling rural poverty has to be one that promotes self-employment, the rural non-farm sector and farm based enterprises.

Expanding Work Force

In the current decade, according to estimates of the Planning Commission, more than 12 million additional people will be seeking work every year. There are about 30 million unemployed or underemployed individuals in the country and more than 75 per cent in the rural areas. Thus, to ensure full employment, more than 15 million new livelihoods will have to be generated every year.

Vulnerability

The rural poor are increasingly becoming vulnerable to spiraling cycles of poverty because of low wages, seasonality and still predominant dependence of agriculture on monsoons. The contribution of the primary sector to GDP has been continuously decreasing. In 1951, it was half of GDP, in 2001, it was less than 1/4th and stood at around 23 per cent, but there has not been a commensurable decline in the number of persons engaged in the agriculture sector. The number of individuals dependent on agriculture and allied livelihoods has gone up from 260 million in 1951 to 650 million in 2001. This sector continues to support more than half-a-billion people, providing employment to 52 per cent of the work force.

Difficulty in Access to Credit and Dependence on Land as Collateral

The dependence of the poor on land is greater because of the lack of access to other productive assets and skills. Even access to credit has a high correlation to the amount of land possessed.

High Correlation between Access to Credit and the Amount of Land Possessed

This correlation exists both in the formal institutional financial sector and the informal sector. Despite efforts made by alternative non-formal financial institutions, access to credit has remained a constraint in the growth in productivity of the small landholdings, thereby diminishing the probabilities of small farmers accumulating capital and assets. This is also a reason why a large number of the small farmers are compelled to do farming at bare sustenance levels. Despite the many government and non-governmental institutions working towards rural development, their impact on rural poverty alleviation has had geographic, sectoral and sociological biases leaving large disadvantaged areas and groups. Owing to the lack of productive assets including skills, the onslaught of privatisation and globalisation will further compound rural poverty unless issues of access to credit through formal financial institutions as banks are resolved. This alone can enable the promotion of self-employment, rural non-farm sector and farm-based enterprises thereby increasing agricultural productivity and increasing agricultural income, diverting surplus manpower from the primary sector to other enterprises.

The Rural Non-Farm Sector (RNFS)

Data on employment over the previous decade shows that employment in the RNFS grew at a much faster rate than in agriculture – 5.4 per cent per annum against 0.7 per cent during the period 1977–78 to 1999–2000 as per NSS data. The data also shows that the average wage rate for workers in the RNFS was higher than that of agricultural workers. The rural market comprises 74 per cent of population, 41 per cent of middle class and 58 per cent of disposable incomes of the country. Of the total rural disposable income, 46 per cent comes from non-agricultural income emphasising both, the importance of the RNFS as well as the need for financial institutions (banks) to penetrate the rural savings market with suitable products.

Financial Exclusion in the RNFS

Studies on outreach of the financial system have shown that the share of non-institutional agencies in the outstanding cash dues of rural households is as high as 36 per cent. Credit dependence on informal sources is higher in case of lower asset groups. Dependence on informal sector was 58 per cent for households with assets lower than Rs 5,000 as per the All India Debt and Investment Survey.

Urban Poverty

The scale of urban poverty in India is staggering. Current estimates suggest that 100 million poor people live in urban settlements constituting about 40 per cent of the urban population. These numbers are expected to increase if the postulates are correct and if the total urban population of India over the next 25 years increases from 26 per cent of total population to over 36 per cent–50 per cent, the number of urban poor could end up between 200–300 million. Hence, urban poverty also needs to be addressed urgently. Self-employment can be an important driver of growth, and economic development provides thorough access to credit from formal financial institutions that improves to keep pace with the growing needs of the urban poor. The National Institute for Urban Affairs estimates that urban India currently contributes more than 50 per cent of the country's GDP whilst accommodating less than a third of its population and this contribution is likely to increase to 60 per cent. The proportion of people living below the poverty line in many states is now higher in urban areas than in rural areas. Developed states such as Punjab and Karnataka, and the less developed states like AP, Kerala, MP, UP and Rajasthan have reported higher levels of urban poverty than rural poverty.

Employment Opportunities

In urban areas, people's main asset is their capacity to sell their labour. They have other assets to build on – their houses may be rented or unfit for habitation, they may not own land or cattle in the town, and the social networks built by households over generations in the village may be less strong in a dynamic urban context where people come and go. The poor are not equipped with the skills and training, to take advantage of newer opportunities in modern industry and rising service sector. The formal wage sector has been unable to absorb the expanding labour force and there has been a massive growth of the informal sector and casual employment. Wages are forced downward, working conditions are unprotected and unregulated, and access to opportunities is mediated by the capacity of individuals.

Access to Financial Services

Access to financial services is a critical aspect of both social development and social protection measures for the poor. These services create an opportunity for access to low interest credit, which can be used for skill enhancement or micro-enterprise, the opportunity for savings and loans as insurance against crisis.

Microenterprise and the Difficulty in Obtaining Credit and Working Capital Loans from Formal Financial Institutions

Much of Asia's vast and growing population forms part of the economy that lies outside the regulatory framework of governments in what is known as the informal sector. The informal sector comprises small-scale and microenterprises producing and distributing goods and services in unregulated but competitive markets. The enterprises are generally independent, largely family owned, employ low levels of skills and technology and are highly labour intensive. All they need is sustainable access to financial services and credit for working capital which they, because of barriers to financial access, are not able to get. They provide income and employment for significant proportions of workers in rural and urban areas by producing basic goods and services for rapidly growing populations. They account for more than 60 per cent of all enterprises and up to 50 per cent of paid employment. With increasing labour force participation among women, a greater number of women depend on them for survival. India has 24 million microenterprises constituting 97 per cent of all enterprises. It provides employment to at least 45 million people. and 63 per cent of all non-agriculture workers. The overall density of employment in microenterprises was 54 workers per 1000 persons. 75 per cent of rural non-agriculture workers are employed in microenterprises against 52 per cent in urban areas. It is increasingly recognised that credit is essential for microenterprise development which forms an essential element in the promotion of broad based growth and improvements in the well being of the poor and women by providing significant income and employment generating opportunities and by encouraging indigenous investment. Access to financial services becomes an urgent necessity for poor households. Poor households are often plagued by fluctuations in income and the need for emergency resources. Microenterprises are often vulnerable to de-capitalisation to meet household consumption expenditures. Often fixed assets, such as a cow or rickshaw may have to be sold, bringing the enterprise to an abrupt halt.

A requirement for any sustainable system of production credit is the existence of consumption credit, and a 'safety net' of essential social services consisting at the very least of basic and emergency health care. It is important that the income of microenterprises be protected from emergency demands on income, that credit extended to such enterprises not be used for lean season consumption and that assets financed are not liquidated. The availability of livestock insurance is also extremely useful.

Access to finance becomes an urgent necessity for poor households. Essentially financial inclusion can assure access to at least some of the critical services required by microenterprises. Microenterprises and their heterogeneity prompt a diversity of financial needs to be met by the formal institutional sector at banks. Some aspects of microenterprise diversity are size, gender, location and sector of activity. Most enterprises are single-owner operated enterprises or slightly larger units engaging one or more family members. A higher proportion of livelihood enterprises tend to be owned and operated by women than growth-oriented enterprises.

The Survival–Viable Enterprise Dichotomy

A survival enterprise is said to be one into which the entrepreneur is often pushed for want of more profitable alternatives, where one is attracted into a viable activity by consideration of profitability and is an entrepreneur by choice. Both benefit through financial credit linkages, however, these are essential viable enterprises. In the former case, the activity is just one of many part-time activities undertaken to support family income. Whereas, in the latter it is usually the main source of family income. Access to credit can definitely help to enlarge its scale and scope.

In case of survival activities, usually no skills are involved, hence very low-entry barriers lead to overcrowding. In case of viable activities, skills and experience are required which restrict entry in the sector. Financial inclusion is very important as primarily what growth oriented microenterprises require is timely access for working capital and fixed investments. Effective technical services on management productivity and quality to raise the firm's competitiveness are also guaranteed through financial inclusion. Credit remains the key factor or rather financial inclusion remains critical as it enables a host of interrelated activities. Promotion of commercial linkages among firms allows economies of scale in production, purchasing and marketing. The key objective is to put at the disposal of small and microenterprises, the different elements to grow and modernize, so that they may use these services according to their entrepreneurial attitude.

Growth of Sustainable Livelihoods and Microfinance

A sustainable livelihood comprises the capabilities, assets and activities required for a means of living. A livelihood is sustainable when it can cope with and recover from stresses and shocks, maintain or enhance its capabilities and assets while not undermining the natural resource base.

In addition to credit, this comprises natural capital, i.e. natural resources. The most important arguably is economic or financial capital which financial inclusion enables. It also prompts and encourages human capital, i.e. skills, knowledge, good health, ability to labour, etc. It also capitalises on the networks of social capital – the social resources (networks, social claims, social relations, affiliations, associations) on which people draw upon and which it buttresses.

Livelihood Promotion: The Challenge of Microfinance

Protective financial services may be critical for poverty alleviation, but do little to help people out of poverty. To enhance livelihoods among poor people, promotional financial services are required. This is a far greater challenge than the mere delivery of microcredit through the formal financial institutions. Microcredit is a necessary but not a sufficient condition for microenterprise promotion. The success of microenterprise depends on a whole range of resources and opportunities. Other inputs are therefore required, which include not just business support and training, but also the identification of livelihood opportunities, establishing market linkages, adapting technologies, organising producers, etc. The challenge for financial inclusion is therefore that microcredit must be coupled not only with business support to individual enterprises among their borrowers, but integrated within sectorally-based technical support which can develop a large number of productive and sustainable livelihoods. The microfinance industry is fixated on microenterprises, as though it alone can obliterate poverty. The reality of mere credit extension is that many microenterprises are not productive, but merely subsistence enterprises. Providing working capital may enable the subsistence enterprise to expand but often at the expense of another growth-oriented microenterprise. Promotion of sustainable microenterprises in access to credit also depends on the availability of basic skill, understanding about the viability of the business, knowledge about market and accessibility of non-financial support services. A market-led locally sustainable curriculum will have to be developed in order to achieve a long-term self-employment movement. Working in remote villages far away from the market centres limits the scope for identifying and initiating income generating (IG) activities through formal financial institutions engaged in the well-defined processes of financial inclusion. It is recommended that credit programmes should focus more on promoting IGAs near markets in semi-urban areas, market centres and larger villages. The savings and credit mechanism cannot by itself be seen as an instrument to promote economic activities.

There are two issues related to marketing that are relevant for the SHGs whether they take up subsistence or profit related, survival or income generating projects using credit from formal sources, banks, NGO, donor funds, or informal sources, such as moneylenders: (i) the marketability of the product or service provided or produced by the group and (ii) market access. In addition to financial inclusion, the Participatory Skill Resource and Market (PSRM) Mapping becomes important in this context. PSRM mapping is a process for identifying various viable enterprises that can be taken up by banks and SHG members based on available, enhanceable skills, local resources and markets accessible to the SHG. It also identifies gaps and bottlenecks so as to arrive at an intervention mix that optimises resource allocation. PSRM mapping is a practical approach to collect ground level information through the involvement of practicing entrepreneurs. It provides critical information towards identifying activities which can be promoted at the village/mandal level. It broadly helps the user understand the geographical area, target group, nature of the sector and characteristics of the enterprise. It assesses ground realities and recommends a detailed plan relevant for each village in ways that enable the villagers to plan and implement the intervention themselves. The process focuses on the market approach for achieving economic growth and it depends on the entrepreneurs' experience and problems faced by them in marketing their own products/services.

Trends in Poverty

Trends in poverty can be examined in two ways: Directly through poverty ratios and indirectly looking at employment/unemployment and wages. The poverty ratios have not shown any trend during 1950/51 to 1973/74 and declined significantly in the late 1970s and 1980s. In the post-reform period, rural poverty has been arrested till 1993–94. On the contrary, urban poverty recorded a sharp decline in the 1990s. Rural poverty also came down between 1993/94 and 1999–2000. However, there are some issues regarding the comparibility of NSS data as between the data for 1993/94 and 1999–2000. The trends in human development which place Sri Lanka ahead of India show that India has a long way to go to attain the levels of even the average of the 'medium' human development category of countries. Convergence of per capita state development product shows that interstate inequalities have been increasing in the 1990s and there are sign of divergence rather than convergence. In the 1990s, poorer states like Bihar, Madhya Pradesh, Rajasthan, Uttar Pradesh and Orissa did not experience any reduction in poverty while richer states as Andhra Pradesh,

Gujarat, Karnataka, Kerala, Maharashtra, Tamil Nadu, West Bengal and Punjab recorded a decline in poverty. Sharp and increasing divergence in these two groups of states is possibly the major reason why overall poverty levels have not declined. Regional disparities in poverty looked at a disaggregated level throw up the following data. Since 1983 all the states have experienced a decline in the proportion of those below the poverty line in both the rural and the urban areas. Inspite of this the regional disparities continue to be high even in 1999–2000 poverty level data. In states like Punjab, Jammu and Kashmir, Gujarat and Andhra Pradesh the incidence of rural poverty was below 15 per cent while in states like Assam, Bihar, Orissa and Madhya Pradesh over 35 per cent of the respective rural population remained mired in poverty. In the post reform period, divergence of trends in poverty rose. For the period 1950/51 to 1997 T.N. Srinivasan has indicated that trends in rural poverty in one group of states – Andhra Pradesh, Gujarat, Karnataka, Kerala, West Bengal and Punjab began to diverge from that in another group of states – Bihar, Madhya Pradesh Rajasthan, Orissa and Uttar Pradesh since 1977–78. In the first set, according to Srinivasan and Mahendra Dev's analysis of data, poverty declined and the decline continued in the post-reform period at a slow pace; while the second group has not shown any such decline. The human development indicators were also better in states with higher per capita income growth. The state of Kerala again provides a different perspective. Income here is not correlated with Human Development Indicators; for e.g., the infant mortality in Uttar Pradesh was five times higher than that of Kerala with both having similar levels of poverty. In the 1970s and 1980s Kerala had higher human development but the economy (both agriculture and industry) was stagnant and unemployment rates were high. Punjab and Haryana had very high per capita incomes but gender inequalities were much higher than southern states. Thus this shows a disjunction between poverty and child mortality in the states of the north, particularly, in Haryana and Punjab where gender bias is very strong, and eastern states like Bihar and Orissa have lower social development.

Financial Deepening as an Imperative for Financial Inclusion

It is evident that wherever per capita income is lower, banking penetration is not high; the banks may be existent but their penetrative outreach and transaction affected by them would be much lower. Hence financial inclusion and the need for mainstreaming remain high as issues on the policy agenda.

Financial Widening

Even in terms of financial widening, the scope for improvement remains. In terms of regional disaggregation since 1991, population per bank office has increased in rural areas from 13,462 in 1991 to 16,650 in 2005 and, as expected, declined in the urban areas from 14,484 to 13,619 over the period. Three regions, North Eastern, East and Central have higher population per office than the all India average and it has increased significantly in the rural areas in 2005 over 1991 (Table 3.16). Consequently, compared to an all India average of 29.9 savings accounts per 100 persons in 1991, virtually all of the states in the eastern and North Eastern regions and several pockets in the Central region had figures lower than this average. In the rural areas, northern and southern region are above the all India average while in the urban areas, northern and western region dominate. In terms of number of credit accounts per 100 persons, the southern states both in rural and urban areas perform above the all India average.

Table 3.16 Regional Level Indicators of Scheduled Commercial Banks.

	Population per Office					
	Total		Rural		Urban	
	1991	2005	1991	2005	1991	2005
Northern	11,002	12,257	10,771	13,043	11,571	10,941
North-East	16,870	26,227	16,335	22,158	21,169	20,318
Eastern	16,441	19,913	16,402	21,208	16,614	15,759
Central	15,786	19,518	15,153	20,264	18,745	17,297
Western	12,771	14,618	12,579	15,526	13,108	13,472
Southern	11,932	12,328	11,276	12,372	13,811	12,243
All-India	13,711	15,680	13,462	16,650	14,484	13,619
Deposits: Number of Savings Accounts per 100 persons						
Northern	40.0	38.3	30.1	29.7	62.6	55.4
North-East	17.8	17.6	16.1	16.4	28.4	24.2
Eastern	21.8	20.5	17.7	16.9	40.0	36.1
Central	23.8	24.5	21.0	22.1	34.7	32.9
Western	35.5	32.5	24.7	23.8	53.8	45.2
Southern	37.0	37.6	34.6	35.5	42.7	41.8
All-India	29.9	29.2	24.5	24.4	45.6	41.6
Credit: Number of Credit Accounts per 100 persons						

(Continued)

Table 3.16 Continued

	Population per Office					
	Total		Rural		Urban	
	1991	2005	1991	2005	1991	2005
Northern	6.4	5.7	6.6	5.1	5.9	6.7
North-East	4.4	3.3	4.4	3.2	4.4	3.9
Eastern	6.6	4.2	7.2	4.2	4.3	4.3
Central	5.5	4.3	5.8	4.2	4.4	4.5
Western	5.7	7.5	6.2	4.2	4.8	12.2
Southern	11.8	14.2	13.6	12.7	7.6	17.4
All-India	7.3	7.0	7.9	6.0	5.5	9.8

Notes: Same as in Tables 3.3 and 3.4.
Source: Reserve Bank of India.

This suggests that banks need to make efforts to mobilise resources from the rural sector, where scope for increase in business is emerging. Further, if the banks are to balance their overall deposit mobilisation and credit extension, as generally robust banking practice would imply, then they would need to devise innovative ways to mop up the resources, particularly in rural areas.

Conclusion

Provision of financial services is instrumental to address the overall development of the poor. Banks need to move beyond mere credit provision to generate capacities within the population to prepare them to address their own problems of development. Efforts have to be made to increase the scope of financial services and their availability in a framework of financial inclusion. Financial deepening remains a key area of concern. Banks need to increase their penetrative outreach in the under-banked states and to address regional inequities in the development process as also the deepening hiatus between rural and urban areas. Banks have to continue to partner the state in the process of unleashing economic growth. Economic growth is essential for reducing poverty. Increasing economic growth translates into increased opportunities for productive employment. It is self-evident that poverty will reduce with higher growth of 8 to 9 per cent. Public resources need to be increased for supporting equity-oriented programmes, since higher growth implies larger outlays.

The growth has to be more in favour of the poor in order to make a dent on poverty levels which continue to be high. In other words, growth has to create opportunities for the poor apart from the middle class and the rich in rural areas. Agricultural growth is considered to be more pro-poor as majority of the population continues to be engaged in agriculture for ensuring basic livelihood support. Diversification of livelihoods is important to shift workers from low productivity to high productivity sectors.

References

Kempson, E. (2006). 'Policy Level Response to Financial Exclusion in Developed Economies: Lessons for Developing Countries', paper presented at the conference on 'Access to Finance: Building Inclusive Financial Systems', World Bank, Washington, D.C.

Connolly, C. and Hajaj, K. (2001). *Financial Services and Social Exclusion*, Financial Services Consumer Policy Center, University of New South Wales.

Treasury, H. M. (1999). *Access to Financial Services*, HM Treasury, London.

Rao, M. Govinda (ed.). (2002). *Development, Poverty and Fiscal Policy Decentralisation of Institution*, Oxford University Press.

Government of India Economic Survey 2005–06.

Chapter 4

Tackling Financial Inclusion and RBI Policy: Responses and Voluntary Initiatives of Banks

Financial exclusion broadly relates to a lack of access to a range of financial services. Several of those who belong to the lower income groups are unable to access mainstream financial products such as bank accounts and bank loans. This financial exclusion imposes real costs on them and their families' implications become graver when they prompt social exclusion and lock families in a cycle of perpetuity of debt, poverty and exclusion. An inclusive financial sector per contra, is one which offers a range of financial services to the entire population of a country and addresses issues of economic growth with equity. The RBI as the Central Bank has always been engaged with building a legal and regulatory environment for the financial sector which broadens access to its services. The processes of globalisation and faster economic growth have spurred the need for affirmative action for inclusive growth and to build social safety nets through increasing financial inclusion. Growth with equity has been the overriding policy concern which has governed the direction of banking policies. In India, in the context of initiatives exercised for extension of the penetrative outreach of the banking sector, the mode of financial sector development discussed in the previous chapters too has been characterised by the following features.

Macro Policy Initiatives

Financial inclusion was sought to be achieved through an increase in bank branches which led to an expanded cooperative network and new organisational forms like regional rural banks. A greater focus on extension of credit for poverty redress led to the stipulation of mandated targets directed at a range of identified priority sectors such as agriculture, the weaker sections of the population, etc.

Interest rate ceilings were also imposed so that credit would not be overpriced for the weaker sections and special schemes as the differential rate of interest scheme were also introduced whereby credit up to Rs 12,000 was to be given at 3 per cent rate of interest, thereby making attempts at greater financial inclusion. During the British rule in India, Nicholson, a British officer in India suggested 'Find Raiffersen in India', i.e., to introduce Raiffersen model of German Agricultural Credit Cooperatives in India. As a follow-up of that recommendation, the first Cooperative Society Act of 1904 was enacted to enable formation of 'agricultural credit cooperatives' in villages in India under government sponsorship. With the enactment of the 1904 Act, cooperatives were to get a direct legal identity as every agricultural cooperative was to be only registered under that Act. The 1904 Cooperative Societies Act was repealed by 1912 Cooperative Societies Act which provided for formation of cooperative societies besides providing credit. Under the 1919 Administrative Reforms, cooperatives were made a provincial subject, making each province responsible for cooperative development. As a key sector of the Indian economy, the Reserve Bank of India has historically allocated a key priority to the agricultural credit delivery. The Reserve Bank of India Act, 1934 envisaged a special developmental role for the Reserve Bank in the sphere of agricultural credit with responsibility, in particular, for financing seasonal operations and the marketing of crops.

The Rural Banking Enquiry Committee (Thakurdas Committee, 1950) stressed the importance for an efficient system of agricultural finance, of a sound cooperative credit structure capable of developing close relations with the Bank. The Reserve Bank followed up the Rural Banking Enquiry Committee with an informal conference. Following the conference's recommendations, the Reserve Bank decided to organise a Rural Credit Survey and constitute a Standing Advisory Committee on agricultural credit.

The All-India Rural Credit Survey, commissioned in August 1951, covered seventy-five districts around the country. Eight villages in each were chosen for the survey, which was based on a sample of fifteen households from each of the selected villages, with a view to recommend practicable policies for the future on rural credit. The survey was completed during November 1951–July 1952, under the Committee of Direction, headed by A.D. Gorwala. Dr D.R. Gadgil was one of members of the committee. The report was submitted in August 1954. The survey was struck by the utter insignificance of cooperatives in providing rural credit. 'Positive and deliberate' measures rather than 'small administrative, functional or other changes' were required to ensure the success of cooperative credit institutions and enable them to become self-supporting. The state's tendency in the past had been to 'over-administer and under-finance' the cooperative movement, but the report pointed out the need for an integrated system of cooperation and rural credit. The report envisaged a key role for the Reserve Bank of India in coordinating the proposed network of cooperative institutions and for its Agricultural Credit Department in over-seeing their functioning.

Developmental Role of RBI

RBI has a unique distinction among central banks of the world with respect to its developmental role especially relating to agriculture and rural areas. This is obvious in our country where two-thirds of the population depends on agriculture and a little below a fourth of the national income is from agriculture. Besides, it is important for the country's industrial exports. RBI's involvement in agriculture and rural credit stems from the statutory responsibility cast on it by Sec 54 of RBI Act 1934. Section 54 of RBI Act states that 'The Bank may maintain expert staff to study various aspects of rural credit and development and in particular it may:

(a) Tender expert guidance and assistance to the National Bank
(b) Conduct special studies in such areas as it may consider necessary to do so for promoting integrated rural development.'

In a sense the effort of financial inclusion can be turned back to the year 1904, when the Cooperative Societies Act was passed. In 1954 the RBI appointed the Rural Survey Committee. The historic All India Rural Credit Survey Committee (AIRCS) established in 1954 confirmed that formal credit institutions provided less than 9 per cent of the rural credit needs in India. Moneylenders, traders and rich landlords accounted for more than 75 per cent of rural credit. Cooperative credit societies had already been in existence for over fifty years but their share in rural credit was still less than 5 per cent.

In 1955, the State Bank of India was created for economic regeneration of rural areas. In 1969, the government nationalised 14 commercial banks, and the RBI appointed the All India Rural Credit Review Committee (AIRCRC), which in its report observed that moneylenders dominated the rural financial markets and amassed considerable wealth. It was realised that there was a need to bring the commercial banking system under social control to align it with the national planning objective of securing economic growth combined with equitable distribution of the fruits of such growth. With the government and RBI beginning to view credit as an integral part of promoting socio-economic development in the rural sector, certain segments of the economy were classified as priority sector credit and intimated to the banks in March 1969. Nationalisation thus saw the introduction of directed credit lending through the introduction of the priority sector concept.

Through the priority sector, the RBI ensured that credit was directed to the hitherto unbanked geographical regions. Secondly, RBI sought to influence the sectoral orientation of bank lending. In 1972 the definition of certain 'priority' sectors was formalised. These included agriculture and allied activities and small-scale and cottage industries. A target of 33 per cent lending to the priority sector was set in 1975, to be achieved by March 1979. In 1979, the target was raised to 40 per cent to be achieved by 1985. In 1980, sub targets were introduced. The share of priority sector advances in total credit of scheduled commercial banks went up from 14 per cent in 1969 to around 40 per cent by the end of the 1980s.

Extending the Horizon to Unbanked Areas

The RBI created a comprehensive list of unbanked locations in India which was circulated every few years to all banks. In 1970, the RBI formulated its branch licensing criteria based on this data. For every new branch in an already banked area with one or more branches, each bank would have to open at least three branches in unbanked rural or semi-urban areas. The RBI directed that all semi-urban locations would have to be covered by the end of 1970. In 1977, the RBI further raised the banked – unbanked license ratio to 1:4. Post nationalisation, branch expansion was deliberately skewed towards previously unbanked or underbanked rural or semi urban areas. The RBI policy was a success in forcing banks to open branches in hitherto unbanked locations. The number of rural branches of banks including RRB increased from a mere 1443 in 1969, to over 35,000. Most of this increase was in the hitherto unbanked locations. The number of banked locations in this period rose from around 1,000 to around 25,000. The share of rural branches went up from 18 to 58 per cent during the same period. Between 1961 and 2000 the average population served by a bank branch decreased from around 1,40,000 to just under 15,000. There is a strong convergence in this figure across states after 1977 and by 1990, all Indian states were below the national target of 17,000. This reflects the fact that bank building intensity was much greater in states with a higher proportion of rural unbanked locations in 1969. Bank branches in unbanked locations really exploded after the 1:4 licensing rule of 1977. That the rule was strictly enforced is clear from the fact that between 1977 and 1990, 80 per cent of all new branches opened were in unbanked locations.

A study conducted by Hans P. Binswanger demonstrated the positive growth and poverty eradicating outcomes of public investment in rural infrastructure. Binswanger undertook a study of 85 randomly selected districts in 1993 and this showed that bank branch expansion accelerated the pace of private investment in agriculture in the 1970s. The demand for fertiliser was also found to be highly correlated with bank expansion. There was thus an explosive growth in rural banking during the period. The Lead Bank Scheme was also introduced by RBI in December 1969 concomitant with the nationalisation of 14 commercial banks. The Lead Bank Scheme emphasised on making banks the key instruments for local deployment by entrusting them with the responsibility of locating growth centres, amassing deposit potentials, identifying credit gaps and evolving a coordinated programme of credit deployment in each district, in concert with other banks and credit agencies. It was expected to assume leadership and to act as a consortium leader for coordinating the efforts of all credit institutions in each of the allotted districts for expansion of branch banking facilities and for meeting the credit needs of the rural economy.

Burgess and Pande (2002) devised an econometric model to study the economic impact of this exponential growth in rural banking during the period 1970–92. They found that bank branch expansion into both banked and unbanked areas had a significantly positive impact on the growth of non-agricultural output. RBI issued detailed guidelines for implementation of the service area approach in March 1988 and the 'Service Area Approach' (SAA) was introduced with effect from 1 April 1989. The crux of SAA was demarcation of service area and preparation of credit plans for systematic administration of credit in the assigned area. The SAA involved five distinct stages:

(i) Identification and allocation of service area for each bank branch: Each rural/semi-urban branch of a commercial bank/Regional Rural Bank (RRB) has been allocated a certain number of villages, which is known as the service area of the bank, by a committee consisting of the Lead District Officer (LDO) of RBI (Chairman), Lead Bank Officer (Convenor) and the concerned officer of NABARD (Member), in consultation with bankers and government officials. Generally 15 to 25 villages are allocated and various Central Government Poverty alleviation programmes are implemented by banks in these villages.

(ii) Survey of villages in the service area for assessing the potential for lending activities and identification of beneficiaries for assistance;
(iii) Preparation of Credit Plan on an annual basis for the service area of each branch; each bank branch is required to prepare a Service Area Credit Plan for all the villages coming under its service area, based on the potential of the area and need of various priority sector activities in the service area. The branch credit plan is aggregated at the block level to form the Block Credit Plan and the Block Plans are aggregated at the District Level to form District Credit Plan and the District Credit plans are aggregated to form the State Credit Plans.
(iv) Coordination between credit institutions and field level development agencies on an on-going basis for effective implementation of the plan; and
(v) Continuous monitoring of the progress in implementation of the plans. The performance under Branch Credit Plan is monitored at three levels viz.: (a) by the branches themselves for each of the villages in their service area, in relation to the Village Credit Plans (b) by the Controlling Offices of the respective banks and (c) by the Block Level Bankers' Committees (BLBCs). At District Level, District Consultative Committee (DCC) and District Level Review Committee (DLRC). At the State Level, State Level Bankers' Committee (SLBC) monitors the overall progress of achievement of targets under the plan.

In 1994–95, public sector banks were advised to formulate Special Agricultural Credit Plans (SACP) with a view to achieve distinct and marked improvement in credit flow to agriculture. The private sector banks have been formulating SACP from the year 2005–06. The Kisan Credit Card (KCC) scheme was introduced from 1998–99 with the objective of providing adequate and timely support from the banking system to the farmers for meeting their credit requirements. Cumulatively, the number of KCCs issued by public sector banks stood at Rs 2.56 crore since its inception.

The public sector banks have been advised to lend up to at least 5 per cent of their net bank credit to women. Public sector banks have also been advised to functionalise at least one specialised small scale industries (SSI) branch in every district and centre having a cluster of SSI units. Banks had been urged in November 2005, to make available a basic banking 'no frills' account either with 'nil' or very low minimum

Table 4.1 Growth of Rural Banking in India 1969–2006.

Year	Number of Bank Offices		Credit Outstanding		Deposits		Credit Deposit Ratio (per cent)	
	Rural	Percent of total	Rural (Rs crore)	Percent of total	Rural	Percent of total	Rural	All Areas
1969	1,443	17.6	115	3.3	306	6.3	37.6	71.9
1972	5,274	36.0	257	4.6	540	6.5	47.7	67.2
1975	7,112	35.5	608	6.0	1,171	8.5	51.9	73.5
1978	12,534	42.5	1,530	8.4	2,664	10.1	57.4	69.1
1981	19,453	51.2	3,600	11.9	5,939	13.4	60.6	68.1
1984	25,541	52.9	6,589	13.5	9,603	13.4	68.6	68.3
1987	30,585	56.2	11,127	15.3	17,527	14.7	63.5	61.0
1990	34,867	58.2	17,352	14.2	28,609	15.5	60.7	66.0
1993	35,360	56.3	22,906	14.1	41,410	15.0	55.3	58.9
1996	32,981	51.2	29,012	11.4	61,313	14.4	47.3	59.8
1999`	32,840	49.3	42,091	11.0	102,697	14.7	41.0	54.8
2002	32,443	47.8	66,682	10.2	159,423	14.2	41.8	58.4
2005	32,082	46.9	109,976	9.5	213,104	12.2	51.6	64.9
2006	30,572	44.5	175,816	8.4	226,049	10.8	56.3	72.5

Source: RBI Basic Statistical Returns (various issues). Quarterly statistics on deposits and credit of Scheduled Commercial Banks (March 2006).

balances as well as charges that would make such accounts accessible to vast sections of the population. Several banks have introduced the no-frills accounts with and without certain value-added features. Regional rural banks have also been advised to allow limited overdraft facilities in 'no frills' accounts, without any collateral. With a view to give an impetus to financial inclusion, all State Level Bankers Committee (SLBC) convener banks have been advised to initiate action for identifying at least one district in their state/union territory for 100 per cent financial inclusion. SLBC convenor banks in several states have since reported achieving 100 per cent financial inclusion in one identified district. Further, in order to ensure that persons belonging to low income groups, both in urban and rural areas, do not face difficulty in opening bank accounts due to the procedural hassles the Know Your Customer (KYC) procedure for opening accounts has been simplified for people with balances not exceeding rupees fifty thousand (Rs 50,000) and credits in the accounts not exceeding rupees one lakh (Rs 1,00,000) in a year. The Reserve Bank has directed banks to make available all printed material used by retail customers in English, Hindi and the regional language concerned. From January 2006, banks have been permitted to utilise the services of NGOs, SHGs, MFIs and other civil society organisations as intermediaries in providing financial and banking services through the use of business facilitator and banking correspondent models.

Banks have been advised to issue general purpose credit cards to eligible beneficiaries. The credit facility extended under the scheme is of revolving credit. The GCC-holder will be entitled to draw cash from the specified branch of bank up to the limit sanctioned. Banks would have flexibility in fixing the limit based on the assessment of income and cash flow of the entire household without any insistence on the security or purpose. Interest rate on the facility may be charged as considered appropriate and reasonable. Banks have been advised that they may utilise the services of local post offices, schools, primary health centres, local government functionaries, farmers' associations/clubs, well-established community-based agencies and civil society organisations for sourcing of borrowers for issuing GCC.

A simplified mechanism for one-time settlement of loans with principal amount up to Rs 25,000 which have become doubtful and loss assets as on 30 September 2005 was suggested for adoption. In case of loans granted under government sponsored programmes, banks were advised to frame separate guidelines following a state specific approach to be evolved by the State Level Bankers' Committee (SLBC). In order to assist the distressed farmers whose accounts have earlier been rescheduled/converted on account of natural calamities, as also farmers defaulting on their loans, due to circumstances beyond their control, banks have been advised in November 2006 to frame transparent One Time Settlement (OTS) scheme for such farmers, with the approval of their Boards. Banks have been specifically advised that borrowers with loans settled under the One Time Settlement scheme will be eligible to re-access the formal system for fresh credit. Banks were advised to retain this facility at all branches to achieve greater financial inclusion.

RBI monitors the implementation of various Central Government sponsored schemes for poverty alleviation and employment generation. These include Swarna Jayanthi Gram Swarozgar Yojana (SGSY) for rural development, Swarnjayanti Shahari Rozgar Yojana (SJSRY) for Urban Development, Prime Minister's Rozgar Yojana (PMRY) for the educated unemployed youth, Scheme for Liberation and Rehabilitation of Scavengers (SLRS) and Differential Rate of Interest Scheme (DRI). Targets are assigned to banks for achievement under these schemes and RBI monitors the performance of banks under these schemes. The Rural Financial Institutions (RFIs) in the country comprise of branches of commercial banks, Regional Rural Banks (RRBs), Local Area Banks (LABs), Cooperative banks and the Micro Finance Institutions (MFIs). While the Reserve Bank regulates and supervises the commercial banks and the LABs, the supervision of cooperative banks and RRBs has been entrusted with NABARD. There is no formal regulation for the microfinance sector in the country at present. The government is contemplating legislation for the microfinance sector and a Micro Financial Sector (Development and Regulation) Bill 2007 is under consideration of the Government.

It has been the endeavour of the Reserve Bank to improve credit delivery mechanisms to the small borrowers, particularly to the agricultural and Small-Scale Industries sector by creating a conducive environment for banks to provide adequate and timely finance at reasonable rates without procedural hassles to different sectors of the economy. The multiagency approach and nationalisation of banks ensured increase in outreach and more and more people got access to the banking services. This enabled a paradigm shift of approach from class to mass banking and helped in financial empowerment of the masses and reduced their dependence on the moneylenders. The policies relating to rural credit are being redesigned to bring about maximum financial inclusion of the poorer sections of the society. It has been decided to include only those sectors as part of the priority sector, which impact large segments of population and the weaker sections, and which are employment-intensive, vis a vis:

- Agriculture (Direct and Indirect Finance)
- Small Enterprises (Direct and Indirect Finance)
- Retail Trade
- Micro Credit
- Education loans
- Housing loans.

A target of 40 per cent of Adjusted Net Bank Credit (ANBC) or credit equivalent amount of Off-Balance Sheet Exposure, whichever is higher has been stipulated for lending to the priority sector by domestic commercial banks. Within this, sub-targets of 18 per cent and 10 per cent of adjusted net bank credit respectively, have been stipulated for lending to agriculture and weaker sections. Weaker sections include small and marginal farmers with land holding of 5 acres and less, and landless labourers, tenant farmers and share croppers; artisans, village and cottage industries where individual credit limits do not exceed Rs 50,000; Scheduled Castes and Scheduled Tribes; beneficiaries under various schemes benefiting BPL families based on income criteria, Swarnjayanti Gram Swarozgar Yojana, Differential Rate of Interest scheme, Swarna Jayanti Shahari Rozgar Yojana, Scheme for Liberation and Rehabilitation of Scavengers; Advances to Self Help Groups; Loans to distressed poor to prepay their debt to informal sector, against appropriate collateral or group security. Foreign banks operating in India are required to lend 32 per cent of ANBC or credit equivalent amount of Off-Balance Sheet Exposure, whichever is higher to the priority sector. Of this, a sub target of 10 per cent is for small enterprises and 12 per cent for export credit. The domestic scheduled commercial banks, both in the public and private sectors, having shortfall in lending to priority sector/agricultural lending target, are required to deposit in Rural Infrastructure Development Fund (RIDF) established with NABARD which has completed its twelfth year of operation. For increased credit flow to the SSI sector, a policy of priority sector landing to banks has been followed, not only for Indian banks but also foreign banks. Foreign banks have 32 per cent of NBC earmarked for priority sector, of which 10 per cent is earmarked exclusively for the SSI sector. Any shortfall in such lending by foreign banks has to be deposited in Small Enterprises Development Fund (SEDF) set up by Small Industries Development Bank of India (SIDBI).

For achieving the objective of inclusive growth, creation of large employment opportunities is of significant importance. SEDF set up through SIDBI focusses on the needs of small and medium enterprises. The objective is poverty alleviation through employment generation and SME development.

The banking sector in the country comprises of:

- Commercial banks (domestic and foreign)
- Regional Rural Banks (RRBs)
- Cooperative Banks (Urban and Rural)
- Local Area Banks.

The Cooperatives are organised with the objective of promoting thrift and self-sufficiency among the middle class/lower middle class population and providing credit facilities to the people with small means in the urban/semi-urban centres.

Several steps are being taken to strengthen the rural sector. They provide medium and long-term loans for making investments in agriculture, rural industries and in housing. NABARD was established on 12 July 1982 with the objectives of facilitating credit flow for agriculture and rural development, promoting and supporting policies, practices and innovations conducive to rural development, strengthening rural credit delivery system through institutional development measures, focusing on poverty alleviation and employment generation and supervising rural financial institutions (co-operative banks and Regional Rural Banks). As on 31 March 2007, the number of commercial banks and RRBs in the country was 85 and 96 respectively. The number of branches of scheduled commercial banks and RRBs are as under:

- Rural – 69,471
- Semi urban – 30,579
- Urban – 12,032
- Metropolitan – 11,304.

Financial Inclusion

Financial inclusion refers to delivery of banking services at an affordable cost to the vast sections of disadvantaged and low-income groups who tend to be excluded from the formal banking channel. Despite widespread expansion of the banking sector during the last three decades, a substantial proportion of the households, especially in rural areas, are at present outside the coverage of the formal banking system. The

Reserve Bank's broad approach to financial inclusion aims at 'connecting people' with the banking system. This does not restrict itself to mere credit dispensation; it also implies mainstreaming of the economically disadvantaged and facilitating their access to the payments system. This can be made possible and secured by incentivising the stakeholders and pursuing them with the notion that financial inclusion is a viable business model and opportunity for profit earning. Efforts towards 'financial inclusion' include sensitising the banks to the banking and financial needs of the common person and ensuring access to basic banking facilities and services.

On an all India basis, 56 per cent of adult population in the country has bank accounts – in other words, 44 per cent of the population is unbanked. There is regional disparity in the performance of the different regions of the country on this count. Further, the extent of credit inclusion is lower in the country at 12 per cent of adult population. To tackle this issue, Reserve Bank has taken the following measures in the recent years towards enhancing access to banking services.

Spread of Bank Branches

The southern region continues to enjoy the dominant share of bank branches at 27.8 per cent followed by the Central region at 19.9%, Eastern region at 17.2 per cent, Northern region at 16.9 per cent and Western region at 15.5 per cent. The North Eastern region had only 2.7 per cent of bank branches. The total number of scheduled commercial banks including RRBs increased from 69,801 at end June 2006 to 71,781 at end of June 2007. These comprised 30,633 branches and 24,838 urban and metropolitan branches. The share of rural branches declined further to 42.7 per cent during 2006–07 from 43.7 per cent of the previous year while the share of all other population groups increased. The decline in the number of rural branches is a definite cause of concern. It points to inadequate financial infrastructure in the rural areas.

To strengthen public redress mechanisms in Banks, the RBI constituted a committee on Procedures and Performance of Public Services audit and as per its recommendations Customer Service Committee of the Board of Banks have been set up. A Customer Services Department has also been set up in the RBI to ensure better customer–bank interface. The RBI's thrust is two-pronged empowerment and protection, along with extension of outreach of banking services. Awareness among the public is being inculcated through financial education using the print and audio-visual media. Protection is ensured through greater awareness of customer rights and through the fair practices code of banks, the work of the newly set up Banking Standards Code Board of India. Grievance and dispute redress is ensured through the Banking Ombudsman scheme.

Financial Literacy

In the context of the focus on financial inclusion and distress amongst farmers, there is a need for the formal financial system to look at increasing financial literacy and financial counselling. As part of the Community Reinvestment Act in the US, banks are expected to contribute towards educating persons from socially and financially disadvantaged groups on matters relating to their financial needs. Indian banks and financial market players should actively look at promoting such programmes as part of their corporate social responsibility. In a cooperative society having linkages to women, SHGs in urban slums, where the borrower was counselled in a full day programme on the implications of the loan, how the interest is calculated and so on, so that she is totally aware of its features. Banks could have similar programmes for their clients including farmers, inclusion of which will lead to the expansion of capabilities of persons to lead the kind of lives they value – and have reason to value. These capabilities can be enhanced by public policy, but on the other hand the direction of public policy can be influenced by the effective use of participatory capabilities by the public. Inclusion is at once the ultimate goal of social and economic arrangements and the most efficient means of realising general welfare. Social institutions like markets and financial institutions play a proactive part in development by enhancing individual freedoms and are in turn sustained by social values. The development of an institution and the freedom it offers to its clients are all closely interrelated; as Amartya Sen famously asks, 'What is the relation between our collective economic wealth and our individual ability to live as we would like?' He emphasizes on incorporating individual freedom as a social commitment to address the social basis of individual well-being and freedom. If economic development and financial inclusion go in tandem, the ends and means of development require examination and scrutiny for a fuller understanding of the development process; it is simply not enough to take as our basic objective just the maximisation of income or wealth. Development has to be more concerned with enhancing the lives we lead and the freedoms we enjoy. Expanding the frontiers of finance implies expanding the freedom that we have reason to value, for all. This makes our lives richer and more unfettered and also allows us to be fuller social persons interacting with and influencing the world in which we live to make it a better place. There are two distinct reasons for the importance of inclusion in the concept of development related respectively to evaluation and effectiveness. First, in the Normative Approach, Substantive Inclusion is taken to be critical. The success of a society is to be evaluated, in this view primarily by the Substantive Inclusion that the members of that society enjoy. This evaluation position differs from the informational focus of more traditional normative approaches which focus on other variables such as utility or procedural liberty or real income. Amartya Sen has attempted an analysis of markets and freedom which is pertinent to any discussion of financial inclusion.

Some of the steps taken to improve financial literacy are:

- The Credit Information Bureau Act passed by Parliament in 2005 will enable credit and personal histories of bank customers to be available and this will serve to further reduce transaction and information costs for banks.
- The State Level Bankers' Committee convener banks have been advised to set up, on a pilot basis, a financial literacy-cum-counselling centre in any one district and based on the experience gained, the concerned lead banks may set up such centres in other districts.
- To increase focused attention towards regional disparities, RBI constituted working groups in different states to suggest measures for enhancing provision of banking services in under-banked regions of the country such as the North Eastern region, Chhattisgarh, Uttarakhand and Bihar. The recommendations of these working groups are under implementation.

Thrust on Agriculture

The RBI has been encouraging banks to provide increased credit to the agricultural sector. With a view to doubling credit flow to agriculture within a period of three years and to providing some debt relief to farmers within the limits of financial prudence, the then Union Finance Minister had announced several measures on 18 June 2004. Reserve Bank/IBA had issued necessary operational guidelines to commercial banks in this regard. As on 31 March 2005, the total credit flow to agriculture by all agencies (commercial banks, cooperative banks, RRBs) was Rs 1,25,309.37 crore (target Rs 1,05,000 crore) which increased to Rs 1,80,485.57 crore (target Rs 1,41,000 crore) as on 31 March 2006 and stood at

Rs 2,03,296.38 crore (target Rs 1,75,000 crore) as on 31 March 2007, which indicates a 12.64 per cent growth in disbursement when compared to the year ending March 2006. During the year 2006–07, the total number of new farmers financed by commercial banks and RRBs together aggregated to Rs 70.69 lakh, which exceed the target of Rs 50 lakh set for the year by the Finance Minister as announced in his budget speech for the year 2006–07.

For focussed attention to agriculture, the RBI initiated the following steps in recent years:

- Advised public sector banks to prepare Special Agricultural Credit Plans (SACP) on an annual basis since 1994–95. The disbursements by the public sector banks to agriculture under SACP for the financial year 2005–06 aggregated Rs 94,277.79 crore constituting 110.88 per cent of the target. For the financial year 2006–07, the disbursements to agriculture from April to September 2006, under this plan was Rs 58,886.92 crore as against a target of Rs 1,18,159.91 crore for the whole year. The SACP mechanism has been made applicable to private sector banks from the year 2005–06. The disbursements to agriculture by private sector banks during the year 2005–06 amounted to Rs 31,199.22 crore, constituting 128.80 per cent of the target. For the financial year 2006–07, private sector banks have disbursed Rs 13,972.71 crore from April to September 2006 as against the target of Rs 40,656.23 crore for the year.
- The Kisan Credit Card (KCC) Scheme was introduced in the year 1998–99 to enable the farmers to purchase agricultural inputs and draw cash for their production needs. During 2006–07 (up to 31 December 2006), public sector banks issued 37.66 lakh KCCs covering limits aggregating Rs 19,781.46 crore. Cumulatively, the number of KCCs issued by public sector banks stood at 2.56 crore covering advances amounting to Rs 88,278.57 crore till December 2006.
- Based on the recommendations of the Working Group constituted under the Chairmanship of Professor S.S. Johl to suggest measures for assisting distressed farmers and in order to assist distressed farmers whose accounts have earlier been rescheduled/converted on account of natural calamities as also farmers defaulting on their loans, due to circumstances beyond their control, banks have been advised to frame, with the approval of their Boards, transparent

One Time Settlement (OTS) policies for such farmers. Such farmers would be eligible for fresh bank finance.

- The Reserve Bank constituted a Working Group to suggest measures to further simplify the procedures, thereby reducing the cost and time for obtaining agricultural loan, especially by small and marginal farmers. Three recommendations of the Working Group, viz., dispensing with No Dues Certificate (NDC) as a requirement, considering opening of counselling centres and extending credit to the landless labourers, share-croppers and oral lessees based on the certificates provided by Panchayati Raj, have been accepted and banks advised to initiate steps accordingly.

Promoting Credit Flow to Small and Medium Enterprises

- SMEs have proved to be a vital element of growth in the global economy.
- Their contribution to the economic development of both developed and developing economies has been well recognised. Throughout India, there is new recognition of the roles played by SMEs in the broader process of economic development as they act as the backbone of national economies.

It is the highest employment generating sector. They are a potential tool of poverty alleviation by creating self-employment avenues, significant contributor to a country's industrial production, exports, national income and GDP. These:

- are born out of individual initiatives and skills
- offer great operational flexibility
- enable low cost of production
- have a high propensity to adopt technology
- have a high capacity to innovate and export
- have high employment orientation
- utilise locally available human and material resources
- reduce regional imbalances despite the common features globally, countries do not use the same definition for classifying the SME sector.

3 parameters generally applied by governments to define SMEs:

- Capital investment in plant and machinery
- Number of workers employed
- Volume of production or turnover of business.

The contribution of SMEs is vital in as much as they, by and large:

make up 80–90 per cent of all enterprises
provide over 60 per cent of the private sector jobss
generate 50–80 per cent of total employment
contribute about 50 per cent of sales or value added
share about 30 per cent of direct total exports.

Table 21 Share of SSI in overall industry.
Source: RBI Annual Report.

Access to finance is very important as compared to many other constraints that impede economic growth. Financial access promotes greater equity. Ultimately the breadth and depth of the entire SSI sector affects individuals, SSI firms and financial growth. SSIs need greater access to finance and greater financial inclusion to ramp up their operations. SSIs enjoy a share of about 30 per cent of direct total exports. There is a regional dispersal of industries. In India, there are more than 3 million SMEs. They produce 50 per cent of industrial output. They contribute about 42 per cent of India's total exports. They contribute 30–40 per cent of value addition in manufacturing and produce a vast range of products, about 8,000 including consumer, capital or intermediate goods. Growth of the SSI sector in India has been rapid as per the table given below. Growth of the SSI sector in India has been rapid as per the figures given in Table 21:

Majority proprietary concerns are about 80.5 per cent, and 16.8 percent as partnership or Private Limited Companies. Rural industries are categorised as:

- Traditional industries based on traditional skills and techniques.
- Modern small-scale industries making use of modern technology.

Traditional industries are further subdivided into:

(a) Handicrafts producing highly selective goods of high skills.
(b) Village and household industries producing common consumer goods and utilitarian products.

Table 4.2 Share of SSI in Overall Industry.

Year	Overall industry	SSI
1998	6.6	8.4
1999	4.0	7.7
1999–2000	6.4	8.2
2000–01	5.2	8.1
2001–02	3.3	6.0
2002–03	5.7	7.7
2003–04	6.9	8.6

Table 4.3 Bank Credit to the SSI Sector, Growth Rate Percent.

1998	21.0
1999	11.4
2000	8.9
2001	6.0
2002	2.1
2003	5.6
2004	9.0
2005	13.3
2006	22.3
2007	29.2

Source: From Table 6.13 as appearing on p. 263 of RBI Report on Currency and Finance 2006–08, Volume II based on data as at end March of respective years compiled from *The Handbook of Statistics on the Indian Economy,* 2006–07.

All these units are non-homogeneous in structure. They produce diverse types of products from traditional handicrafts to high-tech products. They are generally highly labour intensive. They are thus suited for the Indian economic environment with scarce financial resources and large population base. They not only generate income but also ensure a more equitable distribution of national income and wealth since the ownership of these industries is spread wider than large-scale industries. SMEs remain credit constrained and they suffer from the problem of sub-optimal scale of operation and technological obsolescence. SMEs have largely ignored their research and development and have not embarked on new product development and technological upgradation. Today the competition is in terms of new designs, new usages, better services, reduced costs, improved quality, products with higher performance and variety, and all delivered simultaneously to enhance value to the customers. Non-availability of institutional finance on affordable and easy terms constrains SMEs. SMEs also have inadequate managerial skills to deal with day to day problems – of inventory, finances, personnel, suppliers and customers.

The emerging major concerns of the process which serve to increase exclusion, especially financial exclusion, are the impact of globalisation. Non-availability of credit, technology upgradation for differentiation, weak infrastructure support, labour legislations, quality consciousness, inadequate networking capacity, SMEs encounter many obstacles too. They confront problems relating to access to finance, counselling, information, skills, technology and markets. An additional challenge is posed by the policy and business environment in which they operate, which is changing rapidly as a result of market oriented reforms and technological change. What is needed critically is the formulation of a national SME policy. Development of service providers, development of the financial sector, competitive markets, policies and legislation, and suitable financial infrastructure is required. There is insufficient understanding of SME. Chambers of Commerce and trade associations should be included in the policy dialogue of ways to facilitate access to credit for the SME sector.

Rural enterprises need critical financial infrastructure especially adapted in government policies. Rural enterprises also need electrification, telecommunication and access to transportation infrastructure to bring their goods to market and to obtain raw materials and inputs. Extra efforts are required for female entrepreneurs such as providing childcare facilities and ensuring equal rights to assets. Support services for SMEs must be market-oriented.

Earlier programmes were mostly centralised and heavily subsidised and few proved effective. Experience demonstrates that successful business development services should be coordinated and run like a business. When designing a programme for support services, four essential success criteria need to be applied for the provision of these services. First, they should be demand led – reflecting an analysis of genuine need for the support service. Second, businesses like treating end-users as customers rather than beneficiaries. Third, these should be sustainable – provided on a fee-for-service. Fourth, these should be outcome-outreach oriented, going beyond the achievement of outputs to demonstrable and replicable outcomes. Training should be practical.

General awareness training is less useful than training in specific industry skills within a sector. Advisory services are best provided by the local private sector. SMEs need advice on specific business and technical problems. This requires the need of a professional services sector and private sector. Service providers are best equipped to handle this task in the long run. The government should encourage the growth of private sector providers. Cost recovery for services should be actively pursued, but some subsidisation is nearly always required. Subsidising demand for services can be more effective than subsidising supply. Development cooperation should focus on stimulating markets for business services and not on subsidising specific service providers. Services can be made more affordable and effective by letting the SMEs themselves choose among service providers. Where state-sponsored advisory services are deemed necessary, they should retain organisational independence. Dissemination of information can help develop the markets. Small enterprises suffer from a lack of information on available support and market signals. The government needs to foster the flow of information. The development of a national financial sector is a requirement for SME growth. Lack of access to finance can usually be found at the top of any list of problems of small business. Businesses generally start with their own resources and are under-capitalised. This is a major factor in their failure. In developing countries, the financing institutions are usually not able to meet the SME needs for seed money and investment capital as a result of high transaction costs, etc.

Table 4.4 Bank Credit to the SSI Sector.

Period	Percentage of Net Bank Credit
1998	27.0
1999	27.1
2000	26.4
2001	25.6
2002	24.9
2003	20.4
2004	21.0
2005	17.5
2006	16.6
2007	16.9

Source: From Table 6.13 as appearing on p. 263 of RBI Report on Currency and Finance 2006–08, Volume II based on data as at end March of respective years compiled from *The Handbook of Statistics on the Indian Economy*, 2006–07.

One of the major bank credit related factors affecting growth of credit to the SSI sector can be attributed to the high level of NPAs (17.6 per cent to 19.5 per cent) and growing incidence of sickness (1,40,448 number of accounts amounting to Rs 5,215.92 crores). Only 15 per cent of registered units could avail bank credit and of the Small Sector units and only 3 per cent could avail credit. Small Industries Development Bank of Inda (SIDBI) sets up fund of Rs 10,000 crores to assist SMEs at an interest rate of 2 per cent below Prime Lending Rate (PLR) and also venture finances to assist innovative projects.

SSI Finance: What the Future Holds

Credit Guarantee Fund Trust for SSIs is with a corpus of $170 million. Rural Industries Program aimed at setting up new enterprises and employment creation. More intensive initial work is essential to understand the complexity of the SME sector while designing the programs. Involve the private sector in design and implementation. It is crucial to involve the private sector in formulation and implementation since public sector civil servants are not the best placed to advise the private sector on how to develop itself. Programs need to be designed and implemented with other partners. SME development requires action on many fronts such as developing policy that supports the financial sector, providing credit lines and services, developing skills and building capacity. The exhaustive volume of work should be shared and coordinated among partners.

Cluster Development

The concept of cluster development offers new insights into the potential role of SMEs in enhancing their access to new technology. The characteristics of a successful cluster are:

- inter-firm cooperation
- cooperation blended with competition
- importance of local value systems
- flexibility and innovative capacity
- sectoral specialisation
- geographic proximity
- a local pool of skilled labour
- presence of a large number of firms.

There are 400 modern SMEs and 2,000 rural and artisan based clusters. These clusters contribute 60 per cent of Indian manufacturing exports. Some clusters are so big that they produce 70–80 per cent of the total volume of that particular product. Panipat produces 75 per cent of the total woollen blankets. Tirupur produces 80 per cent of the country's cotton hosiery. Agra has 800 registered and 6,000 unregistered small and cottage units making 1.5 lakh pairs of shoes per day with a value of $1.3 million and exporting shoes worth $57.14 per year. State-wise distributions of industrial clusters show that the top six industrially developed states account for 54.3 per cent of SSI units whereas 71 per cent of clusters are located in these states (Maharashtra, Gujarat, Punjab, Haryana, Tamil Nadu and Rajasthan). Location-wise, 65 per cent of clusters are in cities and only 13.5 per cent in small towns and rural areas. In the current decade, according to estimates of the Planning Commission, more than 12 million additional people will be seeking work every year. There are about 30 million unemployed or underemployed individuals in the country, with more than 75 per cent in the rural parts. Thus, to ensure full employment, more than 15 million new livelihoods will have to be generated every year. This is possible only through the SME sector.

Vulnerability of the Poor

The rural poor are increasingly becoming vulnerable to spiralling cycles of poverty because of low wages, seasonality of employment and still predominant dependence of agriculture on monsoons. India has 6,38,000 villages and 5,161 towns spread over 3.2 million square kms as per the census of 2001. The average population in a village was 1,161 which is not a viable figure for providing service delivery unless the population is more than 1,500. There is a significant rural/urban divide in the present population. Migration to urban areas will only compound the problems of urban poverty if employment and self-employment issues are not addressed through the SME sector. Separate initiative for rural industries programme is required for setting up new enterprises for employment creation.

Recognising the critical role and the special needs of the micro, small, and medium enterprises, RBI has instituted steps to promote financial inclusion. The sector touches the lives of the weaker and unorganised sections of the society. More than half of those employed are women, minorities, and the marginalised. Fifty seven per cent of the MSE units are owner-run enterprises with one person. They account for 32 per cent of the workforce and 29 per cent of the value added in nonagricultural, private, unincorporated enterprises. Infusion of appropriate technology, design skills, modern marketing capacity-building and easier access to credit can make this segment an expanding base for self-sustaining employment. The dispersed and decentralised Micro and Small Enterprises (MSE) sector pose special challenge. This sector has the second largest share of employment after agriculture and spans a wide range, including small-scale, khadi, village and coir industries, handlooms, handicrafts, sericulture, wool, powerlooms, food processing, and agro-processing, etc. Sericulture and other village enterprises can check rural-urban migration by gainfully employing people in villages. This is expected to take pressure off agriculture. The MSE sector can open up a window of opportunities. Credit alone cannot lead to promotion of this sector. There is a need to promote this sector creating 'growth poles' and 'business hubs', removal of credit barriers, upgradation of technology, and provision of marketing support. Indeed, credit availability is a major problem for MSEs. Small and Medium Enterprises Development Act 2006 is a step in that direction and should be implemented in spirit. There should be change in the approach from emphasis on loosely targeted subsidies to creating an enabling environment. A Cluster Approach can help increase viability by providing these units with infrastructure, information, credit, and support services of better quality at lower costs, while also promoting their capacity for effective management of their own collectives. The 11th Five Year Plan should restrict subsidies to those needed to create a level playing field and to reflect the costs or benefits to others in the society. The credit flow from public sector banks to medium enterprises is being monitored by the RBI on quarterly basis with effect from March 2006. As at the end of March 2006, the outstanding credit which stood at Rs 61,461.84 crore has increased to Rs 69,043.03 crore at the end of December 2006.

The total credit provided by public sector banks to SSI at the end of September 2006 was Rs 86,465 crore which formed 7.68 per cent of net bank credit and 19.14 per cent of the total priority sector advances of these banks. Out of these advances, advances to cottage industries, artisans and tiny industries amounted to Rs 38,256 crore, constituting 44.2 per cent of the advances to the SSI sector. RBI, as a policy direction, has initiated the following in recent years for the promotion of SME sector in the country.

- Public sector banks are advised to make operational at least one specialised SSI branch in every district and centre with a cluster of SSI units, the idea being to enable SSI branches in clusters to reap the benefits of scale and scope economies and the availability of specialised bank staff skilled in these areas would enable them to assist in swift and correct appraisal, sanction and disbursal of working capital and other facilities. At the end of March 2006, 629 specialised SSI bank branches were functionalised by the banks.
- Sickness is a major issue plaguing the SSU sector. On the recommendations of the Kohli working group appointed to address this issue, The RBI had issued detailed guidelines to banks in January 2002 for detection of sickness at an early stage and taking remedial measures for rehabilitation of sick SSI units identified as potentially viable. As per revised guidelines, the rehabilitation package should be fully implemented within six months from the date the unit is declared as viable/potentially viable.
- A one-time settlement scheme for recovery of Non-Performing Assets (NPAs) below Rs 10 crore for SME accounts was formulated and advised to public sector banks for implementation. These guidelines provide for a simplified, non-discretionary and non-discriminatory mechanism for one-time settlement of chronic NPAs in the SME sector, and for provision of fresh finance to these enterprises.
- A debt restructuring mechanism for units in SME sector was formulated for implementation by all scheduled commercial banks. Accordingly, detailed guidelines were issued to all scheduled commercial banks to ensure restructuring of debt of all eligible small and medium enterprises.

Poverty Alleviation and Employment Generation Programmes

It has been recognised and accepted that along with policies which promote economic growth, direct poverty alleviation programmes are needed which raise the income and purchasing power of the poor, particularly in the short and medium run. These are the targeted poverty alleviation programmes. They are categorised into:

- Wage employment programmes which are the public works programmes. These came to be implemented from the 6th Plan. The Employment Guarantee Scheme is the current scheme.

- Self Employment Programmes – The Swarn Jayanti Gram Swarozgar Yojana and the Pradhan Mantri Rozgar Yojana.
- The Public Distribution System (PDS) and nutrition programmes as the Integrated Child Development Services (ICDS).

India has had long experience in experimenting with labour-intensive public works. After independence in 1947, many schemes were supported by the Central Government such as the Rural Manpower programme in 1960; this was followed by the Food for Work programmes. These programmes provide employment and generate 'public goods' such as physical infrastructure. They also fit into the framework of Nurkse Idea. Nurkse regards surplus labour in low income countries as a potential saving useful for capital formation. In terms of person, days of employment created the Employment Guarantee Scheme is the largest in the world. The Employment Guarantee Scheme (EGS) of Maharashtra was one of the models for the EGS, which has been providing employment to the weaker sections of society in times of distress for the past three decades. Its unprecedented feature is guaranteed employment which makes it unique in the developing world.

The public distribution system, despite all criticism leveled against it, has been effective to some extent. It benefits the poor to a marginal degree. Secondly, there are so many loopholes that PDS ceases to have a significant impact on amelioration of poverty. The other targeted programmes which have achieved a degree of success are those where credit is channelised through banks and the subsidy component is released by the government. Targets are set by the government and the achievement thereof is monitored closely by both the government and the RBI.

Under the SGSY, at the end of September 2006, a total of 5,45,915 *swarozgaris* received bank credit amounting to Rs 408 crore. Under SJSRY, disbursements amounting to Rs 60.34 crore were made in 16,618 cases (out of 24,944 applications sanctioned) for the year 2006–07 as the end of September 2006. Under SLRS, out of the total 4,195 applications received, the number of sanctions and disbursements to 2,261 beneficiaries aggregated to Rs 6.7 crore and Rs 5.11 crore respectively. Assistance under the Prime Minister's Rozgar Yojana (PMRY) scheme as on March 2006 amounted to Rs 11,653.54 crore for 2,67,251 beneficiaries. The outstanding advances of public sector banks under the DRI Scheme, as on the last reporting day of March 2006, amounted to Rs 490.22 crore under 3.89 lakh borrowal accounts, forming 0.07 per cent of the total advances outstanding as at the end of the previous year, as against the target of one per cent.

Promoting Regional Rural Banks

The Regional Rural Banks (RRBs) were set up in 1975 and were expected to combine the local feel of the cooperatives with the efficiency and business acumen of commercial banks. Considering their importance in promoting financial inclusion and inclusive growth in rural and semi-urban areas, several steps have been taken to strengthen the RRBs. These are:

- In view of the importance of the RRBs as purveyors of rural credit, sponsor banks were encouraged to merge, statewise, the RRBs sponsored by them, in order to strengthen them. The Advisory Committee on Flow of Credit to Agriculture and Related Activities (Chairman Professor V.S. Vyas) in June 2004 recommended restructuring of RRBs in order to improve the operational viability of RRBS and allow them to reap the advantages of economies of scale. In order to establish RRBs as an effective instrument of credit delivery in the Indian Financial System of the Government of India, in consultation with NABARD, the concerned state government and the sponsor bank, initiated a state level sponsor. Bank-wise process of amalgamating RRBs was set up in September 2005 to overcome the deficiencies prevailing in RRBs and make them viable and profitable units. Prior to the process of amalgamation, a total of 196 RRBs, sponsored by 27 scheduled commercial banks and one state cooperative bank, in 26 states were operating in the country. With the amalgamation of 147 RRBs into 46 new RRBs, the total number of RRBs all over India, came down from 196 to 95 as on 31 August 2007. The total districts covered by the 45 amalgamated RRBs were 357 as on 31 March 2007 covering 2 to 25 districts. The number of branches of amalgamated RRBs as on 31 March 2007 was 10,563. The network is extensive, varying from 50 to 677 branches. It is expected that this structural consolidation of RRBs will lead to financially stronger and bigger RRBs in terms of size, business volume and outreach. This will pare their business and operational costs. Their penetrative outreach and local feel and familiarity gives them natural advantages. They are, thus, in a better position to achieve the objectives of rural development and financial inclusion.
- Certain measures were announced for RRBs in the Union Budget for 2007–08, proposing, among other things, that the RRBs, which have a negative net worth, would be recapitalised in a phased manner. Modalities for recapitalisation are being worked out in consultation with select sponsor banks and the NABARD.

- Considering the critical role of sponsor banks in positioning the RRBs as partners in development of the rural sector and in order to encourage synergies between the parent bank and the RRBs, the banks which are the sponsor banks of the RRBs need to take steps on issues pertaining to HR, IT and operations of the RRBs sponsored by them. Essentially they have to be allowed a free hand to grant autonomy and beef up infrastructural support in these areas.
- The Boards of RRBs also need greater independence particularly in matters of investments, business development and staffing vis á vis determination of staff strength, fresh recruitment and promotions inter alia. The recommendations of the Task Force, contained in its report dated 31 January 2007, are under consideration of the RBI.

Facilitating Microfinance

The RBI endeavours to create a facilitating environment for the development of the microfinance sector in the country. The interest of the RBI is a major step forward which has led to the promotion and growth of the microfinance sector. RBI advised banks to participate in the SHG-bank linkage programme of the NABARD and to consider financing SHGs as a viable business option by banks. Microfinance is categorised under priority sector lending and lending to SHGs brought under the weaker sections of the priority sector. Lending to the priority sector as the RBI Government dictates, is a mandatory obligation for banks. This enabling provision allows them to lend to the microfinance sector and reap the benefits of priority sector categorisation too. Banks under this dispensation can provide adequate incentives to their branches for financing the SHGs. In April 2005, NGOs engaged in microfinance activities were permitted to access ECBs up to US$5 million during a financial year for permitted end-use, under automatic route. Banks as per directive can use the services of NGOs/SHGs, MFIs and other Civil Society Organisations as intermediaries in providing financial and banking services through Business Facilitator and Correspondent models. The SHG-Bank Linkage Programme is the largest microfinance programme in the country with over 29 lakh SHGs being credit linked at the end of March 2007 with cumulative credit flow to the tune of more than Rs 18,000 crore.

Priority Sector Guidelines Revisited

The government and the RBI view credit as an integral part of promoting socioeconomic development in the rural sector and so certain segments of the economy were classified as priority sector credit. The scope of the priority sector underwent various changes over the years and recently the revised priority sector guidelines have been communicated to banks. The priority sector comprise of agriculture, small enterprises, retail trade, micro credit, education loans and housing loans. A target of 40 per cent of adjusted net bank credit has been stipulated for lending to the priority sector by domestic commercial banks. Within this, sub-targets of 18 per cent and 10 per cent of adjusted net bank credit respectively, have been stipulated for lending to agriculture and weaker sections. Thus, to improve credit delivery mechanisms to the small borrowers, particularly to the agricultural and Small Scale Industries sector by creating an enabling environment for banks to provide adequate and timely finance at reasonable rates without procedural hassles to different sectors of the economy. Thus RBI policies are designed to bring about maximum inclusive growth.

Loans Extended against Gold and Silver Ornaments: Reduction of Risk Weight

Loans against gold and silver ornaments are commonly availed of by the poorer sections of society in both rural and urban areas. These loans entail relatively low risk as they are extended with adequate margins and the collateral (gold or silver) is easily marketable, particularly where the size of the loan is small. Such loans being in the nature of retail (personal) loans attracted a risk weight of 125 per cent. In the Annual Policy Statement of the Reserve Bank of India for the year 2007–08, this risk weight was substantially reduced and hence provide a margin of comfort to the banks. Capital adequacy in India was introduced in April 1992, when all scheduled commercial banks (including foreign banks) were required to maintain a Capital to Risk-weighted Asset Ratio (CRAR) of 8 per cent in a phased manner. The stipulated minimum CRAR was increased to 9 per cent from end-March 2000. Essentially, under the above system the balance sheet assets, non-funded items and other off-balance sheet exposures are assigned. Taking into account the size, complexity of operations, relevance to the financial sector, need to ensure greater financial inclusion and the need for having an efficient delivery mechanism, the capital adequacy norms have been relaxed with respect to extension of loans against the collateral of gold. An enabling provision was made in the NABARD Act, 1981 permitting NABARD to provide microfinance services to the urban poor.

It is the context rather than the message that makes the Reserve Bank of India's recent exhortation to banks to follow inclusive practices particularly significant. Financial inclusion, in the sense of extending banking products at an affordable cost to the vast sections of disadvantaged and low income groups, is not new to India. For more than two decades after the bank's nationalisation, Indian banking consciously sought to position itself as a provider of services to the many unreached sections. The great wave of branch expansion that the government-owned banks undertook was greater than that taken anywhere in the world. That not only had the salutary effect of extending the geographical reach of the mainline banks, but also gave the not-so-well-off sections of the population access to modern banking. In other ways too, public sector banks were in the forefront of reaching out to sections that were once neglected. Designing new, innovative loan products for small-scale and agriculture sectors is an outstanding example. On the deposit side, customers could open savings bank accounts with as little as Rs 5. Indian banks need to lay far more emphasis on inclusive practices. There could be many reasons for this reorientation of their priorities. The reform era's emphasis on profitability and stringent accounting standards seems to have led banks to consolidate before expanding and reaching out to wider sections of society.

To understand the need for inclusion, let us understand financial exclusion as primarily the lack of access to appropriate, low cost, fair and safe financial products and services from mainstream providors for certain consumers and specific sections at the periphery of the frontier are excluded from banking services. An inclusive financial system facilitates efficient allocation of productive resources and thus can potentially reduce the cost of capital. In addition, access to appropriate financial services can significantly improve the day-to-day management of finances. It can also help in reducing the growth of informal sources of credit (such as moneylenders) which are often found to be exploitative. Thus, an all-inclusive financial system enhances efficiency and welfare by providing avenues for secure saving practices and by facilitating a whole range of efficient financial services. In recent years, the importance of an inclusive financial system is widely recognised in the policy circle and financial inclusion is seen as a policy priority in many countries (Kempson et al. 2004). The Government of India has also expressed its precise concern on the issue of overall inclusion in the development process through its various initiatives such as the Rural Employment Guarantee Scheme, the Bharat Nirman Programme, the Sarva Shiksha Abhiyan, among others. Most important, perhaps, is to reorient the attitudes of the operating staff to make them appreciate the benefits of extending the reach to wider sections of the society. Fortunately, all public sector banks now have access to the latest technology, the absence of which had been a constraint on their expansion initiatives.

Focus on Financial Inclusion in India

The Government of India in June 2006, constituted RRC to recommend a strategy to achieve higher financial inclusion in the country. According to the committee on financial inclusion,

'Financial inclusion may be defined as the process of ensuring access to financial services and timely and adequate credit where needed by vulnerable groups such as weaker sections and low income groups at an affordable cost.'

The financial services comprise the complete breadth – savings, loans, insurance, credit, payments, etc. The financial system has to provide its function of transferring resources from surplus to deficit units, but both deficit and surplus units are those with low incomes, poor background, etc. By providing these services, the aim is to help them come out of poverty. Consequently, the RBI has moved to enforce multiple policy and industry changes:

- Banks have been asked to voluntarily make available a 'no-frills' account, and all printed bank material has to be made available in regional languages.
- KYC procedures have been simplified for low income groups.
- Significantly, since January 2006, banks can provide a full range of banking services through 'business facilitator and correspondent' (i.e., MFI partnership) models. Previously, MFIs could only provide credit, but not open bank accounts.
- The Credit Information Bureau Act, 2006, will eventually establish a credit bureau that makes available credit histories of individuals and small businesses. This should lower risk for banks in extending credit further.

The approach to financial inclusion in developing countries such as India, is different from the developed countries. In the latter, the focus is on the relatively small share of population not having access to banks or the formal payments system, whereas in India, we are looking at the majority who are excluded. Financial inclusion can be dealt with in two ways.

One is exclusion from the payments system, i.e. not having access to a bank account and the second type of exclusion is from formal credit markets, requiring the excluded to approach informal and exploitative markets. After nationalisation of major banks in India in 1969, there was a significant expansion of branch network to unbanked areas and stepping up of lending to agriculture, small industry and business. More recently, the focus is on establishing the basic right of every person to have access to affordable basic banking services. The total number of savings account is considered to be a better indicator of banking penetration than other deposit accounts, as percentage of number of households was 137 in rural areas and 244 in the urban areas on the eve of reforms in 1991. The Indian economy in general and banking services in particular, have made rapid strides in the recent past. However, a sizeable section of the population, particularly the weaker sections and low income groups continue to remain excluded from even the most basic opportunities and services provided by the financial sector. To address the issue of such financial exclusion in a holistic manner, it is essential to ensure that a range of financial services is available to every individual. These services are:

- a no-frills banking account for making and receiving payments
- a savings product suited to the pattern of cash flows of a poor household
- money transfer facilities
- small loans and overdrafts for productive, personal and other purposes
- micro-insurance (life and non-life).

Microfinance – Non Banking Finance Companies (MF-NBFCs) could be permitted to provide thrift, credit, micro-insurance, remittances and other financial services up to a specified amount to the poor in rural, semi-urban and urban areas. Such MF-NBFCs may also be recognised as business facilitators of banks for providing only savings and remittance services and also act as micro-insurance agents. Opening of specialised microfinance branches/cells in potential urban centres for exclusively catering to microfinance and SHG-bank is required.

Thus, in consonance with the above approach, the RBI has taken a number of measures in recent years for drawing the financially excluded population into the formal financial system.

The Moneylenders' Act

In order to ensure that the enforcement/administration of the legislation pertaining to the Money lenders' Act is properly monitored, a new section has been proposed which would require the state governments to place an annual report on the administration of the legislation before the state legislature. The state governments should take adequate steps to publicise the maximum rates of interest notified under the Act, the offences under the Act and the dispute redress machinery provided thereunder. A new chapter in the states' moneylending legislations aimed at establishing a link between the formal and informal credit providers, to be called 'Accredited Loan Providers', has been recommended.

The Technical Group has recommended a set of conditions in the agreement between the banks/financial institutions and the 'accredited loan providers' as safeguard measures:

- The advances made by institutional creditors to accredited loan providers may be treated as priority sector lending.
- This would encourage the banks to take up the role of institutional creditors and disburse loans through the linkage with accredited loan providers as an additional business.
- Moneylenders should be registered compulsorily with the state governments.
- Unregistered moneylenders will be penalised.
- The procedure for registration and renewal should be made simple and hassle-free.
- In order to focus the legislation on the regulation of moneylending transactions, banks, statutory corporations, cooperatives, financial institutions, NBFCs and the RBI need to be kept out of the purview of the legislation.
- To provide the state governments with the flexibility of adjusting the rates of interest in accordance with the market realities.
- The maximum rates of interest to be charged by moneylenders should be notified by the state governments from time to time.
- While determining the maximum rate, the range of interest rates and costs and other expenses being charged should be taken into account.
- In order to prevent usury, the rule of damdupat has been recommended.

- Alternate dispute resolution mechanisms such as Lok Adalat and Nyaya Panchayat for speedy and economical dispensation of justice have been recommended.
- Alternatively, state governments may think of setting up of fast-track courts/designated courts to deal with disputes relating to lending transactions by moneylenders and accredited loan providers.

Pilot Project for 100 percent Financial Inclusion

The convener banks of the State Level/Union Territory Level Bankers' Committees (SLBC/UTLBC) in all States/Union Territories were advised on 28 April 2006 to identify at least one district in each State/Union Territory for achieving 100 per cent financial inclusion by:

- providing a 'no-frills' account and
- issue of general purpose credit card (GCC).

They were also advised that on the basis of experience gained, the scope for providing 100 per cent financial inclusion may be extended to cover other areas/districts. The SLBCs/UTLBCs were further advised to allocate villages to the various banks operating in the state for taking the responsibility for ensuring 100 per cent financial inclusion and also to monitor financial inclusion in the meetings of the SLBC/UTLBC from September 2006.

So far, 160 districts have been identified and 100 per cent financial inclusion has been achieved in the whole of Union Territory of Puducherry and in 28 districts in eight States (Andhra Pradesh, Gujarat, Haryana, Himachal Pradesh, Karnataka, Kerala, Punjab and West Bengal). All districts of Himachal Pradesh have achieved financial inclusion. An evaluation of the progress made in achieving financial inclusion in these districts is being undertaken to draw lessons for further action in this regard.

NCAER Survey on Services to Depositors and Small Borrowers in the Rural and Semi-Urban Areas

The RBI's Annual Policy Statement for the year 2005–06 proposed a survey for assessing customer satisfaction on credit delivery in rural areas by banks. Accordingly, the National Council of Applied Economic Research (NCAER) was entrusted with the job of carrying out a study on the quality of services rendered by branches of commercial banks to their customers (both depositors and small borrowers) in rural and semi-urban areas. The NCAER initiated the study in January 2006 and submitted the Report in October 2007. The study covered 930 bank branches across the country from 30 States/Union Territories, and included 9,300 depositors and 13,950 borrowers. Prompt service delivery at the counter and professional attitude of the bank staff in reaching out to the customers emerged as key determinants for customer satisfaction in rural and semi-urban areas.

Credit Counselling Centres

Financial literacy or financial education can broadly be defined as 'providing familiarity with and understanding of financial market products, especially rewards and risks, in order to make informed choices.' Viewed from this standpoint, financial education primarily relates to personal finance to enable individuals to take effective action to improve overall well-being and avoid distress in matters that are financial. Financial literacy goes beyond the provision of financial information and advice. The focus of any discussion on financial literacy is primarily on the individual, who usually has limited resources and skills to appreciate the complexities of financial dealings with financial intermediaries on a day to day basis. Financial literacy is considered an important adjunct for promoting financial inclusion and ultimately financial stability. Both developed and developing countries, therefore, are focusing on programmes for financial literacy/education. In India, the need for financial literacy is even greater, considering the low levels of literacy and the large section of the population, which still remains out of the formal financial set up. In the context of 'financial inclusion', the scope of financial literacy is relatively broader and it acquires greater significance since it could be an important factor in the very access of such excluded groups to finance. Further, the process of educating may invariably involve addressing deep entrenched behavioural and psychological factors that could be major barriers. In countries with diverse social and economic profile like India, financial literacy is particularly relevant for people who are resource-poor and who operate at the margin and are vulnerable to persistent downward financial pressures. With no established banking relationship, the unbanked poor are pushed towards expensive alternatives. The challenges of household cash management under difficult circumstances with few resources to fall back on could be accentuated by the lack of skills or knowledge to make well-informed financial decisions. Financial literacy can help them prepare ahead of time for life cycle needs and deal with unexpected emergencies without assuming unnecessary debt.

The OECD has brought out 'Recommendations on Principles and Good Practices for Financial Education and Awareness'. These recommendations are intended to help countries in designing and implementing effective financial education programmes. The RBI has advised banks to set up financial literacy and counselling centres on a pilot basis.

Use of Intermediaries as Agents through the Use of Business Facilitator and Banking Correspondent Models

In January 2006, the Reserve Bank permitted Banks to utilise the services of non-governmental organisations/self-help groups (NGOs/SHGs), microfinance institutions (other than NBFCs) and other civil society organisations as intermediaries. In providing financial and banking services through the use of business facilitator (BF) and business correspondent (BC) models. The BC model allows banks to do 'cash-in/cash-out' transactions at a location much closer to the rural population, thus, addressing the last mile problem. Banks are also entering into agreements with postal authorities for using the enormous network of post offices as banking correspondents.

The Actual Process

Laptops with suitable software packages were utilised to open accounts at the very doorstep of the target clientele. This was accompanied by doorstep delivery of services. A photographer accompanying the team took photographs, enabling immediate issue of financial inclusion identity cards to the members of the SHGs. 'No frills' savings bank accounts were opened on the spot, the financial requirements were analysed and overdraft, general credit card limits sanctioned, financial education on the usage of these facilities was also provided, coverage with low cost health and life insurance was also extended. Experience gained through the Mangalam project was replicated and a pilot project on similar lines was taken up in all the four regions of the Union Territory and successfully completed within a period of twelve months starting in December 2006. The Union Territory of Puducherry became the first state/Union Territory in the country where all the households were provided with a bank account. In all 1,41,245 'no frills' savings bank accounts were opened on the Mangalam model. All the 144 bank branches of 37 banks operating in the UT of Puducherry were involved in this exercise. In addition, government departments, insurance companies, NGOs and facilitators were involved in the project. The extensive household surveys revealed that the business hours of the banks were inconvenient for the poor. Visiting the bank during daytime meant loss of wages for the poor. Left with surplus funds and in the absence of saving avenues, the poor divert these funds to consumption expenditure. The lower strata of society depend only on informal non-institutional sources for meeting their credit needs. Lack of information and financial illiteracy inhibits them from approaching bank branches. This includes fear of the educated, fear of the literate, fear of the rich, fear of the high caste, fear of the government, fear of the police, fear of the state; myriad complexes contribute to this overall fear which is also prevalent in the towns and is marked in the villages. So who addresses all the small credit needs? Informal relationships, friends, relatives, on the basis of kinship ties, other affinity, informal contracts and for recurrent needs or for larger sums, the ubiquitous moneylender fulfills pressing immediate financial needs. The Indian Bank also replicated its Puducherry successes in Cuddadore in Tamil Nadu. The project was launched in July 2006 and was completed by August 2007 with the coverage of 100 per cent households. This was implemented with success in the Kollam district of Kerala. Most significant has been the success of the Indian Bank in urban replication of the model. This was successfully achieved in Dharavi, in Mumbai. Dharavi, Asia's largest slum has 3 to 3.5 lakh migrant workers working in several units as leather units, chakli factories, etc. The immigrants send money home regularly through relatives, friends returning to their native place and are able to save only through 'Chits'. These are migrant workers who lack a fixed address. Indian Bank introduced Smart Card banking in Dharavi, zero balance, no-frills accounts, Life Insurance, Health Insurance cover was offered. Indian Bank was the first bank to open a commercial bank branch with core banking facility and ATM facilities in the heart of Dharavi. Thus, the migrant worker can now save money from his earnings. The model has been replicated in Tharamani of Tamil Nadu and in Guntur, Andhra Pradesh. To overcome the barrier of digital recognition which is a huge hassle for the illiterate poor, the Bank has set up a first of its kind voice-guided and networked bio-metric enabled ATM. To increase the outreach for the common man, the Bank has embarked on a pilot project on Smart Card banking. These multi-application cards act as customer identity tokens utilising bio-passwords and enable transactions at the door steps of the customers. In Warangal district of Andhra Pradesh, villagers have received wages for the NREGP programme. National Rural Employment Guarantee Programme through savings bank accounts could be opened using smart card technology. The smart cards are fuelled by Radio Frequency Identification (RFID) technology incorporating 'biometric' scan of their fingerprints. Technology initiatives as Smart Cards, Biometric access, Voice recognition technology for ATMs in the rural areas can enable a breakthrough on the lines achieved by ITC's e-choupal. Village Knowledge Centres have been set up by some banks as they provide information on cropping patterns, seeds fertilisers, pesticides and empower farmers by keeping them abreast of the latest technological progress in Agriculture, Crop Management, Cropping Patterns, etc. They acquaint farmers with agro climatic zones and provide inputs on skill development, micro enterprises and formation of SHGs.

The Work of the ICICI Bank Business Model for the Rural Areas

ICICI Bank's agri-banking has created an interface between rural areas and mainstream financial service providers to maximise reach and leverage technology. This reduces the cost of finance delivery, devises customised solutions and offers complete supply-chain solutions for the corporate partner.

No White Spaces' Strategy

Under this strategy, the bank plans to have at least one touch point (collectively referred to as ICICI Bank Grameen Kendras which may belong to ICICI Bank or to partners) every 3–5 kilometres in rural and semi-urban areas. ICICI bank has adopted an entirely new model as a conscious attempt to leverage the strengths of the rural economy. Their business model for the rural areas is based on partnering with existing institutions and local people and offering a suite of products. They are thus attempting to create a distribution base effectively in 600,000 villages in India at one-tenth the cost of business transacted by their bank in urban India. The partner led model is more viable for them than a branch led model. They work with partners who are already present in the local community, RRB, Microfinance agency, fertiliser company, NGO, etc. This strategy allows them to scale up the rural lending model realistically at low overhead costs. Business Correspondents are agents identified by the bank to provide basic banking services such as opening bank accounts, collecting savings deposits, offering insurance products in rural areas. The bank has already launched this service in Orissa and Andhra Pradesh for deposit taking work with a variety of local institutions to provide these services under the Business Correspondent model. Similarly in insurance, ICICI Bank and its group companies – ICICI Prudential Life Insurance Company and ICICI Lombard General Insurance Company work with local institutions for design and delivery of insurance products – under the Bancassurance Model these policies will be sold at the ICICI Bank Grameen Kendras. Given the peculiar challenges of health insurance delivery, it has worked with hospital networks and third-party administrators to coordinate quality of health care as well. In order to facilitate better price discovery and price risk management for farmers, ICICI Bank promoted the National Commodity and Derivates Exchange (NCDEX) in collaboration with National Bank for Agriculture and Rural Development (NABARD), the National Stock Exchange (NSE) and Life Insurance Corporation (LIC). NCDEX along with its affiliate National Commodities Management Services Limited (NCMSL), is attempting to improve access to price derivatives for farmers, facilitate commodity based finance through banks, provide weather stations and improve the warehousing infrastructure. For its work in product development, ICICI Bank has combined its expertise in financial engineering with the insights generated by its partners and allied research institutions.

Till date, ICICI Bank and its group companies have designed and are resorting to scale products including the following: index-based rainfall insurance, catastrophic health insurance, working capital facilities for agriculture traders, working capital facilities for craftspeople and artisans, take-out finance for start-up local financial institutions, warehouse receipt based financing credit to low income households through partnership model and savings to low income households through the banking correspondent model. It is ICICI Bank's belief that in order to improve efficiency in financial intermediation, especially in the context of small unsecured loans, the role of technology is crucial. ICICI Bank's initiatives in technology may be broadly thought of in two categories:

Front-end technology investments – this includes issuance of smart cards with unique identifiers to its clients that help the client track financial services usage data on a real-time basis as well as sharing of credit information across ICICI Bank's network.

Back-end technology investments – this relates to investment in creating better core banking systems among its partner institutions. This enables more efficient data capture and sharing and reduces margin of error on transactions. ICICI Bank has collaborated with FINO – a company that seeks to provide front-end (smart card, point-of-sale terminals), back-end (banking software, performance management and reporting, MIS) and information services (credit bureau) to community-based financial institutions and is now looking to partner with NABARD, State Bank of India and the Credit Information Bureau of India Limited (CIBIL) to try and see if FINO could, as in the case of NCDEX, become a provider of these technology services on a system wide basis particularly to cooperative banks and non-bank finance companies engaged in the business of lending to and collecting savings from small borrowers. The participation of the RBI and NABARD in some of these initiatives that have a systemic benefit would be an accelerator of access to finance. The inability to track credit information or effectively recover collateral poses challenges to every lender in the financial system, forces distortion in product design and may even prevent entry of lenders. NCAER data for top 24 cities in India shows migration to higher income levels growing at over 40 per cent per annum, flexible repayment rates and rising incomes have enabled younger customers to avail of loans. The average age of consumers is coming down. There is a rapid growth in credit availablity, convenience is becoming a strong factor in rural retail with doorstep delivery or at point of sale of asset financed. Indian banking has strong growth prospects driven by demographics, industrial resurgence and deeper penetration of financial services. A paradigm shift in banking service delivery is necessary. ICICI bank has attempted to build a mass banking retail model. Traditional brick and mortar banking was faced with insurmountable overheads, large transaction costs and limited products channels, high costs of delivery and dependence on documentation and financial history coupled with an obsessive concern with inflexible rules and minutiae of documentation (all in detail and preferably in quadruplicate), all of which served as barriers to the extension of services to the rural clientale. Click and Portal banking per contra successfully leverages technology, to offer doorstep banking. Various methods like multiple channels franchisees, internet kiosks, partnerships, simple processes, minimum documentation resulting in penetrative outreach cover the operating costs.

Commercial Banks and Microfinance

Comparative advantage of commercial banks in Microfinance:

- Banks appear well positioned to offer financial services to an ever-increasing number of microfinance clients and earn a profit.
- Commercial banks have several advantages over non-bank micro-lending NGOs.

Advantage of Commercial Banks

- They are regulated institutions fulfilling the conditions of ownership, financial disclosure, and capital adequacy that help ensure prudent management.
- Many have physical infrastructure, including a large network of branches, from which to expand and reach out to a substantial number of micro-finance clients.
- They have well-established internal controls and administrative and accounting systems to keep track of a large number of transactions.
- Their ownership structures of private capital tend to encourage sound governance structures, cost-effectiveness, and profitability, all of which lead to sustainability.
- Because they have their own sources of funds (deposits and equity capital), they do not have to depend on scarce and volatile donor resources (as do NGOs).
- They offer loans, deposits, and other financial products that are, in principle, attractive to a micro-finance clientele.
- All of these advantages could give banks a special edge over micro-lending NGOs in providing microfinance services.

Obstacles

- Banks however lack some key ingredients – most of all, the financial methodologies to reach a low income population.
- There are some key related issues banks need to resolve to enter the microfinance market successfully. These are:
    - *Commitment:* The commitment of commercial banks (particularly the larger banks) to micro-enterprise lending is often fragile, and generally dependent on one or two visionary board members rather than based solidly in its institutional mission.
    - *Organisational structure:* Microfinance programmes need to be inserted into the larger bank structure in such a way that they have relative independence and, at the same time, have the scale to handle thousands of small transactions efficiently.
    - *Financial methodology:* Banks need to acquire an appropriate financial methodology to service the micro-enterprise sector – financial innovations that permit a cost-effective analysis of creditworthiness, the monitoring of a large number of relatively poor clients, and the adoption of effective collateral substitutes.

- *Human resources:* Given that microfinance programmes differ so radically from traditional banking, banks must recruit and retain specialised staff to manage these programmes. Issues of recruitment, training, and performance-related incentives require special consideration.
- *Cost-effectiveness:* Microfinance programmes are costly because of the small size of their loans and because banks cannot operate them with their traditional mechanisms and overhead structures.
- *Regulation and supervision:* Banks must communicate with banking authorities to ensure that reporting and regulatory requirements take into account the specialised nature of microfinance programmes.

Types of Banks in Microfinance

- *Full-service private commercial banks:* Most have a national presence and offer a host of financial products and services through an extensive branch network.
- *State-owned banks:* These large banks provide multiple services according to government priorities. They often act as a channel for government transfers, payments, or receivables and usually serve a large number of deposits.
- *Finance companies and specialised banks:* These smaller financial institutions focus on a particular sector, such as housing or consumer lending, and generally have a regional rather than a national presence.
- *Micro-lending NGOs* transformed into regulated banks or specialised financial institutions. These small institutions have limited regional presence and highly specialised programmes.

Challenges

Two institutional challenges remain in the continuing evolution of these programmes in microfinance. These are:

- The first is the search for the most cost-effective organisational form for large banking institutions to incorporate microfinance in an organisation inherently ill-suited to adapt to the cultural world of the microfinance clientele.
- The second is the most appropriate governance structure for former financial service NGOs evolving into banks. Within commercial banks in the developing world, integrated, separate, or hybrid forms of organisation are emerging through trial and error.

The ICICI Bank

ICICI started as an institutional lender and has grown to become the second largest bank in India. Its move into retail banking started in 1997. It was a newcomer and has had to compete with banks such as SBI with more than 14,000 branches and 200 year old history in retail banking. To compete, ICICI redefined distribution access by moving away from the approach of building branches as the primary source of access to retail customers. ICICI was able to innovate and define access through multiple channels. Today, it is the largest PC-based bank in India with more than 5 million active PC banking customers. ICICI also plans to double its credit card base from 3 million to 6 million by 2010. Much of these additions would come from the southern states with Tamil Nadu being the key market. They have found that credit card spending has been witnessing rapid growth rates in the south. The bank also hopes to double its personal loan disbursement which is now Rs 500 crores every month. In its bid to reach lower middle-class segment, they have introduced the small ticket personal loans ranging from Rs 10,000 to Rs 15,000. They have also set up specialised lending facilities at 30 branches in interior Tamil Nadu to facilitate jewel loans. To reach the interiors they are tying up with the postal department. ICICI also has the largest and fastest growing base of ATMs in India. It has an installed base of 2,500 ATMs. In addition to its own initiatives, in building retail access, ICICI also formed partnerships with large rural marketers such as ITC and EID Parry to access farmers through their networks.

Partnerships

They have also partnered with NGOs towards SHG linkage. Further in acquiring The Bank of Madura (which had built a strong base of rural distribution through SHGs in South India), it gained access to 10,000 such groups involving more than 2,00,000 customers. In a period of six years, through this approach to retail customer access, ICICI has a retail base of 9.8 million customer accounts and is growing at a rapid rate.

Costs of Managing SHGs

ICICI manages with 16 managers, a portfolio of 2,00,000 customers at the BOP. Each project manager supervises the work of six coordinators who are from the local communities in which they work. Coordinators are women who are experienced in the development of SHGs. They help project managers in the approval of loans and help develop new SHGs. The coordinator administers the work of promoters and also trains them. The primary responsibility of promoters is the formation of new SHGs. The promoter must form 20 groups per year. She is rewarded with financial compensation for the successful formation of new groups. The promoters are identified from the local communities and thus have credibility among the village.

The general sales and administration costs of this system are about 5–10 per cent of the costs of a typical bank. This makes the system cost-effective and makes small transactions profitable. Further, this also allows for rapid scaling. ICICI increased from 2000 SHGs in 2002 to 10,000 in 2003. ICICI has also partnered with Aravind Eye Hospital to hold medical eye clinics for cataract surgery. The bank pays the travelling expenses of the surgeons and staff, and Aravind performs the necessary surgery, free of charge. 68,000 villagers have been tested and 4000 surgeries performed in 70 eye clinics. The federation of Joint Meeting Committees (JMCs) represent tens of thousands of women and is chiefly responsible for the handling of emergency funds. Each JMC is run by three female officers and is comprised of 20 SHGs from 10–20 villages. These female officers meet once every 3 months to monitor the internal lending activities of the 200 to 400 women. This internal fund is created by each member contributing Rs 10 and is available as petty cash. The loan is typically used for emergency medical purposes and must not exceed 300 rupees. The JMC is also responsible for the creation and maintenance of an information booth constructed in one of the central villages.

Information Booth

The information booth displays events such as births and deaths in the village and world news. The booth costs 1,000 rupees to create and is monitored in part by the promoter and coordinator assigned to the area.

Welfare Fund Scheme

The WFS is a form of life insurance. Its purpose is to cover the remaining principal of an outstanding loan on the death of a member and to help the family pay for the funeral expenses. The SHG as a single entity becomes eligible for the WPS after 11 months of formation and must decide to participate as a whole. Each member contributes Rs 310 to a common fund held in a fixed deposit account at ICICI. Currently, the aggregate of WFS represents 2,873 SHGs with more than 54,000 members and 15.7 million rupees in deposits. The interest this account collects is paid to a member's family in case of death to assist in funeral arrangements and other adjustments. The WFS is run by seven elected trustees who oversee the application process. Till March 2003, they received 74 applications for disbursement and paid out more than Rs 5,10,000.

Partnership Model

ICICI's objective is to combine the social mobilisation strength of NGOs and MFIs with the financial strength of the bank. The partnership model helps to overcome the constraints faced by NGOs and MFIs in scaling up their activities. This is to increase distribution points and to cost effectively serve the BOP.

Indirect Channels Partnership Model

The model looks to leverage the current infrastructure and relationships that MFIs and NGOs have in place to deliver banking services to the rural poor. By piggybacking on this network, ICICI does not have to implement a costly brick-and-mortar network expansion model. The partnership model essentially looks at microfinance as a viable business activity but with the financial institutions playing a catalytic role of providing cash flow funding for the initial 3 years to the service provider. ICICI provides the MFIs with a line of credit to meet their cash flow deficit for 3 years. In the fourth year the MFI begins to repay the loan within 2–3 years.

Rural Kiosks

ICICI has set up additional partnerships with EID Parry, n-Logue, ITC e-Choupal and BASIX to take advantage of the rural kiosk network that they have established. Each partnership is designed to build on the unique strengths of each organisation and to truly leverage their experiences and relationships.

Future Initiatives

The rural ATM machine placed in kiosks is a simplified version of a regular ATM. With multiple interface and multiple languages, the rural ATM will be accessible to all and is expected to cost Rs 3000.

ICICI is also investigating the possibility of a mobile ATM installed in a truck that would circulate through a number of villages on a specified predetermined route. It is also looking at venture capital to share in the risk with the enterprising poor in ventures of high return. Venture capital would enable the poor to invest in long-term assets.

Conclusions

Financial inclusion has positive externalities and is a public good. Reserve Bank has been closely engaged in formulating appropriate policy responses to spur banks to engage in the processes of financial inclusion facilitation. The formal financial system has to recognise the huge unmet demand for financial services from those who normally tend to be excluded. The focus on financial inclusion comes from the recognition that financial inclusion is imperative. It is to be viewed as a business strategy for growth and banks have to position themselves accordingly. The ICICI Bank has evolved a successful model for rural penetration and it could serve as a replicable model. The RRBs and the cooperative banks who already enjoy penetrative outreach in the rural areas have also to seize the initiative. There are opportunities and challenges and much that remains to be done in this area.

Innovations for Ramping Up Access to the Poor – Branchless Banking – Smart Cards and Mobile Telephony

Through its guidelines on the Business Correspondent – Business Facilitator Model, the RBI created an enabling regulatory environment to foster innovation and increase the outreach of the banking system. Smart Cards and mobile telephony are part of this process which is transformational. Despite the spread of brick and mortar banking, we still have only one bank branch per 16,000 people. Click and Portal banking remains largely an urban phenomena. Yet it is widely recognised that a country which is on a high trajectory of economic growth must ensure growth with equity; hence the policy focusses on financial inclusion. Access to banking mainstreams the poor and helps to bring the unorganised sector within the ambit of the formal financial system. In poorer countries, barriers of illiteracy and geography have been bridged by mobile banking and smart card banking which has helped leapfrog past click and portal and enabled poorer sections to bridge the digital divide and avail the benefits of access to financial services. Banks in collaboration with state governments have successfully leveraged technology to expand the frontiers. The RBI is working in tandem to take banking services to the most far flung and remote corner of the country leveraging small handheld devices and mobile phones. New technologies, smart card, virtual credit card, mobile phones ensure expedient banking services at affordable cost. A smart card or chip card is a pocket sized card with an embedded integrated circuit to store data and process information. Smart card enhanced systems are currently used in several key applications including banking, healthcare, telecommunications, secure identification, and other applications. Under this smart card project, a customer is given a smart card which acts like a bank's passbook. The smart card provides customer's identity, transaction store and biometric data to the bank. It eases services such as opening of no-frills loan accounts, savings accounts revolving general purpose credit, government beneficiary schemes, fund transfer, remittance, recurring deposits, joint accounts, insurance premium collection and utility bill collection.

The main barrier successfully addressed is – lack of access to markets and the last mile problem.

The financial inclusion project commenced on a pilot basis in several areas with active participation from the state government. The approach is to create branchless banking infrastructure by establishing a network of business correspondents – a banking outpost in each village. A Common Service Point (CSP) is identified in the project areas which offer banking facilities. The CSP is manned by a local person familiar with the area and able to communicate fluently and liaise effectively with the local population. A database is maintained with the help of a handheld device and mobile connectivity. The services are utilised on commission basis. Villagers are provided smart cards with biometric identification to access their accounts. The introduction of IT-enabled financial inclusion facilitates easy payments to beneficiaries under various schemes of the state and central governments such as social security pension schemes and the National Rural Employment Guarantee Scheme (NREGS), wages payments which are directly deposited in their bank accounts on the Brazilian Pattern where payments under the 'BOLSA FAMILIAS' programme of the government are made to the recipients entirely through an electronic benefit card (EBT). Public Sector Banks are actively partnering state governments in the financial inclusion project among the Private Sector Banks. ICICI Bank and the HDFC Bank have been the leaders of the pack while Axis Bank and others are also making headway. The Andhra Pradesh government pioneered the initiative by providing an operational framework for increasing outreach of mainstream banking and financial services to the poorest through technology based solutions in August 2006. Rolled out as a pilot project implemented by six mandals of Warangal district and two of Karimnagar through six banks (SBI, SBH, AB, UBI, APGVB, and Axis Bank) payments commenced in May 2007 and are continuing with upscaling of the model – the vision is to achieve Total Financial Inclusion (TFI) through smart cards. Based on the recommendations of the RBI high level committee on the subject the GOAP embarked on the second phase of upscaling since August 2008 using the One District – One Bank model. The success of the project led to the identification of eight other districts where the state government proposes to roll out the project in Medak, Mahbubnagar, Chitoor, East Godavari, West Godavari, Nellore, Krishna and Vishakapatnam districts. The state government's vision is to upscale in a phased manner to all the 23 districts of the state. The project disburses pensions and wages through smart card based IT enabled services provided by participating banks. On 30 November 2008 the smart card project was extended to the entire Krishna district ensuring financial inclusion for 75 per cent of the hitherto uncovered poor. Electronic benefit transfers to social security pensioners under the AP Social Security Pension Scheme (APSSP) and National Rural Employment Guarantee scheme are possible. Under the RBI incentive policy, banks are entitled to receive Rs 50 for every smart card account opened. The Financial Inclusion Fund (FIF) and the Financial Inclusion Technology Fund (FITF) each with Rs 500 crore have been placed with NABARD and Government of India has issued rules for administration of the fund.

Syndicate Bank, SBI and Canara Bank are launching Smart Card Account project in the three districts of Chitradurga, Bellary and Bagalkot in coordination with the government of Karnataka. The smart card will enable farmers to avail government pension, social security payments, National Rural Employment Guaranteee Programme (NREGP), payments and wages. The project is expected to cover the entire state in phased manner. Syndicate Bank is implementing the project on financial inclusion solutions based on iMFAST (Integra's Mobile Financial Applications Secure Terminal) system, a service by Bangalore-based Integra Micro Systems (P) Ltd. iMFAST is a platform designed to handle financial applications specifically targeted at rural customers. PNB for IT-enabled financial inclusion, had identified 27 pilot projects (20 in rural areas and seven in urban areas) to be launched across 13 states in Indo-Gangetic belt.

Out of the 20 rural pilot projects, six pilot projects had already been launched at Neemrana, Rajasthan, Tineri Panchayat, Patna, Bihar, Matki Jharoli, Saharanpur, UP, Gararu, Gaya district in Bihar, Mauli Jagran, Chandigarh Kullu and Himachal Pradesh. Similarly the Indian Bank has been active in Tamil Nadu. SBI's IT-enabled devices and biometric scanners coupled with smart card will provide banking services to far flung areas of the state of Madhya Pradesh. Nine commercial and private banks will be allotted various districts with two blocks each. Banks have responded positively. SBI has also rolled out its Tiny Card in Uttaranchal and in Mizoram in the North East. The Raghuram Rajan Committee on Financial Sector Reforms (CFSR) has advocated the early adoption of m-banking solutions to speed access. The Rangarajan Committee on Financial Inclusion has given a clear strategic direction of the way forward. It is clear that branchless banking represents the wave of the future as it enables banks and users to, on the upside:

- Cut costs
- Eliminate impersonation and fraud thereby plugging leakages in transfers of wages and benefits to the poor
- Promote overall inclusion.

However, on the downside:

- The initial costs involved in setting up electronic infrastructure are prohibitive
- There are also significant costs in building up a rural agent network to disseminate the information and build the competency to enable people to attain the capability of accessing the service
- Whether in the long run this will increase depth and actually promote inclusion remains a moot point.

Though DFID/CGAP have done research in the subject area they have found that the usage of mobile telephony or smart card banking was restricted to:

- Receiving welfare payments
- Making deposits/withdrawals
- Balance enquiry.

Contrary to popular belief while the possession of a mobile or a smart card increases awareness it does not automatically promote access to the entire range of banking services. It also leaves a question mark as to whether people who use the services primarily to get payments under NREGS or other benefits would still continue to use it beyond mere receipt and drawal of wages.

Other technical issues are of meeting the challenge of ensuring:

- Customer safety
- Compliance with AML/CFT guidelines — Anti-money laundering and financing of terrorism guidelines norms as laid down by the Financial Action Task Force (FATF) and the Prevention of Money Laundering Act (PMLA).

In sim/smart card based operations customer data/personal identification data is encrypted on the smart card, service providers merely host this information on behalf of the banks.

Application based security also remain critical. DPSS guidelines issued on 8 October, 2008, have addressed these issues, however they need to be seen in praxis.

These are teething troubles, on a macro perspective, by leveraging technology. We can ensure financial inclusion in the years to come as Nandan Nilekani expresses it-'A key piece of infrastructure atop an interconnected grid is the electronic flow of funds. This requires that each uniquely identified citizen or organization has a bank account into which money can be transferred from the state. This could be an account in a bank, a post office or with a self help group. Within this system the ID smart card can function as a mobile, non transferable, electronic passbook. The impact on inclusive growth and India's savings rate from implementing this would be massive as 80% of Indians do not have a bank account and therefore lie outside any sort of banking system besides perhaps the one represented by the exploitive moneylender and his steel cash box. Linking smart cards to such accounts can open up the banking system to hundreds of millions of people. It also introduces the possibility of offering direct services ranging pension and benefit payments to trading accounts to an unprecedented number of people.'

It is an experiment which is significantly transforming banking across the globe. Russia, Argentina, South Africa (Wizzit), Brazil (Bolsa Familias), Pakistan (Tameer Bank) Phillippines (SMART) and Ghana among others testify to its success.

References

Anand, Adhikari (2006). 'ICICI Bank's Rural Thrust', *Business Today,* June 4, 84–88.

Ananth, Bindu (2005). 'Financing Micro Finance: ICICI Bank's Partnership Model', *Small Enterprise Development Journal,* Vol. 16, No. 1.

Chakraborty, K.C. (2006). *Financial Inclusion: Concepts, Issues, and Roadmap.* CMD Indian Bank Institute for Development and Research In Banking Technology, Hyderabad.

Harper, Malcolm and Kirsten Marie. (2006). 'ICICI Bank and Microfinance Linkages in India', *Small Enterprise Development Journal,* Vol. 17, No. 1.

Helms, Brigit, Xavier Reille (2004). 'Interest Rate Ceilings and Microfinance: The Story So far', CGAP Occasional Paper No: 9, www.cgap.org.

Iyer, Preeti (2006). 'ICICI Bank to Cover 60 Districts by Year-end', *Business Standard,* March 16.

'ICICI Bank Launches New Initiative in Microfinance', *The Hindu Business Line,* July 14, 2006.

'ICICI Bank to Hire More Banking Correspondents', *The Hindu Business Line,* August 2, 2006.

Mohan Rakesh at the Annual Bankers' Conference Hyderabad on November 3rd 2006.

Morduch, Jonathan and Stuart Rutherford (2003). 'Microfinance: Analytical issues for India', Essay for the World Bank, South Asia Region – Finance and Private Sector Development, April 2003.

Rajan, Raghuram (2006). 'Separate and Unequal', *Finance and Development,* Volume 43, Number 1, March 2006.

Chapter 5

Microfinance Experience and Other Institutional Approaches

While the international studies on poverty have been rich and abundant, theoretical and empirical studies have been made on the subject of measuring poverty and targeting the poor for income transfer programmes. Several other strands that deal with specific sets of measures to either protect or promote the poor have also emerged. The growing interest in microfinance as a strategy for poverty alleviation is a case in point. There is a need to identify the key impediments in providing microfinance services to the poor and the necessity of a framework for scaling up the services rendered by various organisations to the poor and the unorganised sector. Introduction of the right incentives and removal of distortions would undoubtedly enable the sector to fulfil its developmental obligations, specifically the enhancement of accessibility of financial services to the poor. While the World Bank has estimated the annual demand for credit support from the 75 million poor households at Rs 450 billion, the extent to which this demand is satisfied by the formal banking sector and by the MFIS has not been ascertained. Several micro level studies however indicate that the poor still continue to depend on informal sources of credit and these sources account for 40 per cent to 60 per cent of household demand. The challenge for mainstream banking institutions and the microfinance sector is how to bridge the gap. The emergence of microfinance brings into sharper focus the need to provide appropriate delivery mechanisms for financial services and the poor are willing to pay for door delivery of reliable financial services. The Indian microfinance sector is characterised by the diversity of approaches. With the patronage of NABARD the SHG – Bank linkage model has grown to be the dominant model of microfinance delivery. A significant number of institutions have also adopted the Grameen methodology. RRBs and cooperatives have made some headway in reaching out to the poor though they have the potential to do much more in this regard. Some private sector banks such as the ICICI have taken the initiative in collaborating with microfinance institutions to ensure continuous flow of funds to members of groups. The rural financial system functions through more than 150,000 retail outlets. Despite the rapid growth of banking network in India and the phenomenal expansion and outreach of the banking system, the poor remain underserved. The All India Debt and Investment survey shows that the share of non-institutional agencies (informal sector) in the outstanding cash dues of the rural households was quite high at 38 per cent (1981). It also showed that households in the lower asset groups were more dependent on the non-institutional credit agencies.

The Development Theology of the Sixties, Seventies and Eighties

Through the 1980s, the policy of a direct frontal attack through the dispensation of subsidised rural credit came increasingly under the scanner due to the disappointing performance of rural credit programmes. Poor loan recovery, prohibitive administrative costs, agricultural cooperative, Regional Rural Banks and rural branches of commercial banks, if evaluated on the profit centre concept, were largely insolvent. The potential for domestic financial markets to act was limited. Between the 1950s and 1970s governments focused their attention on providing credit to small and marginal farmers with the hope of raising productivity and income; efforts to expand access to agricultural credit emphasised government interventions in the form of targeted credit through state-owned development banks at below market rate of interest. In India, these were the decades of the green revolution, but the interest rate subsidy on loans with limited cross subsidisation was not an unqualified success. Populist schemes and announcements of write-offs and loan waiver had an impact on credit discipline. The borrower's perception of loans changed and the loans were treated as state largesse to such an extent that the loanees were termed beneficiaries. Rural Banks suffered a massive erosion of their capital, subsidised lending rates and poor repayment discipline created further iniquities in the rural financial markets as the funds meant for the poor were cornered by the better off farmers.

Financial Systems Approach

A new Financial Systems Approach supplanted the earlier theory. This viewed credit not as a productive input essential for development but as a financial service which needed to be finely priced. It held that interest rate ceilings and credit subsidies retarded development, discouraged disintermediation between savers and investors and benefitted larger producers more than small-scale low income producers.

Strategy for Inclusive Growth and Effective Poverty Alleviation

The 1990s saw a growing enthusiasm for promoting microfinance as a strategy for inclusive growth and effective poverty alleviation. The microfinance sector blossomed in many countries, leading to multiple financial services, firms serving the needs of micro entrepreneurs and poor households. It had two features:

- High repayment rates
- Cost covering interest rates

These enabled the sector to achieve long-term sustainability and extensive outreach among the poor. UN Secretary General Kofi Annan on 29 December 2003 announced 2005 as the 'International year of Micro Credit. Speaking on the occasion he said, 'The stark reality is that most poor people in the world still lack access to sustainable financial services, whether it is savings, credit or insurance. The great challenge before us is to address the constraints that exclude people from full participation in the financial sector… Together we can and must build inclusive financial sectors that help people improve their lives.'

Characteristics of Informal Financial Markets

Informal financial markets are an integral part of all economies. They are more pervasive in the developing countries than in the developed ones (Basu 1994, Besley 1995, Ray 1998, Von Pischke 1991). Large segments of the population do not have access to the formal institutions, though their need for intermediation and other services is high. This demand for services is satisfied by institutions in the informal sector. The popular view of informal activities is that they are primarily those of petty traders, street hawkers, shoeshine boys and other 'underemployed' groups on the streets of big towns. The evidence however suggests that the bulk of employment in the informal sector, far from being only marginally productive, is economically efficient and profitable, though small in scale and limited by simple technologies, little capital, and lack of links with the other formal sector. Within the informal sector we find the entire range of basic skills needed to provide goods and services for a large though often poor section of the population.

Some of their characteristics are:

- An ease of entry groups self select their borrowers
- Reliance on indigenous resources, family, affinity group
- Group ownership of enterprises
- Small scale of operation
- Labour intensive and adapted technology
- Unregulated and competitive markets.

In the budget for the year 2010, the Finance Minister, Pranab Mukherjee, announced that it has been decided to provide appropriate banking facilities to habitatories having population in excess of 2000 by March, 2012. It also committed that 'the government will bring about a major expansion in schemes for microfinance based on self help groups, particularly in the backward and ecologically fragile areas of the country.' Self help groups should graduate from consumption to production credit for starting micro enterprises. As per the NSS survey, 60 per cent of our population does not have access to credit products, which means the bulk of India's population remains unbanked. Efforts needed to be intensified for mainstreaming the populations has been emphasised time and again. The poor are bankable, creditworthy, responsible and reliable borrowers.

Microfinance as a Natural Vehicle for Financial Inclusion

As the penetrative outreach of microfinance enables it to extend credit facilities to the poorest of the poor, the hardcore and assetless poor, in remote and unbanked regions, it is the natural vehicle for promoting financial inclusion. The growth of microfinance and its popularity in India is important for the facilitation of rapid inclusive growth. Micro finance is a positive development in which Indian institutions have acquired considerable expertise and where scaling upholds great promise to expand the nature of financial services offered to micro enterprises and also to make these the springboard for entrepreneurial development.

Let us delve into the meaning of microfinance:

(i) Microfinance is defined as 'the provision of thrift, credit and other financial services and products of very small amounts to the poor in rural, semi-urban or urban areas so as to enable them to raise their income levels and improve their living standards.'

(ii) Microfinance institutions are those that are characterised by their commitment to assisting typically poor households and small enterprises in gaining access to financial service.

(iii) Other financial services can include a broad range of services including credit, savings, insurance and remittances.

Services and Clients

MFIs provide a wide range of services. The best known activity of MFIs is to provide credit to poorer households and small enterprises. Some MFIs offer other financial services such as insurance, advice and training to their clients and this training is often closely linked to the MFIs' main activities. The primary clientele of MFIs consists almost by definition those who face severe barriers in accessing financial products from conventional financial institutions. These barriers comprise mainly high operational costs and risk factors. An MFI's clientele may be distributed in remote locations, possess few negotiable assets and live in an environment where enforcement of formal property rights and other contracts is expensive and uncertain.

MFIs have to be innovative to overcome these barriers. Incentives for loan repayment, dynamic incentives where a borrower initially receives a small sum but as a satisfactory repayment history is established, the borrower may obtain progressively larger sums. The threat to discontinue any further lending when loans are not repaid, strengthen repayment incentives. Small business loans may be a prominent part of MFI activities, but lending and deposit taking to smooth consumption by households may be more important for most MFIs and their clients. Providing saving facilities not only enables households to smooth consumption but is of value in establishing a financial record. One of the lessons of the recent development of the MFI sector is that even the poorest is eager and able to save.

Legal forms of MFIs in India are broadly into 3 categories. These are:

- Not for profit MFIs such as societies, Public Trusts or Section 25 companies
- Mutual Benefit MFIs include cooperative societies, Mutual Benefit Trusts or Nidhis registered under Section 620 of Companies Act 1956
- For profit MFIs that include NBFCs registered under the Company Act.

Operating Models of Retail MFIs

The SHG model: SHGs tend to be homogeneous in nature. The NGO mobilises clients into SHGs and provide savings and credit services. The SHG lends money to its members. Linkages with banks are also arranged for credit purposes.

The Federated SHG Model: SHGs are federated into an institution in the following ways:

- SHGs are registered as cooperatives in states where an enabling cooperative environment exists

- Some small SHGs operate as solidarity groups by adapting the Grameen model and in turn are federated into large cooperatives
- Within this broad structure there can be operating variations depending on the strategy of the promoting NGO.

The Grameen Bank Model: Share Microfin in India is one of the prominent Grameen replicators which has adopted the strategies of the Grameen Bank. Share Microfin Limited (SML) is a Micro Finance Institution (MFI) providing financial and support services mainly to rural women in India.

Urban Cooperative Bank Model: Direct lending to clients in urban areas is done through an Urban Cooperative Bank. Two prominent examples are the SEWA bank, Ahmedabad and the Cuttack Cooperative Bank, Orissa.

Trade based Group Model: The establishment of a structure which manages typically industrial activity.

The NBFC model – for example, Basix.

A Non-Banking Financial Company (NBFC) is a company registered under the Companies Act, 1956 and is engaged in the business of loans and advances, acquisition of shares/stock/bonds/debentures/securities issued by government or local authority or other securities of marketable nature, leasing, hire-purchase, insurance business, chit business, but does not include any institution whose principal business is that of agricultural activity, industrial activity, sale/purchase/construction of immovable property. There are few regulated microfinance intermediaries in the country. Institutions in this category are NBFCs and cooperative banks that have to comply with and fulfil the stipulated regulatory requirements.

NBFCs: NBFCs are registered under the Companies Act, 1956 and regulated by RBI. NBFCs require a minimum Net Owned Fund of Rs 25 lakhs and for a new NBFC, Rs 2 crore. To protect the interest of the depositors, RBI has introduced strict regulations for NBFCs such as maintenance of a minimum standard of NBFC, rating by approved rating agencies, capital adequacy and liquid assets. The prominent NBFCs working with the poor are – Basix, Sarva Jana Seva Kosh, Sangamitra, Share, CFTS.

Cooperative Banks: In the cooperative banking segment, engaged in microfinance among the poor, in addition to SEWA Bank, the latest entrant is the Cuttack Urban Cooperative Bank. Although a cooperative bank has many advantages over NBFCs, the dual control of Registrar of Cooperatives and the RBI has, in many ways, restricted these institutions in achieving their full potential.

Specialised Service Providers: These institutions exclusively work as MFIs with a minimal provision of other services such as health or education. Within this category there exist 2 sub-categories: (a) those that provide retail MF services like savings, lending money and raise funds from members or other financial institutions and (b) those that function as MF Wholesalers or Apex bodies giving financial support to smaller institutions.

Multi-Service Provider: In the Indian scenario, a large number of NGOs registered as societies or trusts have taken up microfinance services as an extension of their community development programmes like providing health services, education, income generation, environment, etc. In this case microfinance is bundled with existing social intervention or occupies a position equal to or less than other programmes.

Retail NGO – MFIs: During the last decade retail NGO – MFIs have come to dominate the retail service landscape with the most widely practiced model being the SHG. Most of them choose to either get credit linkages established through local branches of banks or get credit directly to later on lend the funds to SHGs.

SHG Federations: The several forms of SHG federations make it difficult to classify their operating features around one simple model. In some SHG federations the next level from the SHGs is the cluster which gathers SHGs from a geographic unit and in turn federates them into a larger unit called federation. Certain retail services are undertaken by SHGs, in others by the cluster and in still others by the federations. The point of service in this structure finally determines the point of interface with the local bank. During the past few years, community based organisations are emerging which are directly borrowing from either the government or non-government lenders and are well on their way to becoming full-fledged MFIs.

Mutually Aided Cooperative Societies (MACS)

Andhra Pradesh enacted the Mutually Aided Cooperative Societies Act in 1995. Cooperatives formed under this Act are largely immune from government interventions in their affairs such as fund raising, governance, etc. and over 2000 MACS have been formed so far. These MACS provide savings, borrowings and loan insurance services to their members. Three other states, Bihar, Madhya Pradesh and Jammu and Kashmir have also enacted similar MACS Acts. In Bihar, out of 667 societies formed under the Bihar Self-Supporting Cooperative Societies Act 1996, only 14 were credit cooperatives. In Tamil Nadu the cooperative act allows for a great deal of government intervention. The cooperatives cannot even enact its own by-laws and must adopt the by-laws given by the state. In addition, under certain circumstances, the government can take control of an organisation registered under the Act.

Set of Financial Standards

Indicator	Benchmark
Operational Self Sufficiency (OSS)	At least 100 per cent
Porfolio at Risk (PR) > 60 days past due	Less than 10 per cent
Current Repayment Rate (CRR)	Greater than 90 per cent
Operating Cost Ratio (OCR)	Less than 20 per cent
Total Cost Ratio (TCR)	Less than 30 per cent
Active borrowers per Credit Officer (ABCO)	Between 250–350

Indicators

- OSS = Operating Income/Operating costs + Loan loss + Financing costs
- PR = Unpaid principal balance of past due loans/Total Gross Outstanding portfolio
- CRR = Total Amount collected for the period-repayments/Total amount due
- OCR = Total operating costs/Average outstanding portfolio
- TCR = Total costs/Average outstanding portfolio
- ABCO = Average No. of active borrowers/Average no. of credit officers.

Microfinance in India and Asia

Micro Credit Ratings International Limited (M-CRIL) is based at New Delhi and has been involved in setting rating standards for MFIs in Asia. Rating of microfinance institutions is very important as it gives lenders – both institutions as banks and non-institutions as donors, a level of comfort relating to the soundness and the financial health of the institutions. As microfinance institutions attempt to reach those at the bottom of the pyramid, hitherto denied access to financial services, it is even more important for them to ensure that the services which they provide to the poor are on an ongoing and sustainable basis. Hence, they must have constant financial health checks done. Micro Credit Ratings International Limited (M-CRIL), one of the rating agencies along with rating agencies set up by NABARD fulfills this function. It is based at New Delhi and has been involved in setting rating standards for MFIs in India. M-CRIL has completed 170 MFI ratings covering India, Nepal, Bangladesh, Cambodia, Indonesia, Kazakhstan, Philippines, Sri Lanka and East Timor. The rating of microfinance institutions is done on standard financial parameters – portfolio quality and credit discipline enforced on the borrowers, the nature and variety of penalties and sanctions imposed on the borrower. Assessment of the borrowers' repayment capacity is done keeping in view the income streams of the borrower.

Ideally, the microfinance institution should be able to sustain its operation based on the business it does. Rating agencies also focus on rating the non-financial aspects of the business as the quality of human system – the human resources, the commitment and dedication of those working in these organisations, the systems which have been put in place to monitor loans, to be in touch with grassroots level clients, the handholding of borrowers, and the overall quality of the borrowers affects the overall quality of the loan portfolios. In addition to the quality of the Board, the synergy between its members, their vision and capability, the direction they provide, and their vision for the microfinance organisation is also rated and forms part of the overall governance rating parameter.

Analysis

(i) An analysis of the regional distribution of MFIs: Heavily focused on South India and a sprinkle across India. 60 per cent of Indian MFIs are concentrated in Andhra Pradesh, Tamil Nadu, Karnataka and Kerala.

(ii) Institutional characteristics of sample MFIs: Disaggregated by model and age – In India 60 per cent follow the SHG model, followed by the mixed model, and an equal number of individual banking and Grameen Bank model.

(iii) Institutional characteristics: Though there is a trend widely in India towards profit and formal registration as finance companies or rural banks, there is a constant dominance of not-for-profit institutions. Microfinance activity in Asia is seen as a rural rather than urban activity quite unlike Latin America.

(iv) The sample by portfolio size: There are many small MFIs but the large ones are also increasing. In India, 60 per cent of MFIs have portfolios less than Rs 63 lakhs. There is however, a strong correlation between portfolio size and the age of an MFI.

Client outreach and productivity – Coverage is low in relation to the number of poor people in the region but staff productivity is better than the international average. The number and size of MFIs in India is small in relation to the number of poor people in the country. They cover no more than 10–15 per cent of the 60–70 million poor families.

(v) Outreach: Significant in membership numbers but not substantial in terms of portfolio size. The 110 MFIs covered in the study provide financial services to nearly 2.7 million clients. Of these about 72 per cent (1.9 million) are in India distributed mostly in South India. 64 per cent of total membership is serviced by SHGs, while in other Asian countries the Grameen Bank model takes the lead.

(vi) The ratio of active borrowers to total clients is the highest in the Grameen model where 87 per cent of members are active borrowers, while SHG based MFIs tend to have much lower active borrowers to client ratio (average 28 per cent). The mixed methodology lies somewhere in between at 44 per cent.

(vii) Loans outstanding: Grameen MFIs provide small loans to a large number of clients and Asian MFIs have miniscule outstandings compared to the international average. The Indian MFIs had outstandings of nearly Rs 238 crores. 40 per cent of this is with MFIs using the Grameen model while mixed model MFIs provide 31 per cent. The top 10 MFIs own 32.8 per cent of the portfolio, an indication of the polarised nature of the sector in the region.

(viii) Member savings: Member savings are not always recorded by MFIs with SHG programmes. The 90 Indian MFIs raised some Rs 145 crores but if the actual level of savings made by the members is taken into account then the figure for total savings would increase to Rs 360 crores. This is a low average savings per member as the average savings of 416.50 per MFI client in Asia is miniscule compared to the average savings balance of $269 for the rest of the world.

(ix) Staff productivity: Grameen and mixed programmes are most efficient while social orientation of SHG programmes result in low member staff ratios. The MFIs studied had a staff strength ranging from 3–906 with the average number of staff at about 79 per organization.

(x) Operating efficiency and portfolio quality: Individual banking is spending a lot more per borrower than the SHGs. The cost of delivering micro loans in the region is of the order of $14.40 while the SHG model is most efficient costing just $7 per loan client.

(xi) Operating expense ratio: Typically high costs and the absence of cost-based pricing results in inefficiencies and a gap between the yield and OER. The OER for more than 50 per cent of the MFIs was greater than 25 per cent while in India it was just under 20 per cent.

(xii) Portfolio quality: Grameen programmes are the best performers.

(xiii) Portfolio financing: MFIs are increasingly treating debt and savings as the main sources of funds. Equity investment is constrained by image and regulation.

(xiv) Uses of funds: Sub-optimal deployment of funds in loan portfolio, a few large MFIs face problems of capital adequacy.

(xv) Rating grades achieved by MFIs: Relatively few are creditworthy enough to borrow significant sums of money. The Grameen MFIs rated have been amongst the best of all types, followed closely by the individual banking model. Some of the weakest organisations use the SHG model.

List of some MFIs in India

ASSIST, Guntur, Andhra Pradesh

Spandana, Guntur, Andhra Pradesh

Swayam Krishi Sangam, Hyderabad

Star Youth Association, Velgode, Andhra Pradesh

SHARE Microfin Ltd., Hyderabad

Social Education and Voluntary Action (SEVA), Warangal, Andhra Pradesh

Krishna Bhima Samruddhi Local Area Bank Limited (KBS LAB), Mahboobnagar, Andhra Pradesh

MARI, Hanamakonda, Andhra Pradesh

Pragathi Seva Samiti, Hanumkonda, Andhra Pradesh

Bharti Integrated Rural Development Society (BIRDS), Nandyal, Andhra Pradesh

BASIX, Hyderabad
Bharat Integrated Social Welfare Agency (BISWA), Sambhalpur, Orissa
Darbara Sahitya Sansad, Arapada, Orissa
Gram Utthan, Pimpuri, Orissa
People's Rural Education Movement (PREM), Berhampur, Orissa
Swayanshree, Cuttack, Orissa
Center for Youth and Social Development, Bhubaneshwar
Janodaya Trust, Bangalore
Rashtriya GraminVikas Nidhi (RGVN), Guwahati
Mahaseemam Trust, Madurai, Tamil Nadu
Bullock-Cart Workers Development Association (BWDA), Villupuram, Tamil Nadu
Nav Bharat Jagriti Kendra, Hazaribagh, Jharkhand
New Life, Trichy, Tamil Nadu
Prochesta, Guwahati
Sa Dhan, New Delhi
Rajpur Seva Niketan, Rajapur, West Bengal
Rural Aid Service, Churachandpur, Manipur
Gram Vikas, Mehsana, Gujarat
Holy Cross, Hazaribagh, Jharkhand
Grameen Development Services (GDS), Lucknow, Uttar Pradesh
Grameen Mahila Syamsiddha Sangh (GMSS), Pune
ESAF, Trichur, Kerala
Cashpor, Varanasi, Uttar Pradesh
Bandhan, Kolkata

Role of Microfinance in Expanding Access to Financial Services

In several countries, financial services are available only to a small percentage of the population and the majority of bankable people in the world do not yet have access to them. Various constraints hamper the inclusion of different population groups that need access to financial services, especially women. We know that access to well functioning financial systems can empower individuals economically and socially, allowing them to better integrate into a country's economy and actively contribute to its growth. Microfinance plays a critical role in expanding that access. Significantly, it has a vital role to play as part of the Millennium Development Goals, in which, in 2000, United Nations member states agreed to halve poverty by 2015.

Inclusive Financial Sectors: The Road to Growth and Poverty

Financial services for the poor are an integral part of an Inclusive Financial Sector. The potential for domestic financial markets to act as drivers of growth and poverty reduction over the long-term has been demonstrated. There is an urgent need to place greater value and emphasis on access to financial services by poor households and enterprises. Kathryn Imboden asserts that

> In this context, microfinance, often treated as a social measure distinct from the established financial sectors needs to be taken out of a finance 'ghetto', and become fully integrated into the mainstream of the financial sector. It is necessary to forge partnerships among domestic and international financial sector stakeholders to establish the necessary preconditions, tackle constraints and ensure a favourable policy environment to achieve an integrated financial sector. Micro finance is not an exercise in charity. As the microfinance industry matures, there are more opportunities for domestic and international finance actors to enter this market profitably while contributing to poverty reductions worldwide. Over time the role of the private sector is expected to increase exponentially.

The Concept Underlying Cooperatives and Microfinance

The concept of microfinance is not new. Savings and credit groups have operated for centuries. The concept of the credit union was developed by Friedrich Wilhelm Raiffeisen and his supporters in the late nineteenth century in Austria. It was formed to enable the rural population to break out of the clutches of moneylenders. These credit unions expanded rapidly over the Rhine province. The cooperative banks spread rapidly over Europe, America and the rest of the developing world. In Indonesia, Peoples Credit Union or the Bank Perkreditan Rakyat became the largest microfinance system numbering close to 9000 units.

Formal credit and savings institutions for the poor have been around for decades providing customers who were neglected by commercial banks, a way to obtain financial services through cooperatives. Development finance institutions, an interaction of Savings and Credit groups extending revolving credit facilities include the 'susus' of Ghana, 'chit funds' in

India, 'tandas' in Mexico, 'Arisans' in Indonesia, 'cheetu' in Sri Lanka, 'tontines' in West Africa and in Cambodia and 'pasanaku' in Bolivia. Besides which there are numerous savings clubs and burial societies all over the world.

Rotating Savings and Credit Institutions

In the area of savings mobilisation and credit provision, Rotating Savings and Credit Associations (ROSCAs) are important institutions around the world. An incomplete bibliography identifies more than fifty communities or regions that utilise the institution. In Mexican communities, both in Mexico and the United States, ROSCAs are known under names such as *tanda, cundina, rol, rifa, bolita, mutualista, quincela, vaca, vaquita,* and *ronda*, each name describing a slight variation of the basic institution or a regional/linguistic difference (Valez-Ibanez, 1983). ROSCAs also exist in the developed nations, significantly in immigrant groups, or closely tied communities like the Caribbean people in New York, the Mexicans in Texas and California, and the Chinese communities in the West. ROSCAs remain a popular choice even in countries where the formal institutions have expanded quite rapidly. Besley and Levenson (1996) estimate that 68–85 per cent of the adult population in Taiwan is involved in ROSCAs at any given point in time. Bouman (1995) reported using various sources, that 'membership in Republic of Congo comprises about 50 per cent of the adult population (male and female), and 50–95 per cent in many rural areas in Liberia, Ivory Coast, Togo, Nigeria and Cameroon.' Till recent times, ROSCAs have not been the subject of scholarly attention in economics. Early studies come from anthropology and sociology. The ROSCA form the base of the Self Help Groups. These are essentially pure thrift institutions. They have to transform themselves into institutions which support and promote micro enterprises as income-generating projects which provide livelihood support. In this context, naturally their success depends on choice of products to be produced, the markets to be served, and the creation of an appropriate marketing mechanism.

Starting in the late 1970s, experimental groups in India, Bangladesh and Brazil began extending loans to groups of poor women to enable them to set up small microenterprises and income-generating projects. This micro enterprise credit was based on the principles of solidarity and group lending. They had three distinguishing features. The first feature was credit-led poverty alleviation. These programmes either offered only credit, or offered a combination of credit and training. Credit-led programmes focussed on making low-cost credit available to the poor. Second, practice of peer lending or lending to 'solidiarity groups', and the best example of this method was of targetting loan recipients. Third, they targeted very poor borrowers generally women, whom they helped to set up small income generating self-sustaining livelihood projects.

SEWA Bank

In 1972, the Self Employed Women's Association (SEWA) was registered as a trade union in Gujarat with the basic objective of strengthening its members' bargaining power to improve incomes, employment and access to social security. In 1973, to address their lack of access to financial services, the members of SEWA decided to found a bank of their own. Four thousand women from rag pickers to *beedi* workers contributed to its share capitals from their meager earnings and became its shareholders. Thus the Mahila Self Employed Women's Cooperative Bank was set up in 1974. Since then it has been blazing a trail and providing banking services to poor illiterate self-employed women and has become a viable financial venture providing inclusive banking in the true sense of the word. Self-employed workers are those who earn a living through their own small business or through selling their own labour. These are workers who have no fixed employee – employer relationship and depend on their own labour for survival. They are poor, illiterate and vulnerable. They barely have any assets or working capital but are extremely economically active, contributing very significantly to the economy and society with their labour. This sector of the economy is called the unorganised sector. There are four types of self-employed or unorganised sector workers:

- Hawkers, vendors and small business women selling vegetable, fruit, fish, eggs and other food items, household goods and clothes.
- Home-based workers like weavers, potters, *beedi* and *agarbatti* workers, *papad* rollers, readymade garment workers, women who process agricultural products and artisans.
- Manual labourers and service providers like agricultural labourers, construction workers, contract labourers, handcart pullers, head-loaders, domestic workers and laundry workers.
- Producers.

SEWA considers itself not merely as a workers' organisation, but as a movement. It is in fact, a confluence of three movements – the labour, cooperative and women's movement. Gandhian philosophy is the source of inspiration for SEWA. SEWA has an all India membership of 2,50,000 members today. Over the last 25 years SEWA has organised poor self-employed women using the dual strategy of struggle and development, thus enabling them to enter the mainstream of the economy. In this process, women have become more confident and autonomous. Through its joint strategy, SEWA has helped workers organise around various issues, resulting in their being able to raise with government as well as in the society in general.
Some of the salient features of the bank are:

- (i) It is financially viable and self-reliant from the beginning
- (ii) The bank acts as an instrument to transfer assets to women; it insists that since loans for housing are in the women's name, the house itself should be in her name
- (iii) SEWA has also helped women build their own water structures – wells, hand-pumps, ponds giving them control over natural resources
- (iv) By establishing a relationship of trust, high recovery rates have been established and enabled members to come out of the clutches of moneylenders
- (v) It has helped the members to develop skills to deal with formal institutions and trained them in the habit of banking.

Sewa offers its members the following services:

- Income generation loans
- Limited number of consumption loans
- Housing loans
- Integrated work security scheme on contributory basis, work security insurance, maternity benefits
- Loans to participate in Ahmedabad Municipal Corporation's programme
- A variety of savings products based on recurring deposit principle as also pension scheme
- Comprehensive insurance product
- Personal financial counseling
- Business counselling
- Training programmes on opening and effectively using a bank account.

Clients come to the SEWA Bank through three main sources:

- Through SEWA organisers, who work in the field and are in personal contact with self-employed women
- Through existing members of SEWA and SEWA Bank
- Through word of mouth.

SEWA Bank account holders are made up of approximately 70 per cent urban and 30 per cent rural self-employed women. The urban depositors are engaged in three predominant activities – vend, labour and home based work. The average monthly income of a member of SEWA Bank is Rs 1,500. Savings is mobilised through depositors. SEWA Bank's credit fund comprises additional funds of Rs 2.88 crore from HUDCO for housing loans, additional funds of Rs 2.7 crores from HDFC for long-term housing/infrastructure loans. SEWA Bank has a average loan repayment rate of 94 per cent. SEWA Bank charges 17 per cent interest per annum for loans from its own depositors' fund and 14.5 per cent on loans accessed from finance institutions.
The various types of accounts that SEWA has are:

- Ghar Fund Yojana
- Mangal Prasang Yojana
- Chinta Nivaran Yojana
- Bhavi Suraksha Yojana
- Swapna Siddhi
- Jivan Asha.

SEWA also offers pension products.

None of the products available to formal sector employees are offered to women workers in the informal sector. So, SEWA Bank introduced pension for these women with the objective of giving its clients a certain degree of security in their old age.

Key Features of Urban Banking – SEWA Innovations

- Prevalence of client friendly delivery systems.
- Doorstep banking since the clientele is made up of economically active low income women who cannot go to the bank. SEWA Bank goes to them through two mobile vans covering the city daily and averages a collection of Rs 15,000 each per day.
- Apart from local counters, the latest addition is its team of '*Banksaathis*' who counsel the depositors on all aspects besides aiding in saving collections and loan repayments.

- Rural Banking is done through forming self-help groups at the village level and all savings of these groups are deposited at SEWA Bank.
- The district association organisers visit the villages and motivate rural women to form SHGs and SEWA Bank provides the necessary training to these groups. These groups are federated at the district level and registered.
- SEWA has consciously chosen to promote autonomous district level federations as opposed to opening branches of SEWA Bank in the rural areas – a decentralised approach as opposed to a supply driven, centralised approach.
- Capitalisation is understood as the process of capital formation, sustainability and growth at the level of the group as well as the individual household and the district association. The support to these groups is provided through a Capital Fund which is legally owned by the group and which is the main financial promotion instrument for the strengthening of the group. The fund is divided into two parts:
    - Revolving fund for loans (80 per cent)
    - Development fund for grants (20 per cent).

Financial Counselling

SEWA Bank's close interactions with women workers has shown a need for increased information, dissemination and financial planning among its clients, and thus, have developed financial counselling to plan for their future. The bank's strength lies in its integrated approach, i.e. the provision of financial services in conjunction with social security services and in organising women workers into their own institutions.

Insurance Facilities

Most of the insurance schemes available were not designed for poor people, and since most of the workers are in the unorganised or informal sector, they are unprotected although they contribute significantly to the nation's economy. SEWA Bank thus started an integrated insurance programme for its members in collaboration with insurance companies with three different packages to suit the needs and affordability of the members. SEWA showed the world that poor women can save, the poor do repay their loans and pay market rates of interest. The bank carries out its functions through simple procedures since most of them are illiterate and do not understand complicated procedures. These are the important replicable lessons for financial inclusion which SEWA Bank teaches. Commercial banks and new private sector banks would do well to take a leaf out of SEWA Bank promoted by the Gandhian Srimati Ela Bhatt.

Friends of Women's World Banking

The Friends of Women's World Banking, India is based at Ahmedabad. Its mission is to work towards a society based on equity and social justice where women are active partners in holistic development. It provides financial and capacity-building services to organisations promoting livelihoods and self-reliance of poor women. Through revolving loan fund (RLF), it provides bulk loans to partner NGO/MFIs to reach out to their women members for their sustainable income generation activities. The banks' comparative niche lies in identifying and nurturing nascent organisations by providing them loan and grand funds, and at the same time, building the capacities to become financially sustainable organisations.

The Grameen Bank of Bangladesh

Dr Muhammad Yunus of Bangladesh was the pioneer of micro credit when he started an experimental micro credit enterprise in 1977 after witnessing the cycle of poverty that kept many poor women enslaved to high interest loan sharks in Jobra village. He lent \$27–\$42 to women so that they could purchase bamboo to make and sell stools. Within a short span the women were able to repay the loans while continuing to support themselves and their families. The seeds of Grameen Bank were planted, which works on the very concepts of solidarity and group lending. It targets the poorest of the poor, generally women, as traditionally they are the weaker and the more impoverished. It works on the Joint Group Model, in groups of five members. Grameen Bank is a great step forward in financial inclusion. Through cooperative institutional arrangements of Self Help Groups working on the Joint Liability Group model he helped the poor overcome the institutional trap of poverty. The rural women in Bangladesh were trapped in poverty as local financial markets made them totally dependent on middlemen for short-term finance. Under the then prevailing arrangements the labour and capital markets were interlocked, the poor borrowed money from the local middlemen and sold their output to them at very low prices which left them with a pittance for sustenance. This inability of the poor to access finance and sell output at the right prices traps them into a poverty circle. Grameen Bank intervened exogenously and through its successful initiative broke the interlocked cycle of capital and labour markets, thereby making a significant breakthrough in the processes of fostering financial inclusion. At present, it is spread over more than 34,000 villages and it has more than two million members, organised into subgroups of five members, these are joined together into 40 member centers and is well -known for its innovative banking for the rural poor who are otherwise excluded from formal banking because they lack physical collateral such as land or other immovable property.

Most of Grameen Bank's loans are sanctioned to women and since its inception there has been an astonishing loan repayment rate of over 98 per cent. Some of the functions of Grameen Bank are:

- Homogeneous, affinity groups of five members are formed at village level
- The field worker facilitates the process of forming groups
- All the group members undergo a seven day compulsory training of one to two hours each day
- Some groups undergo the Group Recognition Test which is a screening mechanism between serious and non-serious groups
- Once the groups pass the GRT, then women become members of Grameen Bank by paying a one time member fee
- Eight joint liability groups affiliate to form a center
- Centre meets every week at a defined time and the meetings are very structured and the bank assistant attends the meeting
- Group discipline is enforced through peer pressure
- All loan applications have to be approved by other group members as well as centre members
- The loan disbursement is from Bank fund and not linked to savings
- Loans are of various kinds, general loan, supplementary loan, housing loan, sanitation loan, etc.
- Savings are compulsory for the members and each member saves TK 10 every week and the amount is deposited in the bank
- All loans are repayable within a year in 52 equal installments
- There is a provision of 5 per cent tax on all productive loans
- The group leader collects the loan repayments and savings and hands it to the centre leader who in turn gives it to the field worker–The collected money is never used for fresh loans
- Nominal interest rates are charged on flat basis 15–24 per cent

- The size of the Bank is approximately $100 million in equity; $275 million outstanding loan; has lent more than $2 billion; 2.3 million low income borrowers (94 per cent women)
- The average size of loan is $160 but can range from $1–$300
- Ownership of the Bank is 93 per cent Grameen borrowers and 7 per cent Government
- The number of villages served is 38,951
- Number of employees is 12,000
- Number of branches is 1,128
- Today the micro credit models have spread to over 50 countries worldwide including some advanced countries like U.S.A., Norway, etc.

Social Collateral

The Grameen Bank practices physical collateral free lending relying instead on peer monitoring and peer pressure to enforce loan contracts. It also provides the members with social development inputs, e.g. consciousness raising in health and nutrition training to make the poor both individually and socially accountable for their actions. Providing access to financial services to the poor, as the Grameen Bank believes, would help the poor to be self employed, generate incomes, thus helping them make their own way out of poverty. Further, providing social intermediation inputs would help them to be financially and socially disciplined. The success of microfinance in Bangladesh has attracted great interest around the world and several attempts are being made to replicate its success. Though critics allege that the Grameen Bank is nearer to being a provider rather than a promoter, in that it provides all financial services but gives little control or flexibility to its members/borrowers; hence real control vests in Grameen members and not in the poor, these are issues of intellectual debate. Grameen Bank's contribution to empowerment and the facilitation of inclusion especially financial inclusion has to be acknowledged. The success of Grameen Bank inspired other MFIs in Bangladesh, namely Association for Social Advancement (ASA), Bangladesh Rural Advancement Committee (BRAC) and *Proshika*, an NGO. The changing microfinance landscape of Bangladesh is marked by increasing outreach, market crowding and challenges of innovating – a challenge of moving from doing more of the same to doing it better and doing new.

New Product Line from Association for Social Advancement (ASA)

ASA is one of Bangladesh's leading microfinance institutions working with the poor since its inception in 1978. ASA entered the microfinance market with a more cost-effective version of Grameen model and is the fastest growing MFIs. Since they were only involved in microfinance, they could not compete with Grameen, BRAC and others who were providing other services and thus had to innovate. They introduced a voluntary savings product for two reasons – to increase the volume of savings mobilised and also to increase client satisfaction. They also introduced the concept of open voluntary savings for associate (non-borrowing) members.

Safesave Cooperative

Safesave is a financial service provider that began work in 1996 in two slums in Dacca. Staff from Safesave visit the clients daily and the clients may save or withdraw as much as they like (up to the limits of their saving). Balances that build up attract an interest of 10 per cent a year, payable after five years. Clients may also avail a loan depending on their savings and previous history with Safesave. The loans do not have be repaid in a fixed term or amount. Clients may choose to repay in lump sum. The only compulsory thing is that the interest has to be paid monthly and keeps a computerised account of all transactions of each client and has one mature branch that makes regular monthly surpluses. A total commitment to cost effectiveness is one such lesson that SafeSave learnt from ASA in Bangladesh. It also adapted the principle of combining maximum delegation with maximum standardisation.

First Women Bank Ltd. of Pakistan

First Women Bank Ltd. is a unique financial institution located in Karachi. It is a scheduled commercial bank, and a development finance institution for socio-economic empowerment of women. It was incorporated as a scheduled commercial bank in public sector on November 21, 1986 under Companies Ordinance 1984 and commenced its business on December 2, 1989 with a paid capital of Rs 100 million. 90 per cent of its capital was contributed by five leading public sector banks of the country viz. National Bank of Pakistan, Habib Bank Limited, Muslim Bank Commercial Limited, United Bank Limited and Allied Bank of

Pakistan Limited in varying proportions and 10 per cent from the federal government. In collaboration with ILO, it directly financed women micro-borrowers in rural areas. The project run by the bank identified 42 micro-businesses and provided skill training to 375 rural women. The Bank disbursed micro-credit to 972 women living below poverty line in 64 villages, with 100 per cent recovery rate.

Innovations in Microfinance

Until the late 1990s, most microfinance institutions (MFIs) had the freedom to focus single-mindedly on making the breakthrough in methodology and management, necessary to reach scale and sustainability as they had no competition. But now the above listed organizations have brought microfinance to the threshold of competition. While 'copying' and/or 'replication' remains the main process through which the facilities of microfinance are being extended to the poor, there is growing evidence of innovations in product design and organisational arrangements. NABARD has decided to launch an experiment through five branches of RRBs in Andhra Pradesh and Karnataka. Introducing Processor/ Memory Cards of active clients and SHGs and automation in SHGs is expected to reduce paper work, save time and thus improve the efficiency of the field worker. This will also reduce the scope of manipulation, reduce unintended leakages and also maintain up-to-date books at the SHG level. About 500 such customers would be selected in each bank branch. The first pilot on smart cards has been launched with Sri Visakha Grameena Bank in Andhra Pradesh, which has been one of the forerunner banks in financing SHGs. It is expected that with enhanced use of rural-oriented technology, the bank would be able to provide value addition to services being offered to rural clients and further expand its outreach in a sustainable manner.

Pilot Project for Linking SHGs with Post Offices

The project would test the efficacy of the Department of Posts in providing microfinance services to rural clientele. With more than one and a half lakh outlets, more or less evenly spread all across the country, the outreach of the post offices is unmatched. And it adds to the 'neighbourhood friend' image that the ubiquitous postmen enjoy, especially in the rural areas, which have a near perfect 'doorstep' credit delivery channel waiting to be tapped.

This has prompted NABARD to take up a pilot project on linking SHGs through post offices. A Revolving Fund Assistance of Rs 34 lakhs has been sanctioned to select post offices in Kancheepuram and Pudukottai districts in Tamil Nadu for providing loans to 200 SHGs promoted by NGOs. Grant assistance has also been sanctioned under the project for meeting initial expenditure on publicity and awareness creation. The rate of interest would be 9 per cent, shared between NABARD and the post office in the ratio of 2:1.

Computer Munshi

Professional Assistance for Development Action (PRADAN), an NGO which has promoted more than 4,000 SHGs, have come up with the idea of Computer Munshis. Quality and regularity of bookkeeping is the aspect of linkage banking, which is most affected because of the widespread illiteracy amongst the poor SHG women. The idea involves identification of skilled rural youth for the task of higher order accounting by providing training as Computer Munshis (CM). The trained individuals would be equipped with a computer and software to serve 100–300 SHGs. The SHG level meeting transaction statement will be sent to the CM after every meeting, which will be keyed in by the trained individual to generate outputs like trial balance, member savings and loan balances. The SHG promoter and the banker can access data about the SHGs from the CM on payment of a fee. The software captures all the essential data-financial and non-financial and generates a number of useful reports including 19 different ratio analyses. NABARD has sanctioned a grant assistance of Rs 6.10 lakhs to PRADAN for establishment of 10 Computer Munshis in the states of Jharkhand and Orissa. Later NABARD could consider financing of establishment of MF call centres with computers, which could be financed by banks.

Internal Learning System (ILS)

PRADAN has also introduced Internal Learning System for SHGs. The Internal Learning System is a set of pictorial diaries that are maintained at the level of the SHG members, at the group level, the staff, and at the programme level. The principle in ILS is that the first use of information is at the level where it is generated. It contrasts from the traditional impact assessment systems that are mainly extractive and are used by the outsiders and only selected information flows back to the clients. ILS reverses the system in which the information is generated and used by the clients, and selected information gets collated upwards. ILS is a participatory impact assessment and planning system for NGO development programmes. It is 'internally driven', designed primarily to meet the learning needs of participants and programme staff. Participants use the system to track and analyse changes in their lives; they use the understanding to alter their strategies as they participate in the economy and interact with actors and institutions in the wider community. Programme staff use the system to meet a variety of impact assessment objectives, including 'external proving', that the programme is having its intended impact. The aim of the ILS project was to create a participatory monitoring and impact evaluation system that would respond to the ongoing internal needs of organisations to learn what is working and what is not working, so that changes could be made in a timely manner. This emphasis on the impact assessment objectives of internal learning and improving programme operations is the strength of ILS. The system was also designed to strengthen stakeholder relationships and to build participant understanding and analysis skills.

MF Education Programme

Sa-Dhan has evolved an education programme on perspective-building in microfinance and livelihood promotion. The programme provides an understanding of the multiple models and approaches that are operating in India. The programme has been able to address regional diversities at the national level.

Swayam Krishi Sangam (SKS)

SKS has pioneered a smart card project. The project involves using smart cards and palm pilots at the village level. Smart cards automate field operations reducing transaction costs. The initiative has replaced manual passbooks and collection sheets thereby reducing the cost of delivery, scope of error and fraud and enhancing the speed and efficiency.

Integrated Agriculture Service Provider Model

Under this model, the bank identifies an IASP that has a good relationship with farmers and provides timely and genuine information to farmers through extension services and enters into a tripartite agreement with the IASP and the output buyer. Credit is provided to farmers on the recommendation of the IASP, the farmer pledges his produce to the output buyer at a market based price, the IASP provides inputs to the farmer. Loan processing, disbursement and collection are done by the IASP while the credit decision remains with the bank. At the end of the season, the farmer supplies the crop to the output buyer and the output buyer deducts the loan amount from the sale proceeds and remits the loan amount to the concerned bank in full settlement of the loan amount. The IASP receives a service fee for the loan processing and supervision services (1.5 per cent on recovered loans). The model creates a symbiotic relationship between the input supplier, financier and trader. It reduces transaction costs, reduces the risk exposure of all parties and presents a low-cost way of serving the rural poor engaged in small/marginal farming.

NABARD-CRISIL MFI

NABARD and Credit Rating Information Service of India Limited (CRISIL) have jointly launched a rating for MFIs. This is called the 'NABARD-CRISIL MFI grading scheme.' It is aimed to encourage banks to increase the involvement of MFIs in financial intermediation to enhance credit delivery to the poor. The microfinance grading communicates the ability of the MFI to scale up and sustain operations on an eight-point grading scale.

Rating for MFIs

Banks can utilise CRISIL's expertise to evaluate MFIs and partner with it in their microfinance initiatives through its services at concessional rates. Further, NABARD will be reimbursing banks the grading fees paid to CRISIL. The scheme will support the grading of those MFIs having a loan outstanding between Rs 50 lakhs and Rs 5 crore.

Money Shop

The Philippine Commercial and Industrial Bank (PCIB) in 1973 launched its Money Shop scheme. A Money Shop occupies a stall in the marketplace and provides working capital loans to the vendors in the market. The Money Shop has the same hours as the market and opens early in the morning. Loans are at an interest rate of about three per cent per month. Repayments are collected from the vendors' stalls by a Money Shop officer. In spite of this, arrear levels are high when compared with other lending schemes and the scheme has not been as successful in attracting deposits as the credit unions. Nevertheless, the scheme has grown and is now a major activity of PCIB.

Village Banks

Village banks are intermediaries between the sponsoring agency which gives loans to the village bank and the member/borrowers. Credit to members is linked to savings, and loan sizes to the amount saved by each borrower. Evaluation of village banking programmes indicate that their benefits are both economic and social. The village bank model is of interest because it offers a way to link a larger organisation, such as a commercial bank, with a specialised microfinance institution based at the local level.

The Thrift and Credit Cooperatives promoted by the Cooperative Development Foundation (CDF) is another example of successful inclusion initiatives. The CDF has promoted cooperatives in Warangal and Karimnagar districts of Andhra Pradesh with a total membership of about 10,000, and savings and assets in excess of 200 million. These cooperatives have made a great impact on the local economy and on poverty levels. These cooperatives are patterned on the model of credit unions and have become models for cooperatives in other states. The SHG-Bank linkage programme is the predominant microfinance model in India. SHG banking has been aptly described as a technology for reaching marginal areas and the poor. It recognises that most of the poor, particularly those in marginal areas, have remained excluded from the banking system and it seeks to address this. Credit innovations like microfinance have also evolved as socially significant and commercially attractive models of credit delivery in India. The early 1990s saw the emergence of the Self Help Group concept in India.

The pilot programme started by NABARD in 1992 to promote 500 SHGs was actively supported by the RBI and saw the banks taking a key interest in promoting the programme. As the idea gained acceptance from the banking system and the results were promising, the RBI encouraged this positive initiative by issuing instructions to banks in 1996 to cover SHG financing as a mainstream activity under the priority sector lending portfolio. SHGs were used to promote and facilitate collective decision-making by the poor and to promote doorstep banking. Banks as wholesalers of credit provided the necessary resources and NGOs acted as agencies to organise the poor build their capacities and facilitate the process of empowering them. The SHG-Bank linkage programme has so far become the largest microfinance programme in the country with over 2.9 million SHGs being credit linked as on March 2007 with cumulative credit flow to the tune of more than Rs 140 billion. The SHGs have been linked with 35,294 bank branches of 560 banks in 563 districts across 29 states. About 24 million poor households have gained access to the formal banking system through the programme. RBI issued comprehensive guidelines to banks in February 2000 for mainstreaming micro credit and enhancing the outreach of micro credit providers. Banks were advised to prescribe their own lending norms keeping in view the ground realities and devise appropriate loan and savings products. Banks were advised that micro credit should be included in branch credit plan, block credit plan, district credit plan and state credit plan of each bank. Guidelines stipulated that micro credit extended by banks to individual borrowers directly or through any intermediary would henceforth be reckoned as part of their priority sector lending. Banks were given freedom to formulate their own model(s) or choose any conduit/intermediary for extending micro credit. Banks were asked to delegate adequate sanctioning powers to branch managers and to keep the loan application forms, procedures and documents simple for providing prompt and hassle-free service. The amount collected from the members is deposited in the formal institutional banking system. The evolution of self help groups happened in three stages. At the first stage, poor households use microfinance to meet survival requirements where small savings and loans serve as a buffer in the event of an emergency or to smoothen consumption or even service previous debt to ensure liquidity during lean periods. At the second level 'subsistence' needs are met through microfinance, where a household begins to utilise it to diversify income-generating activities or to meet working capital requirements in traditional activities. At the third level, as households reach a stage where they can assume a higher degree of risk, microfinance is used to invest in setting up an enterprise or facilitating entry into employment in order that the household becomes sustainable. There are three partners viz., SHGs, banks, and voluntary agencies in the SHG–Bank linkage model banks. These banks are those which have the financial muscle, and have the ability to provide credit to the poor who are in need of credit and the voluntary organisations are those which can provide a bridge between the two. Microfinance institutions, played a pioneering role in organising the poor to obtain credit. The majority of MFIs have 500 to 1,500 clients and a few MFIs have attained an outreach of 1,00,000 clients.

Self Help Groups (SHGs)

- Small, economically homogeneous and affinity groups of poor, not exceeding 20, voluntarily formed to save and mutually agree to contribute to a common fund to be lend to its members as per group decision
- All financial decisions are taken by the groups through a consensual approach and inculcates saving and banking habits among the poor
- Secures the poor with financial, technical and moral strength
- Enables availing of loan for consumption and productive purposes and repaying the same over a period of time
- Helps in gaining economic prosperity
- The groups gain from collective wisdom in the financial matters in organising and managing their own finance and distributing the benefits among themselves.

Stages of SHG Development

- Pre-formation: usually one to two months in which the poor are identified
- Formation: two to six months where group leaders are selected, rules are framed, savings and credit starts and systems are put in place
- Stabilisation Phase I: seven to 12 months – regularity in functioning is observed, group level transactions, community issues, linkage with formal financial institutions
- Phase II: 12–18 months and income generating activities start
- Growth and expansion: 18 months and above where bank linkages are strengthened, asset creation for the group, promotion of new groups, attempt cluster formation.

SHG-BANK Linkage Programme

NABARD introduced in 1992 a pilot project for linking SHGs with banks to encourage thrift and savings amongst the rural poor and to supplement their funds to meet credit needs through the banking system. In 1996, this programme was extended beyond the pilot phase and banks were advised to make it a part of their mainstream lending operations.

Criteria for Selecting SHGs

- The group should have been in active existence for at least a period of six months
- The group should have successfully undertaken savings and credit operations from its own resources

- The group should function democratically
- The group should maintain proper accounts/records
- The SHG members should preferably be a homogeneous society
- The interest of the NGO is evident and is helping the SHG by way of training and other ways.

Estimation of Credit Requirements

- The quantum of credit is determined in multiples of the savings pooled by the group and the proportion of savings to credit could vary from 1:1 to 1:4 depending on the assessment of the SHG by the bank
- NABARD provides 100 per cent refinance to all banks for the loans disbursed to SHGs
- The repayment for the loans extended by the SHG to its members is determined by the group and loans extended by banks to the group is discretionary

Interest Rates

The present interest rate structure stipulated by NABARD is:

- NABARD to banks – 6%
- Banks to SHGs – decided by the banks within RBI directives
- Banks to NGO – Banks free to decide
- NGO to SHG – NGO free to decide

Security

RBI has relaxed the security norms and classified such loans as 'Advances to Weaker Sections' since in most cases SHGs are not in a position to offer any collateral security other than their savings. Peer pressure among members is the alternative form of collateral.

Eligible Agencies

For this programme of Bank–SHG linkage, all commercial banks, regional rural banks, cooperative banks, primary agricultural societies and MFIs are eligible.

Models of Credit Delivery

- Financing of SHGs directly by banks without any intervention/ facilitation by an NGO
- Financing of SHGs directly by banks with intervention of NGOs
- Financing of SHGs directly by banks with intervention of government agencies

- Financing of SHGs with financial intermediation of NGOs
- Financing of SHGs with financial intermediation of NGO/MACS/ Cluster Associations.

Network of SHGs

New coalitions and networks are fast emerging due to the proliferation of a large number of thrift and credit groups. Mature SHGs network to obtain synergies through sharing of information, resources and wisdom. The groups get together at village, cluster or mandal level and later graduate to form a formal and structured federation.

Monitoring of SHGs according to NABARD Study

The monitoring indicators include number and spread of SHGs, amount of credit disbursed, number of loanees, deposit mobilisation, repayment performance, expenditure on awareness, training programmes, cost of management, etc.

Study Findings

- Emergence of SHG–Bank linkage as mass social mobilisation programme
- Strength of SHGs is reflected in group cohesion and vibrant behaviour
- Development of leadership qualities and increased confidence in interactions with goverment agencies
- Improvement in access to credit
- Financing of unique and non-traditional activities
- Definite shift in loaning pattern of the members from consumption to productive activities
- Improvement in loan volumes of SHGs through internal capitalisation
- Very good repayment of loans at SHG level
- Interest rates at group level are adjusted to market conditions
- Greater awareness of the need to graduate to higher economic operations
- Creation of common and community assets
- Reduction in transaction cost for banks and borrowers alike
- Simplified loaning procedure and documentation
- SHGs help banks to expand good clientele base among rural poor

- SHGs provide enabling environment for conscious leadership development, decentralised decision making, peer pressure and sustainability of group actions
- Participation in socio-economic development programmes have contributed to overall empowerment of the poor.

Negative Findings

- Irregular group meetings
- Irregularity in savings
- Lump sum contribution in savings to attain eligibility for higher loans
- Large loans to only a few members
- Absence of proper and up-to-date record keeping
- Repayment of bank loans instalments by raising loans from other sources
- Absence of rotation in leadership positions
- Lack of confidence among bank branches in extending loans to SHG in absence of NGO
- Lack of proper understanding and internalisation of SHG concepts among bank and govt. agencies
- Complacency on part of banks about recovery of SHG loans and absence of follow up leading to growing NPAs.

Future Perspective

- There is an imperative need to enlarge the coverage of SHGs in the advances portfolio of banks as part of their corporate strategy
- To recognise perceived benefits of SHG financing in terms of reduced default risk and transaction costs
- The banks may have to devise suitable policy guidelines for proper appraisal, monitoring and supervision of SHG advances together with necessary documentation
- Number of new SHGs formed by agencies: 92,774
- Number of SHGs formed by NGOs: 1,06,228
- Number of SHGs financed by banks: 3,61,731
- Number of SHGs provided repeat finance: 1,71,669.

Highlights of SHG Linkage in AP during 2004–05

- Number of SHGs financed by banks: 2,61,254
- Amount of finance: Rs 1,017.71 crores

- Number of fresh groups: 1,07,351
- Number of repeat groups: 1,53,909
- Number of participating branches: 4,096.

First 3 districts in credit linkage

- East Godavari: 30,850 groups
- West Godavari: 19,818 groups
- Chittoor: 15,659 groups.

First 3 commercial banks in linkage

- Andhra Bank: 50,841 groups
- State Bank of India: 50,290 groups
- State Bank of Hyderabad: 22,545 groups.

First 3 RRBs

- Sri Visakha Gr. Bank: 13,936 groups
- Rayalseema Gr. Bank: 9,724 groups
- Sri Venkateswara Gr. Bank: 6,611 groups.

Challenges

Enormous challenges remain like reaching out to the remaining 150 million rural poor in India, expanding into states where coverage is still minimal, assuring adequate financial deepening, finding profitable microenterprise investment opportunities and making financial services sustainable in the long run.

Sustainability

Sustainability of SHG banking in the long run is an unresolved issue. Given the flexibility of SHG banking in India, there may be different routes to the sustainability of access to formal financial services. One is *direct access of individuals* to bank services, based on the growth of their microenterprise activities and the track record provided by their SHGs. Another option, presently developing in Andhra Pradesh and neighbouring states on a growing scale is the *formation of federations*, some with and others without financial intermediation functions, indirectly giving legitimacy to the member SHGs. A third option may lie in the *integration of credit* of NGOs and MFIs with their SHG clientele, into the formal financial sector.

The least promising option of sustainability in the long run is the continued existence of *informal groups* with full access to bank services.

When is Microcredit Successful?

Success requires both client discipline (timely repayment) and institutional discipline (practices that lead to sustainability). Microcredit is best implemented as a professional banking activity by a strong, local microcredit organisation dedicated to operational self-sufficiency. Transforming a non-financial organisation into a sustainable microfinance institution requires technical assistance and institutional development. Progress on performance should be monitored using clearly defined microcredit performance indicators.

When May Microcredit be Inappropriate?

Microcredit may be inappropriate in post-emergency environments, severely disadvantaged rural areas and as an intervention for the chronically destitute. Clients with debilitating illnesses and extremely dispersed and highly mobile are generally not suitable for microcredit programmes. Microcredit is rarely sustainable where the regulatory environment creates significant barriers to sustainability (interest caps, etc.). In 2005, mainstream financial institutions took a notably greater interest in microcredit as a core part of their long-term growth strategy. Several of the largest commercial banks, including Citigroup, Deutsche Bank, Credit Suisse, HSBC, ING and ABN-AMRO have invested in the sector. According to estimates, demand for loans from poor but creditworthy people in India alone could amount to 40 billion dollars. In 2008, ICICI Bank nearly doubled its MFI portfolio to Rs 2,600 crores and expects the segment to grow by at least 20 per cent in 2009–10. The strategy it has adopted is to work closely with 30 top MFIs to finance their projects. The bank is also training various other MFIs through its sister organization – ICICI Foundation. Citigroup is also investing heavily in microfinance initiatives. The bank has already established relationships with MFIs in 20 countries with another 10 waiting in the pipeline. A milestone was also hit in 2005. Global micro-financier ACCION International announced that the active loan portfolio managed by its MFI partners rose above \$1 billion. The group has also formed an alliance in India with units to reach out to 15 million new households within the next 10 years.

During the year 2006–07, 6,86,408 new SHGs were credit linked with banks taking the cumulative number of SHGs credit linked to 29,24,073 as on 31 March 2007. Since inception of the microfinance (MF) programme, it has enabled an estimated 409.5 lakh poor households to gain access to MF from the formal banking system. NABARD continued to emphasise scaling-up of the SHG – Bank linkage programme in 13 priority states, which have large population of the rural poor. The cumulative number of SHGs credit linked in these states increased from 10.05 lakh during 2005–06 to 13.75 lakh during 2006–07 constituting 54 per cent of the number of SHGs credit linked across the country during the year. The regional spread of the programme reveals that the share of non-southern regions improved significantly from 29 per cent as on 31 March 2001 to 48 per cent as on 31 March 2007. A grant assistance of Rs 1,403.96 lakh was sanctioned to promote 59,662 SHGs to eight cooperative banks, one RRB, 352 NGOs and 23 Individual Rural Volunteers (IRVs)during the year, taking the cumulative sanction to Rs 4,749.96 lakh for the promotion of 3.09 lakh groups. An amount of Rs 1,980.77 lakh was released and 1,52,928 SHGs were credit linked as on 31 March 2007.

Under NABARD's capacity-building programmes for its partner institutions, 70 exposure/field visits to SHGs and institutions pioneering in MF for 1,864 bank/NGO officials, 682 training and awareness programmes for 23,964 participants from banks and NGOs, 155 sensitisation programmes covering 6,395 government officials and elected members of Panchayati Raj Institutions PRIs were arranged during the year. NABARD also extended support for conducting 3,494 awareness creation and capacity building programmes covering 2,01,854 SHG members. To motivate and assist members of matured SHGs to take up income generating activities on a sustainable basis, NABARD continued to promote micro-enterprise development by SHG members. Under the Micro-Enterprise Development Programme (MEDP), 297 such programmes covering 7,579 SHG members were conducted during the year. The pilot project launched during 2005–06 for developing micro-enterprises, in partnership with Marketing and Research Team (MART), is being implemented in nine districts across nine states involving 14 NGOs as 'microenterprise promotion agency (MEPA). During the year MEPAs completed detailed surveys of the project districts and identified existing opportunities and demand/supply patterns for farm/non-farm activities in consultation with

SHG members that could be taken up for sustainable income generation in the project area. Action plan finalised by each MEPA on the basis of the survey findings is being implemented.

To facilitate matured SHGs to meet their credit requirements of production and investments in agriculture and allied activities and to enable them to diversify their income generating activities, NABARD introduced a new line of refinance for scheduled commercial banks, RRBs and co-operative banks. Under the scheme, cent per cent refinance is provided to banks under ARF for financing term loan and cash credit limits sanctioned by them to SHGs. To support the MF programme, NABARD selectively extends Revolving Fund Assistance (RFA) to MFIs for on-lending to SHGs. During the year, RFA of Rs 1 crore was sanctioned taking the aggregate support to Rs 27.98 crore as on 31 March 2007 for 31 agencies. In addition, to enable rating of MFIs and empowering them to intermediate between the lending banks and the clients, NABARD provides financial assistance to commercial banks and RRBs to avail the services of credit rating agencies for the purpose. The Bank also introduced a scheme to provide capital/equity support to MFIs during 2006–07 to enable them to leverage capital/equity for accessing funds from banks; providing financial services at an affordable cost to the poor, and achieve sustainability in their credit operations over a period of three to five years. During 2006–07, three agencies were sanctioned total capital support of Rs 3 crore. NABARD continued to implement the pilot projects launched during the earlier years. Based on its experience and in response to the Union Budget 2006–07 announcement for financing of tenant farmers by banks, NABARD formulated the scheme for financing Joint Liability Groups (JLGs) of such farmers. It designed a pilot project for collaboration with post offices for financing SHGs which is under implementation in five districts of Tamil Nadu. As on 31 March 2007, 530 SHGs have opened saving bank accounts, of which 46 have been credit linked by the participating post offices. A pilot project for proving a social security system for SHG members was also sanctioned for implementation in two villages covering 500 poor households from Betul district of Madhya Pradesh and is being implemented through an NGO, the Organisation for awareness of Integrated Social Security (OASIS) with a grant assistance of Rs 8 lakh. During the year, Rs 11.18 crore was utilised from the Micro-Finance Development and Equity Fund (MFDEF) for MF related activities. The Micro Financial Sector (Development and Regulation) Bill 2007 was introduced in the Lok Sabha on 20 March 2007.

Other Agencies and Models

As the profitability of microfinance increased, SIDBI, Friends of Women's World Banking (FWWB) and Rashtriya Mahila Kosh (RMK) began extending finance to SHGs in addition to the commercial banks. This led to the transformation of the larger and medium MFIs to NBFCs and Section 25 companies and of one into a Local Area Bank. The passage of the Mutually Aided Cooperative Societies Act in states like Andhra Pradesh led to the transformation of SHGs to MACS. Thus, microfinance provision has assumed a diversity of forms but microfinance activity remains concentrated in the southern states and the MFIs. The bulk of loans outstanding may be concentrated in the top 20 MFIs. MFIs of all legal forms have as their major source of funds debt from banks. Thus banks have become key players in the microfinance sector. SHGs JLGs Grameen replications supplement bank loans with donor grants and funds. Section 25 not for profit companies with equity investments and promoters, capital cooperatives with shareholdings and with retained earnings in case of all categories raise compulsory savings through a variety of arrangements such as small weekly contributions measured either in terms of cost per borrower added on to the loan repayment installment.

Microfinance in Andhra Pradesh

Andhra Pradesh is the microfinance leader in India, and gained momentum with a scheme called Podupu Lakshmi which involved daily savings collection from women and was the forerunner of the SHG movement. The Government of Andhra Pradesh has played a proactive role in encouraging SHG activity for more than four decades. It identifies the poor and organises them into SHGs. Mainstreaming is taken care of as they are organised into village organisations which in turn form *mandal samakhyas* and these then go up to *zila samakhyas* so as to enable these federated entities to take care of the marketing requirements as also procure goods and self regulate themselves. The Andhra Pradesh Mahila Abhivruddhi Society, APMAS, is a public–private partnership working towards financial inclusion and empowerment. The MFIs operating in AP are registered under the MACS Act, some are NBFCs and one is a Local Area Bank. Over 5,00,000 SHGs federated with very large government support and consequent control have bank loan outstandings of Rs 1,500 crores to SHGs. The MFI sector is also active in the state. It has about Rs 1,000 crore outstanding, it relies on donor/bank support and on self generated incomes. The dominant model in Andhra Pradesh as in the rest of India is the SHG Bank Linkage programme where 1,000 plus NGOs are involved with more than 2,000 cooperatives. Owing to the success of the Andhra Pradesh model, governments have embraced the SHG Bank linkage model in several states and even in states of north India where SHG activity traditionally has not been as strong as it has been in the south and west of India. In Rajasthan, Madhya Pradesh and Uttar Pradesh the government-sponsored poverty alleviation programme of the SGSY also adopts the SHG methodology. While government support has undoubtedly been useful in terms of helping to garner additional resources and scaling up low quality, a target chase subsidies with endemic leakages and consequent non repayment by borrowers have introduced portfolio contamination. This needs to be guarded against in the MFI sector since there is a problem of high interest rates. Both in the government SHG – Bank linkage programme and the MFI sector there is a rush to grow at all costs which leads to poaching of members, breakage of groups over lending and sometimes coercive collection practices.

Exclusion

The Joint Liability Group has been criticised as it fosters exclusion to the extend that all members are denied loan even if only one member faults in the instalment. Shahidur Khandkar in his study of Grameen Bank has also criticised the Joint Liability Group Model (JLG Model) where a fresh loan cannot be extended till the last member has repaid her loan. This increases peer pressure, prompts domestic violence, and leads the defaulting borrower to approach the moneylenders on occassions. Sometimes fines are imposed, the security deposit is adjusted against the loan outstanding but defaulting borrowers suffer abuse and social ostracism. Thus, this model of financial inclusion also suffers from very real problems though on the whole it has been found to be a successful model.

The problems in the model lead to exclusion, where exclusion may also occur for other reasons. The phenomenon of exclusion has kept the extent of outreach to 51 per cent. Self-exclusion as well as exclusion by self-help promoting agencies is practiced for much the same set of reasons—anticipated difficulty in meeting savings obligations and in keeping up with loan repayments:

The following factors also contribute to self-exclusion:

(i) Lack of understanding and confidence in group processes
(ii) Need to go outside the village for daily work which makes it difficult to attend weekly meetings.

The issue of inability to save regularly by households with variable and uncertain incomes can be addressed by introducing lower and more flexible savings in keeping with varying cash flows. Despite its reckoning process costs, microfinance still manages to score very highly as a participative approach and can give a very big thrust to financial inclusion. As far as the MFIs go, the rates of interest have been a cause for concern. The rates should be cost covering but attempts should be made to pare down the costs and introduce greater efficiencies in the delivery of services. This is preferable to the alternative of loading a fee on to the interest rate charged to the borrower. The higher interest rates charged were bound to attract adverse attention. The dispensation of SRO among the MFIs to put their own house in order saved the day in Andhra Pradesh where this controversy erupted in 2006.

Credit Counselling

There is a need for face to face money advice. The levels of literacy in our country are relatively modest at 65.4 per cent in 2001, with wide differentials between urban and rural areas. In 2001, the proportion of rural illiterate was about 59 per cent as compared with 80.3 per cent in the urban areas. Additionally, organised sector employment comprises less than 10 per cent of the workforce leaving the vast majority of the working population with irregular income streams and paucity of defined safety net making them susceptible to unforeseen contingencies. Penetration of formal finance is not very high and even where loans are availed from banks there is a need to supplement these with informal finance. Credit counselling is generally ex-post but if it is ex-ante it is definitely more useful as it can help avert loan delinquency. As potential borrowers grow more market savvy they may actually prefer to pay small installments rather than allow them to accumulate to insurmountable debt. On pilot basis the Bank of India has started credit counselling centres called Abhay.

SHG Case Studies

Purana Sahi Mahila Self-Help Group, Orissa

This group consists of 15 women in Dublabeda village of Mayurbhanja district which is one of the most backward districts of Orissa. The village is tribal dominated and livelihood is based on traditional agriculture and wage labour. There was no provision for credit except the village money lender and livelihood of the villagers was under the control of nature. The group was formed in January 2001 and linked with Baitarani Gramya Bank in July 2001. All the women members are married and five of them are literate. With the support of Gramin Vikas Trust, the group diversified from traditional agriculture replacing local varieties of paddy by high yielding varieties. The group adopted Golden Grass trading, processing and cultivation. Some of the members entered into livestock enterprises of piggery, goatery and cattle. To address the irrigation problem, they purchased one diesel set and dug wells. They also received 12 iron ploughs from the government.

Enterprise

- In the initial year, the group traded in Golden Grass by purchasing it at Rs 220/40 kg and selling it at Rs 270/40 kg and traded 40 quintals.
- Subsequently they started processing the grass by making ropes and this was done individually with each member earning Rs 1,000.
- Once the group realised the profitability of the business they started cultivation of the grass.
- A total of 30 acres of land was covered under Golden Grass with an average yield of 1,000 kg and earning of Rs 6,250 per acre.
- The net annual benefit from 30 acres after deducting for expenses was Rs 1,54,500.
- The group has been regularly supported by Gramin Vikas Trust who has provided one sprayer machine, one diesel pump, and tarpaulin. The NGO has also constructed a threshing floor for the group with the support of the group.
- The average annual income from rental of the above was about Rs 5,500.

Bank Linkage

- The group also took a loan of Rs 15,000 in June 2003, from the bank for the Golden Grass business and repaid it in seven months.
- The bank sanctioned another loan of Rs 30,000 to the group looking at the requirement and repayment.
- The group is functioning well and the linkage with the bank is now strong.

Dharamveer SHG, Orissa

This group of 14 like-minded farmers was formed in August 1999 with the motivation of GVT, in Manikpur village of Manikpur Gram Panchayat of Mayurbhanj district. All the members belong to the BPL category. The group linked up with Bank of India in October 1999.

Enterprise

- The group went into income-generating activities like goatery, leaf plate making, cattle herding and agriculture with the support of the government who was instrumental in providing the necessary training, revolving fund and pump set to the group.
- The group also availed loan from the Bank of India to the tune of Rs 8,000 in February 2000.
- This loan was repaid in eight months by the group.
- The group has been successful in using the revolving fund and loan to their advantage as also renting out the pump set.
- The use of high yielding variety of paddy seeds has been instrumental in increasing the productivity and income.
- The other activities of goatery and duckery have been expanded since the group has also linked up with DRDA who has given another revolving fund of Rs 10,000.

Building Institutional Strength

- The group made an assessment of the village and approached Nehru Yuvak Kendra, Mayurbhanj. 25 women of the village were provided with training in tailoring.
- The group also linked up with State Social Welfare Board, Bhubaneshwar, to conduct an awareness programme. 25 women were trained on health, education, social welfare and consumer rights. The women later became trainers for the village.
- The group approached State Civil Supply Corporation to run the retail center at Manikpur Gram Panchayat which was lying vacant. The centre now runs successfully and all villagers are benefitted.
- The leadership of the group is efficient and effective and the benefits of the group has percolated into the village.

The 11th Plan must ensure that our policies are sufficiently flexible to support the development of microfinance. The interest rates in the microfinance sector are higher than in the banking sector. These are generally stated to be lower than rates charged by moneylenders and therefore provide competition to the moneylenders. There have been incidents of state governments imposing restrictions on microfinance institutions. The adverse selection aspect of interest rates is a consequence of different borrowers having different probabilities of repaying their loan. The expected return to the bank obviously depends on the probability of repayment, so the bank would like to be able to identify borrowers who are more likely to repay. It is difficult to identify good borrowers, which is why a bank uses a variety of screening devices, including the interest rate. Those who are willing to pay high interest rates may be at worse risks; they are willing to take higher risks to gain higher returns if successful, but such high returns are generally associated with a higher probability of failure, making it less likely that the loans will be repaid. This is known as 'moral hazard'. As the interest rate rises, the average of risk of those who borrow increases, possibly reducing the bank's profit. Similarly, as the interest rate and other terms of the contract, such as collateral requirements, change, the behaviour of the borrower is likely to change. Stiglitz and Weiss show that higher interest rates lead to 'moral hazard', that is, they induce firms to undertake riskier projects with lower probability of success but higher payoffs when successful. In a world with imperfect and costly information that leads to adverse selection and moral hazard problems, the expected rate of return to the bank will increase less rapidly than the interest rate and, beyond a point, may actually decrease. Self Help Groups are informal associations of up to 20 women who meet regularly usually once a month, and save small amounts typically Rs 10–50 per month. They are formed either by the members themselves as affinity groups who self select their members or with the help of an intermediary as an NGO or other Self Help Promoting agency. After six months of small periodic recurrent and regular savings a group corpus is built up and the group now reaches level 2. The funds are used by members for lending among themselves. Small amounts are lent on interest and the amount recovered is again ploughed back into the group corpus. The members now learn the importance of basic bookkeeping and maintenance of proper records and then graduate to level 3. They are now linked through a bank under the NABARD Bank SHG programme. The activities of the groups are the taking up of livelihood sustenance or income-generating projects. This model is *swayam bhu* and unique to India.

The microfinance model is one where the MFI acts as an intermediary much like the SHG and borrows a much larger quantum of funds generally from private banks who lack the outreach which the public sector banks enjoy in the rural areas. Lending to groups entails the joint and several liability of all members which is more moral than legally binding and is exercised through group pressures and the possibility of being denied future loans in the case of SHGs. It is a single loan made to the group which then allocates it to its members while an MFI loan is given directly. The SHG model has created a lasting impact in terms of the participation it has engendered in millions of poor rural women of which nearly half are below the poverty line. It also spreads much faster as it is able to leverage India's penetrative network of bank branches and potentially the network of the primary agricultural credit societies PACs. The loan size however remains moderate as it is linked to the loan cycle of other members. Every member under the JLG model must wait till the last member has repaid her loan before it can repay its loan to the Bank.

Microfinance has been successful in many continents as it fulfills one or two prerequisites of success which have been explained as two virtuous cycles:

- The first virtuous cycle is one of sustainability, wide and deep outreach with marked and encompassing results. Impact outreach with impact results in exponential and sustainable growth.
- The second virtuous cycle is of institutional and enterprise viability where growth leads to the seeding of viable enterprises which in turn fuel economic growth. Any model of microfinance can be successful only as long as the microfinance enterprises are able to mobilise their own resources through savings and repay their loans and cover their costs from their operational income and finance their expansion through their profits.

Emerging Challenges of the Microfinance Sector

The emerging challenges of the Microfinance Sector are:

(i) **Regional imbalances**

The first challenge lies in the skewed distribution of SHGs across states. About 60 per cent of SHG credit linkages in the country are concentrated in the southern states. However in states which have a larger share of the poor, the coverage is much lower. There are various reasons adduced for this. First, some state governments have extended greater patronage to the programme, second there is a skewed distribution of NGOs, and third, local culture and practices.

(ii) **Limited loan size**

The second and major issue engaging attention is that the total disbursement of credit is very limited and per household credit made available is very small. As on 31 March 2003 the average loan was Rs 28,600 per SHG and Rs 1,760 per household. If a serious impact on the economic conditions of the poor has to be made, larger credit outlays to support an enlarged production base are required.

(iii) **Reaching the poorest**

The third challenge is of reaching the poorest. Microfinance does serve very poor clients, although in general, they do not participate in very large numbers. Though very poor people are present in most programmes, the majority of clients are from the moderately poor and vulnerable non-poor categories, i.e. those just below the poverty line. Evidence from poverty assessments conducted by the Consultative Group to Assist the Poorest (CGAP) on a number of MFIs indicates that though all those surveyed were reaching some very poor clients (defined as those in the bottom third of the population), few were reaching larger numbers from this group. Most MFIs were biased towards less poor clients or at best reflected the general population distribution. The CGAP experience demonstrates that MFIs do not automatically reach large numbers of very poor clients by using conventional design features such as small loan sizes. Those MFIs that use active poverty targeting to focus on the needs of the very poor are the only ones with significant outreach who are working towards inclusion.

Absolute or Relative Poverty Targeting to Ensure Financial Inclusion

Poverty outreach can be seen both in absolute and relative terms. Three levels have been defined:

(i) Those that are very poor compared to their neighbours: The CGAP poverty assessment looks at the poverty level of incoming clients and divides the population in an MFI's operational area into thirds and defines the bottom as very poor, the middle as poor, and the top third as non-poor. This definition does not take into cognizance the relative poverty of the MFI's operational area vis-a-vis the rest of the country.

(ii) Using a national definition of poverty, the poorest are defined as those people living at below half the national poverty line. This population allows for accurate comparisons within a country but does not capture how poor the country is on an international comparison.

(iii) The international definition of absolute poverty is of the poorest, as those living at or below US$1/day per person (adjusted for the purchasing power of the local currency).

To enquire whether MFIs reach very poor clients, it is important to understand how these are defined. In a poor country such as India, the poorest are defined as those living below less than a dollar a day, thus, most persons reached will be living below the US$1/day per person level (adjusted for the purchasing power of the local currency). So, this does not mean that they necessarily include large numbers of the poorest clients relative to national poverty.

The Case for Poverty Focussed Microfinance

A market-based approach is hugely inadequate for inclusive development. Those engaged in the microfinance industry often adopt the 'Financial Systems Approach' – they see the primary goal of MFIs as developing strong institutions that can sustainably meet the needs of the markets they choose to serve. Their argument is that if the services were not catering to a demand or if for instance, the services were too expensive, or interest rates were too high, there would be no clients for the services. Thus, client demand for services is used as an ultimate justification. They argue that steps to limit access through eligibility criteria or targeting, raise the cost of operations and distort the market. Microfinance should offer appropriate market based approaches to deliver the right services to the right people. They further argue that the increased costs incurred by poverty-focused MFIs undermine their financial performance and result in services that are inappropriate to the market needs. For their inclusion, the very poor require state transfers. These arguments are backed by economic logic. There is a strong case for poverty-focused microfinance that actively work with poor and very poor clients, attempts to understand their needs and design services specifically for them and which monitors and assesses the success of the programme in meeting these needs, thus reducing poverty. Most MFIs have far to go in finding ways of reaching extremely poor households. Their contention is that the very poor can only be benefited through welfare or that programme sustainability is incompatible with the inclusion of the very poor. This possibly belies a lack of understanding of the dynamics of poverty and the opportunities that exist for the provision of financial services to the extremely poor. Till date, there has been inadequate exploration of financial products and low cost service delivery mechanisms that would allow MFIs to include extremely poor households without compromising their sustainability objectives.

Is Microfinance Viable?

From a developmental perspective, many support the view that microfinance is inadequate on its own to combat poverty, given its limitations and the multidimensionality of poverty. Particularly prevalent is the view that credit is not an appropriate service for the poorest. Much of the work, looking at risk and vulnerability, points to the important role of savings and other financial services for the livelihoods of the very poor (Rutherford 1999). This work does not negate the role of credit but seeks to redress the overemphasis on credit. It terms savings as the forgotten half of microfinance. This is distorted and represented as reflecting credit inappropriate for the very poor, or that the needs of the very poor are separate from mainstream microcredit. Marguerite Robinson, for instance, argues that savings rather than credit, are better able to reach the poorer section, and that the extreme poor, whom she defines as the majority of those below the poverty line, need subsidised poverty alleviation programmes, not financial services.

Table 5.1 Microfinance within Ranges of Different Income Groups.

Income Level	Commercial Financial Services	Subsidised Poverty Alleviation Programmes
Lower Middle Income	Standard Commercial Bank Loans Interest bearing savings accounts for small savings and full range of savings services Commercial micro loans	
Economically active poor official poverty line		Poverty programmes for such purposes as food and water, medicine and nutrition, employment generation, skills training, and relocation
Extremely Poor		

Source: Poverty Tool Kit, Marguerite Robinson, 2001.

To understand the role that microfinance can play in inclusion, it is important to have a clear conceptual grasp of the mechanisms by which financial services can affect the lives of the poor. The poor are vulnerable to high risks and changing environment. They need to be able to avail and take advantage of opportunities that lead to an improvement in income or status to protect themselves against risks or shocks and crisis and cope with these when they arise. Poverty reduction is in part a process of increasing income and economic stability, which lead to improved fulfillment of basic needs and access to services. Financial services smoothen and increase income. Stuart Rutherford (1999) has outlined how the biggest financial need for people is to assemble "'lump sums' of money to make muckles from mickles that can be used to cope with opportunities or demands." Despite their small income, the poor are often faced with expenditure needs which are large in relation to the sums of money that are immediately available to them. These 'lump sums' can be acquired either through credit or savings. Understanding why 'lump sums' are needed by poor people provides an understanding of how financial services may be useful and what positive or negative impacts these may have on poor people's lives. There are broadly four areas where the need for 'lump sums' may create hardship and hassles and where a poor person's livelihood is strengthened through credit, savings and other financial services.

Opportunities

Poor people need lump sums in order to invest in opportunities-economic or social. Money may be invested as working capital or as productive assets for an income-generating activity. Other opportunities may not be related to economic returns.

Consumption

There is often a difference between people's consumption patterns and their income. Household consumption patterns, for example, may necessitate regular purchase of food items or bulk purchase or outlay on purchase of material for house repairs, roof repairs, etc. Income may be evenly spread throughout the year or its patterns may be skewed and erratic. In both cases, money may not be available when needed in case of inefficient management of household finances.

Life Cycle Needs

All people have major predictable occurrences throughout their lives which are termed as their lifecycle needs, such as birth, marriage, school fees, retirement, etc. These require relatively large sums of money.

Crisis and Emergencies

Unpredictable events such as illnesses, death, accident, fire, natural catastrophe are common for all and more common for the very poor, which is also more vulnerable to their negative impacts. Microfinance thus enables financial inclusion and impacts directly and significantly on economic poverty. It leads to stabilisation of income and expenditure smoothing. Credit invested in an income-generating enterprise as working capital or for productive assets, leads to establishment of a new enterprise or growth of an existing one. Profit from the enterprise provides increased income and a general strengthening of income sources. Microfinance helps clients accumulate or retain physical assets. Assets are increased either through direct loan, used as a benefit of income smoothing or through the use of profits generated through the investment of a loan. The poor invests in three types of assets:

- (i) Household assets which contribute to quality of life, and may also provide security and possible income in case of future need.
- (ii) Household assets which are primarily held as savings in kind, such as livestock.
- (iii) Productive assets which are used to generate income such as land/houses for rent or equipment for a business.

There are two types of exclusion which arise in the absence of access to finance. These are the formal and informal exclusion which need immediate redress.

- (i) **Formal exclusion:** MFIs may take a decision to provide services only to a specific group of clients. For example, many MFIs only provide loans to clients with established micro enterprises.
- (ii) **Informal exclusion:** Whilst the MFIs may commit themselves to cater to the very poor, these may both choose not to join or be prevented by other members. This is most often the case when there is a mix of very poor and less poor clients.

Self Exclusion

The lack of confidence of the poor constrains their capacity to believe that microfinance can be beneficial, or have the perception that the services by MFIs are not intended for them. An example of these is seen in Nyesegiso, a cooperative in Mali where the very poor people exclude themselves most often because of 'the poverty of their household' or 'lack of experience or means for starting an income-generating activity: fear of tainting their reputation or the trust of others if they cannot repay the loan amount and pressure to meet immediate consumption need such as food and clothing.' (Ntezigyaremye, 2001, pp. 2–3).

Exclusion by Other Members

In group-based lending (solidarity groups, self-help groups, village's banking cooperatives) there is a tendency for stronger people in the community to exclude those who are poorer. There is often a negative perception by the community of the poor (useless, lazy, unlikely to be able to repay a loan), resulting in other members not wanting them in their group. This is particularly apparent where group liability is operated, and group members are encouraged to exclude any person who may be bad credit risk.

Client Exit

Where policies are not oriented to the needs of the very poor, it is likely that they will experience a greater proportion of problem, and therefore be more likely to choose to leave the programme, or to be pushed out by other members.

Informal Exclusion by MFI

Whilst intending to reach a defined set of clients, the MFIs unintentionally exclude people who should not be formally excluded. This is a result of a complex inter play of factors at all levels of the organisation.

Exclusion by Staff

Loan officers may have explicit or implicit incentives to exclude the poorest. This may be based on a perception that the poorest are problematic and will create an increased work burden. This can be exacerbated by an organisational culture and incentive schemes that emphasise financial targets above the need to work effectively with the poorest. This will encourage loan officers to focus on greater productivity, increasing portfolio outstanding and reaching larger number of clients rather than achieving greater poverty impact.

Exclusion by Design

Many aspects of the methodology design of a microfinance programme may deliberately or inadvertently exclude the poorest. These may include entry fees, rules that exclude people who do not have an existing business, inappropriate or inflexible loan terms, automatic loan size increases, inaccessible or compulsory saving, group liability rules, providing services from central offices rather than in community based situations, or locating the programme in accessible rather than remote areas. Other aspects of programme design may not exclude the poorest, but may be biased towards the less poor.

Mechanism for exclusion of the very poor:

Action	By whom and Why
Formal Exclusion by MFIs Through eligibility criteria	Deliberate and considered MFI policy
Informal Exclusion Self exclusion of very poor people	Lack of confidence and negative perceptions of MFI processes

Impact on Risk and Vulnerability

Recent studies of the impact of microfinance have placed a much greater emphasis on the role of financial services in reducing client risk and vulnerability (Sebstad and Cohen, 2000; Snodgrass and Sebstad, 2002; Wright, 1999). Financial services have the capacity to interact with many aspects of the client's lives, not just to develop a micro enterprise. Microfinance is thus an important enabling input. It has the potential to create an impact on poverty in a holistic way, supporting client livelihoods, reducing vulnerability, fostering social and economic empowerment, and releasing people's potential to achieve their goals.

Even where there are no net gains in income, significant impact in terms of reduced vulnerability can be achieved through the establishment of more regular, reliable, diversified and resilient income sources, consumption smoothing, increased savings and assets, expanding options for credit, and improving household money management (Snodgrass and Sebstad). The combined effect of these changes reduces risk of crisis and emergencies occurring, and increases the ability of clients to cope, if they occur. Diversified incomes, managed by MFI clients with increased skills are less likely to fail due to mismanagement or as a result of an external shock. Savings reduce vulnerability, allow for planning and management of household finances, consumption smoothing, and accommodating predictable life cycle needs as well as for coping with unpredictable negative event and responding to opportunities. Insurance can provide lump sums that can be used to pay for unexpected needs. Increased investment in food, health, housing, education, etc., lead to healthier, more skilled people. Capital developed through group-based interaction may mean there is an increased network of people to assist in the case of a crisis. Empowerment in turn improves poor people's ability to seek outside support and demand the services and support they may be entitled to.

Key to the impact of financial inclusion on poverty is the enabling effect of economic improvements. Increased income and economic security give clients access to improvement in many aspects of their well-being and basic needs. Thus, financial inclusion impacts basic needs and capabilities (Murdoch and Haley 2002). Financial inclusion through banks which provide financial services helps by contributing to the incomes and economic security helps to stabilise lives of the poor.

Growing Enthusiasm for Microfinance

The 1990s have seen a growing enthusiasm for microfinance and the sector has blossomed in many countries leading to multiple financial services firms serving the needs of micro entrepreneurs and poor households. Today there is increasing focus on expanding financial markets for the poor in frontier markets and on the integration of microfinance in financial systems development. The recent introduction of the financial systems approach which emphasises favourable policy environment and institutions is certain to improve the overall effectiveness of the financial inclusion strategy but several gaps remain in rural and agricultural finance and other frontier markets. Poverty eradication and alleviation require addressing the multiple dimensions of poverty. For the community this means reaching specific Millennium Development Goals (MDGs), education, women's empowerment, and health among others.

International Experience of Financial Innovations in the Microfinance Sector

Prodem, Bolivia's third largest Microbank, has introduced a combination of biometric fingerprint technology to deliver financial services to its clients. Biometric technology measures an individual's unique physical or behavioural characteristic such as fingerprints, facial characteristics, pattern and gait to recognise and confirm identity. Although the technology is still growing, awareness of the importance of data security is increasing. Prodem's fingerprint verification has reduced fraud error and repudiation of transactions. As in other systems, the illiterate customers find it difficult to remember pin numbers leading to unauthorised use of card accounts.

Prior to introduction of credit scoring models, Unibanka, a commercial bank in Latvia found microfinance loans too costly to deliver. Bannock Consulting helped design a credit scoring model based on qualitative design as quantitative data was not available. Unibanka with reduced cost of review found microfinance profitable through the credit scoring model.

- In Nyeri district, Kenya: Accumulated Loan and Savings funds. World Council of Credit Unions (WOCCU) is the global trade association and developmental agency for credit unions. WOCCU promotes the growth and development of credit unions through technical assistance programmes. The Cooperative Insurance Company (CIC) also stepped in to provide insurance to over half of Kenya's more than one million credit members who subscribe to policies through their credit unions
- In South Africa, a network of 8000 armoured trucks equipped with thumb recognition and smart card technology offer pension payments of about USD 60 to 4.5 million South Africans
- In Brazil, a joint venture between the post offices and the large bank, Bradesco, offers banking and payment services through its network branches in the remote and poorer areas of the country since March 2002. Thus there is much to be learnt from the international experience
- In India, Corporation and Canara Bank have shown the way by partnering with NGOs to provide salaried low income workers access to savings. They have established automated teller machines in factories
- Hatton National Bank, a small commercial bank in Sri Lanka avoids the costs of full ledged branches by serving rural areas with small one or two person sub offices
- Hatton Bank, Sri Lanka, launched its microcredit program called Gami Pubuduwa Upadesika (village awakening) in 1989 with the aim of poverty alleviation
- It had been established more than 100 years ago and has a long history of rural finance through banking services to small farmers,

dairy operators, fisheries developers and agricultural product processors

- It operates through a network of 108 branches plus 38 customer centres and 6 mobile units
- It is the largest privately owned bank in Sri Lanka
- They have 72 GP field officers who report directly to the branch managers
- The GP officers work closely with village leaders and potential clients to identify areas of talent for start-up businesses and opportunities for business expansion
- The GP program is fully integrated into HNB's operation as an additional product offered by the bank
- Loans range from USD 244 to 7,320
- There is a GP portfolio in 84 of the 108 total branches
- As on 30 June 2004, GP had almost 11,000 outstanding borrowers with a portfolio of approximately USD 7.4 million. The savings contributed by GP clients totalled over USD 8.8 million
- Loan portfolio and client targets are set by the Development Banking Unit
- The GP program makes use of HNB's head office departments including human resources, marketing, legal operations, information technology and other centralised functions
- This structure leverages HNB's market presence, infrastructure, funding capabilities and management support and gives GP programme a competitive edge over other microfinance providers
- GP consists of a single microloan product partly due to HNB's understanding of GP clients as comprising a small niche market and the programme is intended to graduate microfinance clients into larger loans
- However they are reviewing the possibility of introducing two new products – one involving remittances and the other for retirees who may want to stay active and start a microenterprise
- The estimated profitability in the GP operations of the bank shows that it was marginally profitable
- This is also largely a result of the comparatively low interest charged on GP loans 9–14 per cent against 20 per cent charged by NGOs and others
- GP field officers manage on an average 203 loans each.

In Bangladesh, mobile collections are made on bicycles by SafeSave, thus a great deal of innovation is required to promote access, and in India, a beginning has been made with the Banking Correspondent Model. Recognising the potential of microfinance to positively influence the life of the poor, the Reserve Bank has been making efforts to create an environment for its orderly development. The Reserve Bank conducted a joint fact-finding study in May 2006 with a few major banks. The study revealed that some of the Micro Finance Institutions (MFIs) financed by banks or acting as their intermediaries/partners appeared to be focusing on relatively better banked areas. They were also operating in the same area trying to reach out to the same set of poor resulting in multiple lending. Further, many MFIs supported by banks were not engaging themselves in capacity building and empowerment of the groups to the desired extent. Also, some banks, as principal financiers of MFIs, did not appear to be engaging them for improving their systems, practices and lending policies. An advisory was, therefore, issued to banks in November 2006 communicating these findings and advising them to take corrective action at their end. The microfinance sector has gained momentum in recent years and this has brought into focus the issue of its regulation. A draft Microfinancial Sector (Development and Regulation Bill, 2007) is under consideration of the Union Government, which envisages regulation of the microfinance sector. The Bill was tabled in the Lok Sabha on 20 March 2007. As C.K. Prahlad puts it 'Fortune lies at the bottom of the pyramid'.

The Other State Sponsored Initiatives for Financial Inclusion

The programmes aimed at directly helping the poor are the State Sponsored Programmes of Poverty Alleviation. The main objective of the programmes is inclusion – they are the State's attempt at a direct frontal attack on poverty. They have been designed to directly target the poorest of the poor on the Antyodaya concept, with a view to assist the poor and improve their economic, financial and social conditions. The programme for the poor in India can be broadly categorised as wage employment programmes, for e.g., public works, credit and subsidy based self-employment programmes where credit is released by banks and proportional subsidy by government as the Swarn Jayanti Gram Swarozgar Yojana (SJGSY) and the Pradhan Mantri Rozgar Yojana (PMRY), general access programmes like the Public Distribution Systems and Nutrition Programmes as the Integrated Child

Development Services (ICDS). There is a plethora of schemes in existence – Total Village Employment Scheme, Sampoorna Grameen Rozgar Yojana, Prime Minister's Total Village Self-Employment Scheme, Prime Minister's Village Development Scheme, Pradhan Mantri Gramodaya Yojana, Prime Minister's Village Development Rural Housing Scheme, Pradhan Mantri Grameen Awas Yojana, Pradhan Mantri Gramodaya, Grameen Drinking Water Yojana, Food for poorest families scheme, Antayodaya Anna Yojana, Food Security for senior citizens, Annapoorna, Indira Awas Yojana, Indira Dwelling units scheme, Swarna Jayanti Shahri Rozgar Yojana (SJSRY), Valmiki Ambedkar Awas Yojana, Bharat Nirmaan and the Employment Guarantee scheme.

In addition to the centrally sponsored poverty schemes, there are several state sponsored schemes. If Andhra Pradesh is taken as the pioneer state, it has several state schemes of note. Andhra Pradesh is synonymous with the SHG movement which is group based lending. The precursor of the present SHGs are the 'Podupalakshmi' – grow through savings program, 'Velugu' – grow through literacy, 'Neeru Meeru' – water for all, 'Janmabhoomi' – sustenance through Motherland, 'Phani Ahar Padakam' – food for work programme. A comparison between public works programmes and the Integrated Rural Development schemes in Maharashtra shows that participation in public works programmes is the highest for the poorest households and it tapers off with rising expenditure levels. The transfer efficiency is higher under Employment Guarantee Schemes (EGS). The benefit cost ratio in the case of public distribution and general access schemes has turned out to be only half of that in employment guarantee programmes.

Wage Employment Programmes

The wage employment programmes are considered superior to other programmes as they result in additional benefits such as asset creation, increase in agricultural wages and insurance benefits. As regards credit based self employment programmes, group lending has been found to be more successful than lending to individuals. As far as inclusion goes, EGS has been found to have been very successful, and EGS has promoted financial inclusion as benefits under State Sponsored Programmes received through bank accounts opened for the purpose. An analysis shows that in terms of targeting success, self targeting schemes like rural public works score over income based and general access schemes. By now it is well recognised that rural public works programmes (RWPs) have become important instruments for alleviating poverty and hunger. The poverty programmes also fit into the idea of Nurkse (1957) who regarded surplus labour in low income countries a potential saving useful for capital formation. The objective of Rural Works Programmes is to provide employment and to generate public goods such as physical infrastructure. India has a long experience in experimenting with labour intensive public works. After independence in 1947, many schemes were transferred by the Central Government, beginning with the rural manpower programme in 1960. EGS has received acclaim from several sources. It is a particularly interesting example because of its unprecedented feature of guaranteed rural employment which makes it a model throughout the developing world. In terms of person days of employment created, India's rural public works programmes are the largest in the world. The Employment Guarantee Scheme has reduced unemployment, has increased the incomes of many participating households; it acts as an insurance mechanism and has an impact on agricultural growth and wages has made the rural poor a political force and has had a considerable impact on the employment of women. The major criticism against public works is that they are relief oriented and are not creating durable public assets. The major issue is how to generate productive assets without diluting the primary objective of employment guarantee and poverty alleviation.

Conclusions

Microfinance and other approaches have emerged as significant for poverty redress and financial inclusion. Informal financial arrangements are generally robust. However, microfinance, whether through the SHG Banking model, which is the predominant model or through commercial microfinance institutions cannot supplant the efforts of Commercial Banks, Cooperatives and Regional Rural Banks, who also have penetrative outreach and can supplement their efforts positively. It is necessary as it caters to the needs of the extreme poor. It has been almost conclusively established that informal financial arrangements are pervasive and very successful in providing some types of financial services to the poor. They are timely, reliable and extend small loans for short periods of time. Despite their valuable contributions they do suffer from certain limitations. As they are grounded in the local economy they are limited by local demand and income stream constraints as also the covariant risks of the local environment. As a result, their frontier remains narrow, they do not go far enough in scope geographically, over time, and across products. Informal finance provides valuable services, but in small amounts over short periods of time. The loans remain small in size and as they are cost effective only in the immediate geographical vicinities they are unable to overcome market segmentation and do not contribute much to the most important function of finance; the integration of markets. There are several major advantages which banks possess in their efforts to reach marginal clientele. They operate with a national scope, under a clear regulatory framework and they can leverage their equity with deposits from the public to reach economies of scale and scope. Banks, however, need a genuine technological revolution. MFIs in contrast possess informational and enforcement advantages. Decentralisation certainly improves performance through better use of information though the difficulties of upscaling remain as challenges. Financial inclusion recognises the strengths of both institutional and non-institutional approaches and assigns due importance to both.

References

Kimenyi M.S., Robert C. Wieland and J.D. Von Pischke (eds.). *Strategic Issues in Micro finance: Towards a Sustainable Micro finance Outreach in India, Experiences and Perspectives*, NABARD GTZ SDC 2006.

National Bank for Agriculture and Rural Development Annual Report, 2006–07.

WOCCU a technical guide to Rural Finance Exploration *WOCCU Technical Guide* 3, December 2003.

CGAP IT Innovation Series Credit Scoring.

Johnson, Susan, Nthenya Mule, Robert Hickson, and Wambui Mwangi (2001). *The Managed ASCA Model Innovations: Kenya's Micro finance Industry* Africa: Microsave.

Khandekar, S.R. (1999). 'Grameen Bank Impact, Costs and Program Sustainability' *Asian Development Review*, Vol. 14, No. 1. pp. 97–130, Asian Development Bank.

Rutherford, Stuart (1999). *The Poor and their Money*, Practical Action Publishing.

Joshi, Rajeev (2006). Study of Hatton National Ban Joshi Rajeev Monograph on Grameen Bank Bangladesh.

Pant Joshi, Deepali (2006). *Social Banking*, Foundation Books, New Delhi.

Imboden, Kathryn (2005). 'Building Inclusive Financial Sectors: the Road to Growth and Poverty Reduction' *Journal of International Affairs* Vol. 58.

Chapter 6

Policy Response Committee on Financial Inclusion

In order to address the issues of financial inclusion, the Government of India constituted a 'Committee on Financial Inclusion' under the Chairmanship of Dr C. Rangarajan. The Committee submitted its final report to Union Finance Minister on 4 January 2008.

The terms of reference of the committee included:

(i) studying the pattern of exclusion from access to financial services disaggregated by region, gender and occupational structure
(ii) identifying the barriers confronted by vulnerable groups in accessing credit and financial services including supply, demand and institutional constraints
(iii) reviewing the international experience in implementing policies for financial inclusion and to examine their relevance applicability to India.

The committee further suggested:

(i) a strategy to extend financial services to small and marginal farmers and other vulnerable groups, including measures to streamline and simplify procedures, reduce transaction costs and make the operations transparent for growth
(ii) measures including institutional changes to be undertaken by the financial sector to implement the proposed strategy of financial inclusion
(iii) a monitoring mechanism to assess the quality and quantum of financial inclusion including indicators for assessing progress.

To suggest measures to extend the reach of the financial sector to such vulnerable groups by minimizing, if not eliminating the formal and informal barriers to access encountered by such groups.

In the report that Dr Rangarajan submitted, it was maintained that access to finance by the poor and vulnerable groups is a prerequisite for poverty reduction and social cohesion. This has to become an integral part of our efforts to promote inclusive growth. In fact, providing access to finance is a form of empowerment of the vulnerable groups. Financial inclusion denotes delivery of financial services at an affordable cost to the vast sections of the disadvantaged and low-income groups. The various financial services include credit, savings, insurance, payments and remittance facilities. The objective of financial inclusion is to extend the scope of activities of the organised financial system and to include within its ambit people with low incomes. Through graduated credit, the attempt must be to uplift the poor from one level to another to rid them of poverty.

Extent of Exclusion

NSSO data reveal that 45.9 million farmer households in the country (51.4 per cent), out of a total of 89.3 million households do not access credit, either from institutional or non-institutional sources. Further, despite the vast network of bank branches, only 27 per cent of total farm households are indebted to formal sources (of which one-third also borrow from informal sources). Farm household's not accessing credit from formal sources as a proportion to total farm households is especially high at 95.91 per cent, 81.26 per cent and 77.59 per cent in the north eastern, eastern and central regions respectively. Thus, apart from the fact that exclusion in general is large, it also varies widely across regions, social groups and asset holdings. The poorer the group, the greater is the exclusion, thus reflecting an inversely proportional relation.

Demand Side Factors

While financial inclusion can be substantially enhanced by improving the supply side or the delivery systems, it is also important to note that many regions, segments of the population and sub-sectors of the economy have a limited or weak demand for financial services. In order to improve their level of inclusion, demand side efforts need to be undertaken including improving human and physical resource endowments, enhancing productivity, mitigating risk and strengthening market linkages. However, the primary focus of the Committee has been on improving the delivery systems, both conventional and innovative.

National Mission on Financial Inclusion

The Financial Inclusion Committee has recommended that the task of financial inclusion must be taken up in a mission mode as a financial inclusion plan at the national level. A National Mission on Financial

Inclusion (NaMFI) comprising representatives from all stakeholders may be constituted to aim at achieving universal financial inclusion within a specific time frame. The Mission should be responsible for suggesting the overall policy changes required to achieve the desired level of financial inclusion, and for supporting a range of stakeholders – in the domain of public, private and NGO sectors – in undertaking promotional initiatives.

A National Rural Financial Inclusion Plan (NRFIP) may be launched with a clear target to provide access to comprehensive financial services, including credit to at least 50 per cent of financially excluded households, say 55.77 million by 2012 through rural/semi-urban branches of Commercial Banks and Regional Rural Banks. The remaining households, with such shifts as may occur in the rural/urban population, have to be covered by 2015. Semi-urban and rural branches of commercial banks and RRBs may set for themselves a minimum target of covering 250 new cultivator and non-cultivator households per branch per annum, with an emphasis on financing marginal farmers and poor non-cultivator households.

Development and Technology Funds

There is a cost involved in this massive exercise of extending financial services to hitherto excluded segments of population. Such costs may come down over a period of time with the resultant business expansion. However, in the initial stages some funding support is required for promotional and developmental initiatives that will lead to better credit absorption capacity among the poor and vulnerable sections and for application of technology for facilitating the mandated levels of inclusion. The Committee has therefore proposed the constitution of two funds with NABARD – the Financial Inclusion Promotion and Development Fund, and the Financial Inclusion Technology Fund with an initial corpus of Rs 500 crores each to be contributed in equal proportion by GoI/RBI/NABARD. A Financial Inclusion Promotion and Development Fund (FIPDF) with NABARD for meeting the cost of developmental and promotional interventions has to be introduced. The FIPDF shall support 'developmental and promotional activities' with a view to securing greater financial inclusion, particularly among weaker sections, low income groups and in backward regions/hitherto unbanked areas, so as to enable these segments of the population to increase their incomes, acquire capital, invest their savings, manage their risks and ultimately work their way out of poverty within a reasonable time frame. The activities to be supported by FIPDF shall involve capacity-building, improving credit absorption capacity, reduction of transaction costs, simplification of procedures, development of innovative products/processes, supporting measures for awareness creation/publicity for improving financial literacy/education, undertaking counselling activities, R & D proposals, suitable pilot projects and viability gap, etc. A Financial Inclusion Technology Fund (FITF) has been constituted to meet the costs of technology adoption. The FITF shall be utilised to enhance investment in Information Communication Technology (ICT) aimed at promoting financial inclusion, stimulate transfer of research and technology in financial inclusion, increase technological absorption capacity of financial service providers/users and encourage an environment of innovation and cooperation among stakeholders. The FIPDF will focus on interventions like, Farmers' Service Centers, Promoting Rural Entrepreneurship, Self-Help Groups and their Federations, Developing Human Resources of Banks, Promotion of Resource Centers and Capacity-Building of Business Facilitators and Correspondents, while the FITF will focus on funding of low-cost technology solutions. This recommendation has already been accepted by GoI.

Business Correspondent Model

The RBI had examined the issues relating to:

(i) allowing banks to adopt the agency model by using the infrastructure of civil society organisations
(ii) appointment of banking correspondents to function as intermediaries between the lending banks and the beneficiaries
(iii) identification of steps to promote MFIs.

Based on the recommendations of the group and with the objective of ensuring greater financial inclusion and increasing the outreach of the banking sector, banks have been permitted to use the services of specified intermediaries such as post offices as business facilitators and correspondents.

Extending outreach on a scale envisaged under NRFIP would be possible only by leveraging technology to open up channels beyond branch network. Adoption of appropriate technology would enable the branches to go where the customer is present instead of the other way round. This, however, is in addition to extending traditional mode of banking by targeted branch expansion in identified districts. The Business Facilitator/Business Correspondent (BF/BC) models riding on appropriate technology can deliver this outreach and should form the core of the strategy for extending financial inclusion. The Committee has made some recommendations for relaxation of norms for expanding the coverage of BF/BC. Ultimately, banks should endeavour to have a Business Correspondent touch point in each of the 6,00,000 villages in the country.

Procedural Changes

Procedural changes like simplifying mortgage requirements, exemption from stamp duty for loans to small and marginal farmers and providing agricultural/business development services in the farm and non-farm sectors respectively, will help in extending financial inclusion.

Role of RRBs

RRBs, post-merger represent a powerful instrument for financial inclusion. Their outreach vis-à-vis other scheduled commercial banks particularly in regions and across population groups facing the brunt of financial exclusion is impressive. RRBs account for 37 per cent of total rural offices of all scheduled commercial banks and 91 per cent of their workforce is posted in rural and semi-urban areas. They account for 31 per cent of deposit accounts and 37 per cent of loan accounts in rural areas. RRBs have a large presence in regions marked by financial exclusion of a high order. They account for 34 per cent of all branches in the North East, 30 per cent in eastern and 32 per cent in central regions. Out of the total 22.38 lakh SHGs credit linked by the banking industry as on 31 March 2006, 33 per cent of the linkages were by RRBs which is quite impressive to say the least. Significantly the more backward the region the greater is the share of RRBs which is amply demonstrated by their 56 per cent share in the North East, 48 per cent in central and 40 per cent in eastern region.

RRBs are thus the best suited vehicles to widen and deepen the process of financial inclusion. However, there has to be a firm reinforcement of the rural orientation of these institutions with a specific mandate on financial inclusion. With this end in view, the Committee has recommended that the process of merger of RRBs should not proceed beyond the level of sponsor bank in each state. The Committee has also recommended the recapitalisation of RRBs with negative net worth and widening of their network to cover all unbanked villages in the districts where they are operating, either by opening a branch or through the BF/BC model in a time bound manner. Their area of operation may also be extended to cover the 87 districts, presently not covered by them.

SHG-Bank Linkage Scheme

The SHG-Bank Linkage Programme can be regarded as the most potent initiative since independence for delivering financial services to the poor in a sustainable manner. The programme has been growing rapidly and the number of SHGs financed increased to 29.25 lakhs on 31 March 2007.

The spread of the SHG-Bank Linkage Programme in different regions has been uneven with southern states accounting for the major chunk of credit linkage. Many states with high incidence of poverty have shown poor performance under the programme. NABARD has identified 13 states with large population of the poor, but exhibiting low performance in implementation of the programme. The ongoing efforts of NABARD to upscale the programme in the identified states need to be given a fresh impetus. The Committee has recommended that NABARD may open dedicated project offices in these 13 states for scalingup the SHG-Bank Linkage Programme. The state governments and NABARD may set aside specific funds out of the budgetary support and the Micro Finance Development and Equity Fund (MFDEF) respectively for the purpose of promoting SHGs in regions with high levels of exclusion. For the North East, there is a need to evolve SHG models suited to the local context of such areas. NGOs have played a commendable role in promoting SHGs and linking them with banks. NGOs, being local initiators with their low resources, are finding it difficult to expand in other areas and regions. There is, therefore, a need to evolve an incentive package which should motivate these NGOs to diversify into other backward areas.

The SHG-Bank Linkage Programme is now more than fifteen years old. There are a large number of SHGs in the country which are well established in their savings and credit operations. The members of such groups want to expand and diversify their activities with a view to attain economies of scale. Many of the groups are organising themselves into federations and other higher level structures. To achieve this effectively, resource centres can play a vital role. Federations of SHGs at village and taluk levels have certain advantages. Federations, if they emerge voluntarily from amongst SHGs, can be encouraged. However, the Committee feels that they cannot be entrusted with the financial intermediation function.

Extending SHG-Bank Linkage Scheme to Urban Areas

There are no clear estimates of the number of people in urban areas with no access to organised financial services. This may be attributed, in part at least, to the migratory nature of the urban poor, comprising mostly migrants from the rural areas. Even moneylenders often shy away from lending to the urban poor. The Committee has recommended amendment to the NABARD Act to enable it to provide microfinance services to the urban poor.

Joint Liability Groups

SHG-Bank Linkage has emerged as an effective credit delivery channel for the poor clients. However, there are segments within the poor such as share croppers/oral lessees/tenant farmers, whose loan requirements are much larger but who have no collaterals to fit into the traditional financing approaches of the banking system. To service such clients, Joint Liability Groups (JLGs), an upgradation of the SHG model, could be an effective way. NABARD had piloted a project for formation and linking of JLGs during 2004–05 in 8 states of the country through 13 RRBs. Based on the encouraging response from the project, a scheme for financing JLGs of tenant farmers and oral lessees has also been evolved. The Committee has recommended that adoption of the JLGs concept could be another effective method for purveying credit to mid-segment clients such as small farmers, marginal farmers, tenant farmers, etc. and thereby reduce their dependence on informal sources of credit.

Micro Finance Institutions – NBFCs

Micro Finance Institutions (MFIs) could play a significant role in facilitating inclusion, as they are uniquely positioned in reaching out to the rural poor. Many of them operate in a limited geographical area, have a greater understanding of the issues specific to the rural poor, enjoy greater acceptability amongst the rural poor and have flexibility in operations providing a level of comfort to their clientele. The Committee has, therefore, recommended that greater legitimacy, accountability and transparency will not only enable MFIs to source adequate debt and equity funds, but also eventually enable them to take and use savings as a low cost source for on-lending.

There is a need to recognise a separate category of Micro finance–Non Banking Finance Companies (MF–NBFCs) without any relaxation on start-up capital and subject to the regulatory prescriptions applicable for NBFCs. Such MF–NBFCs could provide thrift, credit, micro-insurance, remittances and other financial services up to a specified amount to the poor in rural, semi-urban and urban areas. Such MF–NBFCs may also be recognised as Business Correspondents of banks for providing not only savings and remittance services but also to act as micro-insurance agents.

The Micro Financial Sector (Development and Regulation) Bill, 2007 has been introduced in Parliament in March 2007. The Committee feels that the Bill, when enacted, would help in promoting orderly growth of the microfinance sector in India. The Committee feels that MFIs registered under Section 25 of Companies Act, 1956 can be brought under the purview of this Bill while cooperative societies can be taken out of the purview of the proposed Bill.

Revitalising the Cooperative System

Though the network of commercial banks and RRBs has spread rapidly and they now have nearly 50,000 rural/semi-urban branches, their reach in the countryside both in terms of the number of clients and accessibility to the small and marginal farmers and other poorer segments is far less than that of cooperatives. In terms of number of agricultural credit accounts, the Short Term Cooperative Credit System (STCCS) has 50 per cent more accounts than the commercial banks and RRBs put together. On an average, there is one Political Action Committee for every six villages; these societies have a total membership of more than 120 million rural people making it one of the largest rural financial systems in the world. However, the health of a very large proportion of these rural credit cooperatives has deteriorated significantly.

For the revival of the STCCS, the Vaidyanathan Committee Report has suggested an implementable Action Plan with substantial financial assistance. The implementation of the Revival Package would result in the emergence of strong and robust cooperatives with conducive legal and institutional environment for it to prosper. A financially sound cooperative structure can do wonders for financial inclusion given its extensive outreach.

Micro Insurance

Micro-insurance is a key element in the financial services package for people at the bottom of the pyramid. The poor face more risks than the well off. It is becoming increasingly clear that micro-insurance needs a further push and guidance from the regulator as well as the government. The Committee concurs with the view that offering micro credit without micro-insurance is self-defeating. There is, therefore, a need to emphasise linking of micro credit with micro-insurance.

The country has moved on to a higher growth trajectory. To sustain and accelerate the growth momentum, we have to ensure increased participation of the economically weak segments of the population in the process of economic growth. Financial inclusion of hitherto excluded segments of population is a critical part of this process of inclusion. A major development challenge currently faced by us is how we can make one institutional setting more conducive to growth and poverty reduction. This is the key to better development outcomes. The challenging question is how to move from dysfunctional institutional settings to those with greater development effectiveness. The organised banking system, despite the impressive branch expansion in rural and semi-urban areas, had not penetrated the society enough. The exclusion is estimated to be between 50 per cent to 70 per cent. The Committee has defined financial inclusion as 'the process of ensuring access to financial services and timely and adequate credit where needed by vulnerable groups such as weaker sections and low income groups at an affordable cost.'

Experience has shown that in the initial phases of real and financial sector reforms, there is a need to build in adequate provisions ensuring that the economically weak segment of the population have increased participation in the process of economic growth and social development. Reforms in financial systems need to be complemented by measures that encourage the institutions, instruments, relationships, and financial arrangements to be properly gearing for providing sound, responsive financial services to the majority of the people who do not have such access. Financial inclusion implies ensuring a range of financial services available to every individual and enabling them to understand and access those services. Apart from the regular form of financial intermediation, this includes a basic, 'no frills' bank account for making and receiving payments, a savings product suited to the cash flows of a poor household, money transfer facilities, small loans and overdrafts for productive, personal and other purposes.The Committee scanned the data forward out by NSSO in the situation assessment survey on inbebtedness of farm households (2003) and noted that the definition of inbebtedness as adopted in the survey referred to farmer households having outstanding loans from institutional or non-institutional sources in cash or kind having a value of Rs 3000 or more at the time of transaction. As per NSSO data, 45.9 million farmer households out of a total 89.3 million households in the country do not access credit either from institutional or non-institutional sources. Only 27 per cent of total farm households are indebted to formal sources of which one-third also borrow from informal sources. In other words 73 per cent of farm households do not have access to formal credit sources. Financially excluded households are defined as those not having any debt to formal credit sources. Farm households not accessing credit from formal sources as a proportion to total farm households is especially high at 95.91 per cent, 81.26 per cent and 77.59 per cent in the North East, eastern and central regions respectively. In terms of absolute numbers, these regions taken together account for 64 per cent of farm households not accessing credit from formal sources.

Level of Indebtedness to Institutional Sources

Only 27 per cent of the total farm households were indebted to institutional sources. Data disaggregated by states indicates that indebtedness among the more 'inclusive states' of the southern region show a high recourse to non-institutional sources of finance. This is particularly the case in Andhra Pradesh and Tamil Nadu.

Table 6.1 Level of Indebtedness across Regions.

		Incidence of indebtedness to both formal & non formal sources		Indebtedness to institutional sources	
Region		Lakh HHs	(Percentage to total HH)	Lakh HH	(Percentage to total HH)
Northern	109.46	56.26	51.39	27.42	25.05
North East	35.40	7.04	19.88	1.45	4.09
Eastern	210.61	84.22	40.01	39.47	18.74
Central	271.33	113.04	41.66	60.81	22.41
Western	103.66	55.74	53.77	45.59	43.98
Southern	161.56	117.45	72.70	69.07	42.75
Group of UTs	1.48	0.49	33.10	0.150	10.14
All India	893.50	434.24	48.60	243.96	27.30

Source: Report of the Committee on Financial inclusion.

Table 6.2 Level of Non-indebtedness across Marginal Sources – Small Farmer Households.

Category of farmer HH	Size class of land owned (Ha)	Total farmer HH (No lakh)	Non indebted farmer HH (No lakh)	Incidence of exclusion by both formal and nonformal	Proportion of non indebted (HH) (Percentage)
Marginal	<1.00	589.06	324.04	55.0	70.6
Small	1.01–2.00	160.60	78.68	49.0	17.1
Semi-medium	2.01–4.00	93.50	39.10	41.8	8.5
Medium	4.01–10.00	42.58	14.84	34.9	3.2
Large	10.00+	7.76	2.60	33.6	0.6
All sizes		893.50	459.26	51.4	100.0

Table 6.3 Level of Indebtedness across Marginalised Societies

Households	Scheduled Tribes	Scheduled castes	Other backward castes	Others	All
Total No. of farmer HHs (lakhs)	119.24	155.93	370.43	247.90	893.50
Non-indebted farmer HHs(lakhs)	75.94	77.60	179.96	125.76	459.26
Proportion of non-indebted farmer HHs (%)	63.69	49.77	48.58	50.73	51.40

It can be seen from the table above that 87 per cent of all non-indebted farm households belong to the marginal (70 per cent) and small (17.1 per cent) farmer categories. The NSSO estimates of the year 2003 show that only 45 per cent of marginal farmer households had access to both institutional and non-institutional credit. There is no data to show the finance extended exclusively to marginal farmers by institutional sources. Marginal farmers who account for 66 per cent of all farm holdings remain by and large excluded from the formal financial system, and by rough approximation as noted by the Rangarajan Committee, only around 20 per cent of these households access credit from the formal banking sources. The proportion and level of inability to access credit increases with the decline in size of farm holdings. Thus those who need credit the most are denied access to the same. The highest levels of non-indebtedness to both formal and non-formal sources is observed among Scheduled Tribes (ST) with 63.7 per cent followed by Scheduled Castes (SC) with 49.8 percent as detailed above.

Incidence of financial exclusion among all non-cultivator households was 78.2 per cent which comprises 78.8 per cent of agricultural labourer households, 71.4 percent of artisans, and 79.7 percent of other rural households. Of 5.96 crores non-cultivator households, 4.66 crores were estimated by the Committee to be financially excluded. The number of non-cultivator households affected by financial exclusion was the highest for 'Others' category (2.44 crores) followed by agricultural labour households (1.67 crores) and artisans (0.55 crores) as given in Table 6.4.

Table 6.4 Level of Exclusiveness across Agricultural Labour Household

Households	Agricultural labourers	Artisans	Others	Total Non-cultivators
Number of households (crores)	2.12	0.77	3.06	5.96
Number of households facing financial exclusion (crores)	1.67	0.55	2.44	4.66
Incidence of financial exclusion (%)	78.80	71.40	79.70	78.20

Source: AIDIS Report of household indebtedness in India (59th round) NSSO

In this context, the Committee, under the package for Doubling Flow of Agricultural Credit, had assigned commercial banks and RRBs had been assigned to target 100 new farmers in the rural/semi-urban branches per annum. This target was achieved, indeed exceeded. Taking heart from this, the Committee is of the view that the semi-urban and rural branches of commercial banks and RRBs may set for themselves a minimum target of covering 250 new cultivator and non-cultivator households per branch per annum, with an emphasis on financing marginal farmers and poor non-cultivator households. The national targets would have to be disaggregated state wise with adequate emphasis on districts having a large percentage of population not accessing bank credit, as indicated in the following table:

Table 6.5 Disaggregated State-wise Nature Targets

S. no.	State	No. of districts	Range of credit gap
1	Arunachal Pradesh	5	98.3–99.3
2	Assam	19	96.1–98.5
3	Bihar	37	95.0–98.6
4	Chhattisgarh	15	96.5–98.0
5	Dadra &Nagar Haveli	1	97.6
6	Gujarat	7	95.7–98.1
7	Haryana	5	95.4–96.9
8	Jharkhand	12	95.6–97.8
9	Madhya Pradesh	30	95.3–98.3
10	Maharashtra	20	95.1–98.0
11	Manipur	9	97.9–99.2
12	Meghalaya	1	99.0

(Continued)

Table 6.5 Continued.

S. no.	State	No. of districts	Range of credit gap
13	Mizoram	1	98.3
14	Nagaland	6	98.2–99.3
15	Orissa	2	95.2–95.3
16	Rajasthan	14	95.2–97.8
17	Uttar Pradesh	58	95.1–98.6
18	West Bengal	14	95.2–97.1
	Total	256	

Source: Report of the Committee on Financial Inclusion.

The per branch annual coverage envisaged under the plan is quite high in certain states of the North East, eastern and central regions. The various recommendations made by the Committee have kept this in view for providing the required support including financial assistance on a region-specific basis to banks operating in the above regions. The strategy for achieving the above goal would comprise mapping out on a state-wise/district-wise basis, rural households having no access to formal sources of credit. This task should be assigned to the District Level Consultative Committees (DLCC) of Banks on a priority basis, with instructions to proceed with the mapping exercise on a block-wise/district-wise basis. The task would require, inter alia, the lead bank and the district administration placing appropriate personnel and material at the disposal of the DLCCs so that the task is complete at the earliest. At the end of the exercise, each DLCC should be in a position to draw up block-wise/village-wise maps of households not having access to formal credit sources. This information should be disseminated widely and transparently by the DLCC in the district. Thereafter, at the state-level, a financial inclusion document (State Level Rural Financial Inclusion Plan – SLRFIP) should be prepared jointly by the State Level Bankers' Committee (SLBC) and NABARD, for arriving at the target of financial inclusion for the state. The target should clearly indicate the number of rural households not having currently any access to formal sources of credit and based on the mapping, indicate the number of households that will be provided such access by 2012. With a minimum target coverage of 50 per cent of currently excluded households states will be free to set themselves higher targets. The target will thereafter be allocated institution-wise, with each bank—commercial banks and RRBs. Other institutions like cooperative banks, NBFCs and MFIs may also be asked to join in the task of financial inclusion with self-set targets. The committee has recognised correctly and candidly that target setting by itself will not be sufficient. There is a need to bring about coordinated efforts of all the above players. Appropriate support instruments for achieving these targets have to be designed. The progress in implementation shall be reported and monitored at the District Level Coordination Committee meetings (DLCC) and the State Level Bankers' Committee Meeting (SLBC).

In addition, the Committee on financial sector reforms has suggested, 'The poor need efficiency, innovation, and value for money, which can come from motivated financiers who see the poor as profitable, but who also have the capacity of making decisions quickly and with minimum paperwork.' The process by which the mandates are implemented should be reformed to emphasise efficiency and ease of compliance, and once the new process is in place, the mandate should be strictly enforced. The focus should be on actually increasing access to services for the poor. On the eve of the 11th Plan, our economy is in a much stronger position than it was a few years ago. After slowing down to an average growth rate of about 5.5 per cent in the Ninth Plan period (1997–98 to 2001–02), it has accelerated significantly in recent years. The average growth rate in the last four years of 10th Plan period (2003–04 to 2006–07) is likely to be a little over 8 per cent, making the growth rate 7.2 per cent for the entire tenth Plan period. Though, this is below the Tenth Plan target of 8 per cent, it is the highest growth rate achieved in any plan period. This performance reflects the strength of our economy and the dynamism of the private sector in many areas. Yet, it is also true that economic growth has failed to be sufficiently inclusive, particularly after the mid-1990s. Agriculture lost its growth momentum from that point onwards and subsequently entered a near-crisis situation. Jobs in the organised sector have not increased despite faster growth. The percentage of our population below the poverty line is declining but only at a modest pace. Malnutrition levels also appear to be declining, but the magnitude of the problem continues to be very high. Far too many people still lack access to basic services such as health, education, clean drinking water and sanitation facilities without which they cannot claim their share in the benefits of growth. Women have increased their participation in the labour force as individuals, but continue to face discrimination and are subject to increasing violence, one stark example of which is the declining female child sex ratio. Despite these problems, most of the ordinary people have tried to cope with their livelihood issues. Many have participated in collective action to improve their social and economic conditions. Empowerment of Panchayati Raj Institutions (PRIs) is ongoing but much remains to be done. Civil Society Organisations have gained strength and are trying new experiments to reach the unreached, often in partnership with Panchayati Raj Institutions. Women are participating in Panchayati Raj Institutions and leading group actions for a better life.

SHGS, NGOs and Rural Development Estimates

- In the current decade, according to estimates of the Planning Commission, more than 12 million additional people will be seeking work every year.
- There are about 30 million unemployed or underemployed individuals in the country of which more than 75 per cent belong to the rural parts.
- Thus to ensure full employment, more than 15 million new livelihoods will have to be generated every year.
- The rural poor are increasingly becoming vulnerable to spiraling cycles of poverty because of low wages, seasonality and still predominant dependence of agriculture on monsoons.
- Contribution of the primary sector to GDP has been continuously decreasing. In 1951 it was half of GDP, in 2001 it was less than one fourth. In all economies in transition, the share of agriculture in GDP tends to decline, while that of manufacturing and services tends to increase. The decline of the share of agriculture in GDP per se is not so much a cause for concern, as the fact that the share of labour force in agriculture is not coming down commensurably.

Sustainable Livelihoods and Microfinance

- A livelihood comprises the capabilities, assets and activities required for a means of living.
- A livelihood is sustainable when it can cope with and recover from stresses and shocks, maintain or enhance its capabilities and assets, while not undermining the natural resource base.

Microenterprises

- Promotion of sustainable multiple microenterprises depends on the availability of basic skill, understanding about the viability of the business, knowledge about market and accessibility of non-financial support services.

- A market led, locally sustainable curriculum will have to be developed in order to achieve a long-term self-employment movement.
- Working in remote villages far away from the market centres limits the scope for identifying and initiating Income Generation (IG) activities. It is recommended that programmes should focus more on promoting income generating activities near markets in semi-urban areas, market centres and larger villages.
- The savings and credit mechanism cannot, by itself, be seen as an instrument to promote economic activities.

Conclusions

Financial inclusion is the extension of the frontiers of formal institutional finance to include the hitherto excluded. This is the thrust of growth with equity which alone can empower the poorest of the poor and the weakest, and most vulnerable groups. Financial services denote the entire gamut of services and include credit, savings, insurance, payments and remittance facilities. The objective of financial inclusion is to extend the scope of activities of the organised financial system to embrace within its ambit those hitherto excluded due to uncertain income streams. Through access to credit, attempts must be made to help the poor work their way out of poverty. For growth to be real, it must be informed by equity issues relating to financial exclusion, particularly in the rural sector. These have become a key policy concern, and devising strategies for inclusive growth has become the guiding principle of public policy.

References

Report of the Committee on Financial Inclusion, 2008.

Committee on Financial Sector Reform – Planning Commission Draft Document 11th Plan.

Chapter 7

International Experience in Promoting Financial Inclusion and Policy Responses

In developed countries, there is a greater awareness of the positive role financial inclusion can play in empowering the low income groups. Official policies in these countries actively promote inclusive practices, going as far as to give them statutory sanction. In UK, a dedicated fund has been set up to encourage inclusion, and banks and credit unions have been assigned definite responsibilities. In the US, the Community Reinvestment Act prohibits discrimination by banks against low- and moderate-income groups, while in France, it is a legal right for anyone to have a bank account. Clearly, there is much to learn both from international developments and from the experience gained within the country during the first two decades after bank nationalisation.

A Goal Relevant to All Economies

Building inclusive financial systems and allowing access to them is a goal that is relevant to economies at all levels of development. The primary objective lies in making financial systems available to all and ensuring that as many people as possible enjoy access to the financial system, thereby tapping the full potential of the economy. Attention needs to be devoted to enhancing the quality, reach and range of financial services and products credit, savings, insurance payment systems for sustained growth and productivity. It is axiomatic that well-functioning financial systems boost economic growth which reduces poverty. Financial market imperfections as high transaction costs flowing from asymmetry of information are addressed by well-functioning financial systems. All countries need to improve financial access. In several countries (developed and developing) barriers to access potentially exclude a significant share of population from using banking services.

World Bank Research

According to the World Bank survey, in systems that are predominantly government owned, customers pay lower fees but also face greater restrictions in terms of where to apply for loans and how long it takes to have applications processed. These policies have important implications for policy reforms to broaden access. A World Bank survey conducted in 2007 revealed that only 87 per cent of the adult population had a bank account as opposed to 48 per cent in Andhra Pradesh and Uttar Pradesh, 41 per cent in Bogotá and Colombia, and 25 per cent in Mexico. To open a bank account in Cameroon an amount of over $700 is needed, which is higher than GDP per capita of that country while in South Africa and Swaziland, no minimum amounts are required. Fees to maintain a checking account exceed 23 per cent of GDP per capita in Sierra Leone while there are no such fees in the Philippines. The fees for transferring $250 internationally is $50 but only 30 cents in Belgium. While most people in the developing world take access to banking services for granted, there are barriers which bar people in large parts of the developing countries from using and accessing formal banking services. The poor cannot afford to spend more than 2 per cent of their household income on bank charges. The fees observed in many countries prevent them from using such accounts. Similarly, the requirement of a physical address or a formal sector job as eligibility criteria to open an account excludes the majority of people in many developing countries where a large percentage of the population lives in rural areas and works in the informal sector. Affordability, eligibility, transaction costs and information asymmetries – all serve as tangible barriers to financial inclusion.

Outreach Considerations

Financial exclusion can retard economic growth and increase poverty and inequality. A large body of empirical literature has established the importance of the broadening of the banking sector into the interiors for economic development and poverty alleviation. While banks in 19 countries do not impose any minimum balances for checking accounts, such balances are higher than 105 per capita than in others. While in five countries only one document is needed to open a bank account, four documents including Identity Card, Payment Slip and Proof of Domicile are required in six countries effectively preventing large parts of the population from accessing these services.

Barriers to Financial Inclusion

Attempt has been made to document and analyse banking barriers using surveys of 193 banks in 58 countries. The data shows significant variations to banking across countries. Barriers like high minimum deposit balances, minimum loan amounts and fees can lead to exclusion by making these products unaffordable for a large share of the population, for e.g., high fees on savings and checking accounts effectively exclude more than 305 per cent of the population from having a checking account in 10 of the 58 countries surveyed. Strict documentation requirements and long processing time exclude households and firms which cannot provide these documents that depend on faster loan decisions. Geographic centralisation of deposit and loan decisions at headquarters reduces physical access and increases the opportunity costs for households and firms to access financial services. In their paper, 'Access to finance – An Unfinished Agenda', Horsten Beck and Asli Demigurc Kunt argue that financial exclusion is likely to act as a brake on development as it retards economic growth and increases poverty and inequality. Without access to financial services, households will not be able to invest in their human capital. As Jonathan Murdoch has so well expressed it 'the poor need secure and sustainable finance'.

Price and Non-price Barriers

Price and non-price barriers were again responsible for financial exclusion which was both voluntary on the part of the borrowers, who don't trust banks, and want to keep personal records private. A bank located at a distance and lacking faith in borrowers without fixed income or job addresses, may possibly lead to financial exclusive the underprivileged fraction of the underprivileged fraction of the population. An interesting feature which emerges from the international practice is that the more developed the society is, the greater the thrust on empowerment of the common person and low income groups. Let us look at various countries for their experiences.

United Kingdom

The United Kingdom (UK) government has taken certain initiatives concerning financial inclusion, among which seven initiatives are of most significance:

- Identification of three priority areas for the purpose of financial inclusion, namely, access to banking services, access to affordable credit, access to free face-to-face money advice
- Establishment of a Financial Inclusion Fund to promote financial inclusion
- Assignment of responsibility to banks and Credit Unions to remove financial exclusion

- Introduction of a 'No Frills' basic bank account
- Creation of Post Office Current Account for those unable or unwilling to access a basic bank account
- Introduction of a 'Savings Gateway' for those on low-income employment
- Setting up of Community Finance Learning Initiatives to promote basic financial literacy among housing association tenants.

United States of America

In the United States of America (USA), between 9.5 per cent and 20 per cent of households lack a bank account. Further, the US evidence is that 22 per cent of low-income families (8.4 million families earning less than US$25,000 per annum) do not have a current or savings bank account. To correct this situation, a civil rights legislation known as the Community Re-investment Act (CRA) has been enacted. The CRA prohibits discrimination by banks against low and moderate-income neighbourhoods and obliges banks to serve the credit and banking service needs of all communities in which they are chartered. Some states have gone beyond the CRA mandate and placed an obligation on banks to provide basic banking low cost accounts with minimum facilities to all citizens. The CRA and the Home Mortgage Disclosure Act require banks to disclose details of peoples' and groups to whom services have been currently offered. This important step was originally introduced as a response to banks reclining areas and refusing to do business with residents of certain neighbourhoods. The Act also require banks to serve the convenience and needs of communities in which financial institutions have been given charters and licenses to business. The legislation has had the effect of ensuring that banks meet their social objectives, encourage the community to access banking services and change their own commercial behaviour; for example, banks now provide money to community development funds in order to ensure positive scoring when lending is disclosed under the enactment.

Indonesia

In 2001, the financial deepening in Indonesia was 101 per cent. In the same year, the number of MFIs in Indonesia was around 53,000 – seven times the number of branches of commercial banks. Thus MFIs are playing a very important role in extending credit outreach and making financial inclusion a reality in Indonesia. The rural financial institutions are largely owned by government at village and provincial levels. In 1983, in the wake of financial sector reforms undertaken by the Indonesian government, the Bank Rakyat Indonesia transformed its Unit Desa network from loss making channeling agent for the government subsidised credit programme for rice cultivation (BIMAS) into commercial micro finance intermediaries. This turnaround which has greatly facilitated outreach to poorer borrowers and increased credit off-take, facilitating the exponential growth of financial inclusion is at the heart of the Indonesian model. The Unit Desas have achieved profitability with high outreach to the poor.

Brazil

Regulations have allowed banks to offer a new type of account designed specially for the poor. Anyone with a national identity card can open an account, new accounts are available at corner groceries, post offices and gas stations. A banker only needs a computer or a magnetic card reader to handle transactions such as bill payments, deposits and withdrawals and can earn fees for each transaction. Overheads are minimal since there are no bank branches. Cost of capital is close to zero since regulations have allowed banks to use up to 2 per cent of their reserve requirement to make small loans to the poor. The interest charged on such loans cannot exceed 2 per cent a month compared to the 10–12 per cent that others bear. The contractors get a cut of the bank's revenues as do owners of shops and other outlets offering the service. Each new account costs the bank just 55 cents to open compared to US$17 at other commercial banks. The amount of loans is also capped at US$110 for individuals and US$370 for small businesses. The biggest is Banco Postal which operates out of post offices and boasts of 2.8 million accounts. The first branch was opened in March 2002 followed by Banco Popular Do Brasil that opened in February 2006 and already has more than one million accounts. It farms out the work of running the retail network to financial services companies.

Commonalities Observed in the Various Approaches Applicable in the Indian Context

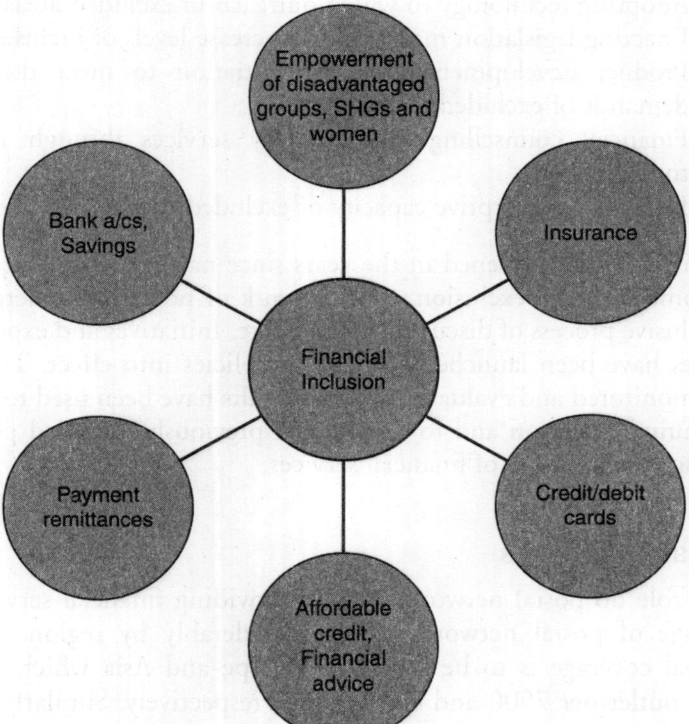

Financial inclusion implies making available all of the above services to all individuals irrespective of their financial and social status. This requires the following steps:

- Identification and geographical demarcation of excluded areas and segments of society formulating suitable policy to facilitate inclusion
- Regulation is a must, even if it is 'regulation by exception'
- Strategy to be adopted through interaction with stakeholders
- Inclusive efforts have a cost to be met by Government and banks
- Institutional reforms are a must, for only strong institutions can serve social mandate in full

- Effective participation and coordination among Government, private service providers, financing banks and members of civil societies
- Adopting technology to widen outreach in excluded areas
- Enacting legislation mandated to increase levels of inclusion
- Product development and differentiation to meet the varying demands of excluded segments
- Financial counselling and advisory services through identified touch points
- Improving absorptive capacity of excluded segments.

A great deal has happened in the years since nationalisation of banks to overcome financial exclusion. A framework of policy has emerged from an inclusive process of discussion and debate. Initiatives and experimental services have been launched to put the policies into effect. These have been monitored and evaluated and the results have been used to establish continuing provision and to ensure that previously excluded people are making beneficial use of financial services.

Postal Networks

What role do postal networks play in providing financial services? The coverage of postal networks varies considerably by region. The best regional coverage is to be found in Europe and Asia which have one postal outlet per 7500 and 4350 people respectively. Similarly, while it is estimated that around 15 per cent of the world's adults, some 390 million people, have a postal savings or transmission (or Giro) account, the regional penetration varies from a high of 20 per cent in Asia, owing to popular financial service offerings in India and China, to a low of less than 1 per cent in Latin America, where the postal network is less pervasive.

In addition to geographical penetration, the range and types of postal financial services offered also differ considerably by region. Most post office deposits were often invested in government bonds (as commonly in Africa); or through the sale of Treasury bonds to the public, acting as an agent of the government (as in India and Pakistan). In some cases, postal financial services also included insurance and retail credit distributed on an agency basis (In Morocco, Poste Maroc developed a partnership with Wafa Assurance to distribute a pension insurance scheme through postal outlets). In the developing countries,

Table 7.1 Percentage of Inhabited Villages in Selected States Having Posts and Telegraph Offices and Telephone Connections (1991).

State	Any Postage and Telegraph facilities	Post Office	Telegraph Office	Telephone Connections
Andhra Pradesh	55.49	52.35	6.67	12.82
Karnataka	31.62	30.30	9.06	16.05
Kerala	98.70	94.73	53.83	59.39
Tamil Nadu	55.72	47.93	7.53	14.09
Gujarat	55.58	46.22	4.00	28.62
Maharashtra	28.91	25.60	2.64	6.08
Rajasthan	51.08	48.83	2.00	8.06

Source: www. indiastat. com.

postal networks already offer several basic financial services, such as money transfers and savings accounts. Moreover, postal networks have widespread coverage even in rural areas which the formal financial sector usually does not directly reach. There are almost twice as many post offices and postal agencies (5,00,000) as commercial bank branches (2,75,000) in the developing world. How to make best use and develop these large networks for expanding access to financial services is an important question for policy makers to consider. Ensuring long-term sustainability of current initiatives and tackling new forms of exclusion and marginalisation as they arise is the best way to deal with arising teething problems. Post offices in India do not provide credit services, but they do provide savings services. In a recent World Bank NCAER study on penetration of post offices it was found that Andhra Pradesh and the southern states had better connectivity.

Thus if financial inclusion is treated as a key objective of public policy the post offices have an important role to play in creating an enabling environment to facilitate the process.

The European Scenario

France and Belgium have undertaken initiatives to committing banks to open an affordable account with bare minimum facilities. 'Call Deposit Account' in Belgium offers three basic types of transactions: money transfers, deposits, withdrawals, and bank statements.

However, individual banks may opt to offer other services if they wish to do so. In Germany, a voluntary code was introduced by the German Bankers' Association in 1996. This makes provision for an 'everyman' current account, offering basic banking transactions, without an overdraft facility. Likewise, access to basic banking in the United Kingdom and Australia has been achieved through voluntary arrangements with banks and has not involved formal charters. In the United Kingdom, for instance, a Banking Code has been drafted which requires banks to inform customers about their basic bank account and its suitability for their needs. A Financial Inclusion Taskforce, instituted in April 2005, monitors access to basic banking services.

Several countries have also introduced specific legislation that gives both a universal right to a bank account and spells out the precise nature of banking services to be provided. In France, the law on exclusion of July 1998 reiterated the right to an account first set out in the 1984 law and has since then simplified the process of exercising the right to an account. In Belgium, a banking Bill was enacted which has been implemented since October 2003. In addition to setting out the minimum standards for basic bank accounts, it also specifies the ceiling on charges and a minimum number of free face-to-face transactions. In many ways, the policy response in Canada combines the best of developments in other countries. The relevant legislation, enacted in June 2001, requires all banks to provide accounts without minimum opening balances to all Canadians, regardless of employment or credit history, with minimum identification requirements. A Financial Consumer Agency of Canada has been established to monitor whether financial institutions adhere to their public commitments. Typically, countries with low levels of income inequality tend to have lower levels of financial exclusion, while high levels of exclusion are associated with the least equal ones. In Sweden, for example, less than 2 per cent adults did not have an account in 2000 and in Germany, the figure was around 3 per cent (Kempson, 2006). In comparison, less than 4 per cent of adults in Canada and 5 per cent in Belgium, lacked a bank account (Buckland et al., 2005). Countries with high levels of inequality record higher levels of banking exclusion. In Portugal, about 17 per cent of the adult population had no account of any kind in 2000 (Kempson, 2006).

The policy responses to such exclusion have been varied in Sweden, for example, banks cannot refuse to open a savings or deposit account under Section 2 of the Banking Business Act of 1987; in France, Article 58 of the Banking Act, 1984 recognised the principle of the right to a bank account; in the US, federal government introduced the Community Reinvestment Act in 1997, partly in response to concerns about bank branch closures in low-income neighborhoods. Under this legislation, federal bank regulatory agencies rate banks on their efforts to serve low-income communities. These early legislations were designed to ensure access to a deposit account but did not spell out the nature of banking services that should be on offer. Refinements in this area have actually taken place in the latter half of the 1990s, resulting partly from a wider concern regarding social exclusion (Caskey et al., 2006, Kempson et al., 2000).

South Africa

A South African IT initiative worth emulating is the Mzansi account, a National 'no frills' Bank Account (NBA) product that caters to the unbanked population of South Africa, established to leverage existing networks of banks, government and other bodies. The Mzansi initiative which was launched in 2004 has setup service banking within almost 15 kilometres of all citizens and an automatic teller machine within 10 kilometres of their homes. By the end of August 2005, more than 1.5 million Mzansi accounts were opened including within the ambit of financial services majority of people who had not availed of banking facilities before. The Mzansi is the first of two first order savings/transmission products aimed at penetration of banks into first order markets. Access to the NBA product is provided through a combination of existing point outlets and physical branch outlets including own and shared ATM offices and merchant POS, etc. There is a money transfer service associated with Mzansi account which facilitated money transfer among customers of all banks offering the Mzansi services. It is a technology leveraged product which has dramatically reduced service costs. It may, thus, be noted that financial inclusion is a concern even in developed countries and legislative or regulatory measure to achieve it are a common feature.

Table 7.2 Country-wise Composite Index of Financial Inclusion and Percentage of Population with Access to Financial Services.

Country	Composite Index FI percentage with access to FS	Poverty percentage Pop B. P. L.	Unemployment During 2000–04 (per cent)	Gini Index
India	48	28.6 (1999)	4.3	32.5 (1999)
Bangladesh	32	49.8 (2000)	3.3	31.8 (2000)
Brazil	43	22.0 (1998)	9.7	58.0 (2003)
China	42	4.6 (1998)	4.0	44.7 (2001)
Indonesia	40	27.1 (1999)	9.9	34.3 (2002)
Korean Republic	63	15.5 (1989)	3.5	31.6 (1998)
Malaysia	60	36.8 (1997)	3.5	49.2 (1997)
Philippines	26	25.0 (1995–95)	9.8	46.1 (2000)
Sri Lanka	59	25.0 (1995–96)	9.0	33.2 (1999–0)
Thailand	59	13.1 (1992)	1.5	42.0 (2002)

Source: World Bank (2006) and (2008).

Conclusion

Financial exclusion is a subset of economic exclusion; thus, for financial inclusion to happen, economic inclusion becomes a necessary precondition. Policies of economic inclusion focus on equity and distributional objectives. Financial inclusion is an international concern. A better world order can only be ensured with the participation of all. This will also enable all citizens to reap the manifold benefits accruing from the processes of globalisation. Both developed and developing countries have been actively engaged in this discourse and in the formulation of policies which will serve to subserve the equity objectives besetting India. The government's concern has been articulated in bringing financial inclusion centerstage through setting up of a special committee under the chairmanship of Dr Rangarajan to look into, consider and make policy recommendations on all aspects of the issue. Policy makers are now bound by the recommendations of the committee and the banking sector has a critical role to play in extending outreach, leveraging technology, and empowering microfinance groups to ensure widespread availability of credit to the poor at reasonable rates of interest. Large segments of the poor and disadvantaged groups remain out of the pale of the formal financial institutions. The costs of exclusion are wide ranging and the solutions necessitate coordinated efforts of public private and voluntary sectors.

References

Buckland, J. and B. Guenther (2005). 'There Are No Banks Here, Financial and Insurance Exclusion in Winnipeg' North End', *Social Sciences and Humanities Research Council of Canada.*

Caskey, J. P., C. R. Duran, and T. M. Solo (2006). 'The Urban Unbanked in Mexico and the United States', World Bank Policy research Working Paper 3835.

Connolly, C. and K. Hajaj (2001). 'Financial Services and Social Exclusion', Financial Services Consumer Policy Center, University of New South Wales.

Government of India: *Economic Survey* (various years), Government of India, New Delhi.

Treasury, H.M. (1999). *Access to Financial Services*. HM Treasury, London.

Kempson, E. (2006): 'Policy Level Response to Financial Exclusion in Developed Economies: Lessons for Developing Countries', paper presented at the conference, Access to Finance: Building Inclusive Financial Systems, World Bank, Washington, DC.

Kempson, E., J. Caskey, C. Whyley, and S. Collard. (2000). *In or Out*? Financial Services Authority. London.

King, R.G. and R. Levine (1993). Finance and Growth: Schumpeter might be right, *Quarterly Journal of Economics* 108, 71737.

Financial Services Authority, May 2004, Building financial capability in the UK.

Chapter 8

The Way Forward – Determinants and Macro Policies

The Future

With decades of rapid growth behind us, and very positive prospects ahead, India is enjoying an unprecedented position of influence in the global economy. The years ahead should be years of growth and opportunity that will enable us, as important members of the global community of nations to make further progress in the struggle against poverty and move towards the attainment of the Millennium Development Goals.

Policy for All Inclusive Growth

The challenge of extending India's growing prosperity to the poorest sections of society remains pressing and immediate. Without a significant increase in investment, the region will fall short of achieving several millennium development goals, particularly with regard to health, water supply, and sanitation, primary education and the environment. Financial inclusion starts with the vision that the poor are bankable and experience has shown that poor people can be enabled to have access to credit and other financial services, the services when effectively used by them will enhance their contribution to the economy. These can be delivered in a financially sustainable way. Much has been done and much remains to be done. What is important is that by recognising this we seize the opportunity to take on the many arduous challenges that remain and forge ahead. This is critical. We have concluded that growth, per se, is not enough.

Growth with Equity

We have to broaden the base of growth and through the processes of financial inclusion, we have to address the problems of poverty by redirecting our investments and development efforts towards the poor to promote equity with efficiency. We need to put in place necessary infrastructure for expediting these processes and an effective framework of policies and strategies to ensure this is required.

Financial Inclusion

Financial inclusion is the key for overall economic development of the country though financial access has significantly improved in the last three and a half decades. But the basic question which remains to be answered satisfactorily is, whether this is adequate. The quantum of deposit accounts (current and savings) held as a ratio to the adult population has not been uniformly encouraging. There is a tremendous scope for greater financial coverage where banks have to exercise the initiative if we have to work on equity considerations which have guided public policy in India for the last five decades.

The Role of Institutions in the Process of Financial Inclusion

- Institutions influence economic performance through socially credible commitment to given rules and their enforcement mechanism.
- Affects costs and uncertainties associated with transacting through positive interventions.
- Enables economic and political flexibility in adapting to new paradigms.
- Opening up the economy to international trade and investment enables faster rate of growth by improving competitiveness of the economic structure and expanding opportunities for mutually beneficial exchange, and at the same time makes the corresponding pairs of adjustment sharper.
- International experience shows that rapid growth has been sustained, living standards improved, and poverty reduced only in open economies.
- No closed economy has sustained growth for long periods. Kuznets (1972) emphasised the institutional adjustments are required in society and polity for ensuring mobility of resources and evolving mechanisms for equitable sharing and alleviation of the pains of structural adjustments in order to reap the benefits of economic growth.
- Historically, all the rapidly growing economies that managed to bring about successful institutional arrangements did manage to reap the benefits of new technologies, expanding opportunities and international trade and those that did not consequently experienced economic stagnation or slow growth.

Financial Access

Financial access rests on accessibility to all. Banks have to offer their services in a way that does not prohibitively increase transaction costs. Internet kiosks and mobile vans provide a ready solution to the problems of geographic dispersal and distance. To be effective, the internet kiosks/bank branches/mobile vans should be near the geographical area to be served and the service must be quick and the time convenient to the target clientele.

Macro Policy Responses

Reaching these depositors requires low cost delivery systems that bring services closer to places that depositors frequent. Bank clients are concerned first about the safety of their funds, secondly with liquidity, i.e., if they invest in the savings product of a bank for example, in a fixed deposit with a bank, and there is an urgent need for money, they should be able to exit the fixed deposit scheme and obtain the funds. Liquidity means the ability to quickly obtain the funds, if required, and third is that, the security deposit made with the bank should be secure; there should be an assurance that the borrowers can get their funds back. For the banker too, these three words are critical but have a different meaning. Safety means the ability of the banker to critically assess the clients' ability to repay the amount lent to him. Liquidity for the banker means the ability to get the advances liquidated, and security implies that the advance extended should be backed by adequate security, or the income stream of the borrowers should be such that the advance is not imperiled. Borrowers need to be confident that saving in a bank is backed by safety funds for future unforeseen expenses while being able to access them in case of emergency. The poor use savings to manage sudden crisis, to avail it during lean times, invest when opportunity strikes, and accumulate lump sums for school and other expected expenses. If depositors lack other comparable savings options, returns take a distant fourth place to these other criteria. When other criteria are met, returns play an important role in attracting clients. Access, security, liquidity returns – this is the order in which most of the poor rank their preferences.

Growth in Agriculture—The Key to Inclusive Growth

Broad based economic growth is the only means whereby the poor and the disadvantaged can be provided livelihood and food security as two-thirds of the population is engaged in agriculture or agriculture-related activities. Agriculture also has supply and demand linkage with industries and is a force multiplier for economic growth.

There is a need for complete paradigm shift in our thinking on agricultural policy. Agricultural growth through direct subsidies (fertiliser, electricity, water) or indirect subsidies, as increase in minimum support prices, is no longer sustainable. The key areas for action lie in creating an enabling environment which will improve productivity and efficiency of agriculture rather than focus on increasing subsidies. There has to be a greater focus on improving rural infrastructure. Banks are essentially institutions which survey credit. Increase in credit is important for agriculture which leads to greater employment in agriculture and help in poverty alleviation. The philosophy of nationalisation was that direct involvement of banks is essential to strengthen the credit delivery system for agriculture and poverty alleviation. Nationalisation of banks led to improvement in access of the rural poor to bank credit on concessional rates. Nationalisation was described as the reservation of entitlement for previously disadvantaged groups. However, credit was cornered by middle level cultivators and landed population. The poor repayment of bank loans led to non-profit making assets. The banking system was not able to adapt to the task of poverty alleviation. Despite all the shortcomings in the direct involvement of the banking system in affirmative action for increasing the flow of credit to the weaker sections, and for eradication of poverty, involvement of banks in the process remains important. The availability of institutional credit and greater financial inclusion helps to reduce dependence on the moneylender and reduce vulnerability of risks. Studies have shown that the share of non-institutional agencies in the outstanding cash dues of rural households is as high as 36 per cent and that credit dependence on informal sources is higher in the case of lower asset groups. Dependents on the informal sector were as high as 58 per cent with households having assets less than Rs 50,000. There should be greater thrust towards providing for the various credit needs of small borrowers and households as part of financial inclusion.

Table 8.1 Percentage Share of Credit Agencies in Cash Borrowings of Cultivator Households.

Sources of credit	1971–72	1981–82	1991–92	2002–03
Non Institutional of which	68.3	36.8	30.6	40.5
Moneylenders	36.1	16.1	17.5	29.1
Institutional of which	31.7	63.2	66.3	59.5
Cooperative societies/Banks	22.0	29.8	35.2	31.0
Commercial Banks	2.4	28.8	35.2	24.5
Unspecified	–	–	3.1	0.0
Total	100	100	100	100

Source: AIDIS 2006.

Table 8.2 Percentage Share of Different Crecit Agencies in Cash Borrowings of Rural Households.

Credit Agency	1971–72	1981–82	1991–92	2002–03
Institutional				
Government	3.1	4.2	3.9	2.7
Coop societies/banks	14.9	26.3	25.7	2.8
Commercial banks	1.7	23.1	20.7	22.7
Insurance	–	0.1	0.3	0.3
Provident fund	–	0.8	1.3	1
Financial corporation/Institution	–	–	–	0.6
Financial company	–	–	–	0.8
Other	–	–	1.4	1
All institutional	19.7	54.5	53.3	57.1
Non institutional				
Landlord	6.4	3.8	3.9	0.6
Agricultural moneylender	18.7	9.7	8.1	9.6
Professional moneylender	15.9	7.8	13.3	20.6
Traders	14.9	5.9	4	2.9
Relatives and friends	11.4	12.4	8.9	7.4
Others (doctors, lawyers, etc)	12.9	4.7	4.2	1.7
All non institutional agencies	80.2	44.3	42.4	42.8
Unspecified	–	1.2	4.4	0

Source: NSSO/AIDIS,NSS Fifty-ninth round January–December 2003.

The results of the All India Debt and Investment Survey (2002–03) reflect a marginal increase in the incidence of borrowing in rural households over 1991–92 and 2002–03. There has been an overall increase in the share of institutional sources in cash borrowings of rural households from 53.3 per cent in 1991–92 to 57.2 per cent in 2002–03. This increase has been driven largely by cooperative banks and commercial banks who account for 50.7 per cent of all institutional cash borrowings. The share of co-operative banks exceeds that of commercial banks by 5.3 percentage points. In the initial phase after nationalisation of banks, there was a jump from 19.7 per cent share in household cash borrowings to 54.5 per cent in the immediate post-nationalisation phase spanning 1971–72 and 1981–82. Thereafter, there has been stagnation. The nationalised banks need to renew their commitment to financial inclusion and to make all efforts to institute necessary steps to make this a reality.

National Rural Employment Guarantee Programme

This NREGP is the major wage employment programme and will help increase income of the poor directly and reduce expenses incurred on distress migration. The emphasis on expanding access and improving quality of public sector schools and health facilities may also help by reducing the need to pay privately for this services. Improved rural connectivity envisaged through the Bharat Nirman programme is also expected to trigger growth.

Expanding the Frontier – Extending the Scope of Financial Inclusion

The scope of financial inclusion can be expanded in two ways.

- Through state-driven intervention by way of statutory enactments (for instance the US example, the Community Reinvestment Act and making it a statutory right to have bank account, as in France).
- Through voluntary effort by the banking community itself for evolving various strategies to bring within the ambit of the banking sector the large strata of society.

The RBI has accorded a great deal of emphasis on financial inclusion. The banks need to change the mindset that aggressive competition policy and social inclusion are mutually exclusive. Mass banking, with no-frills, etc., can become a win-win situation for both. Basically banking services need to be 'marketed' to connect with large population segments and these may be justifiable promotional costs. The opportunities are plenty.

- India is emerging as one of the largest microfinance markets in the world especially in the growth of women's savings and credit groups (SHGs) and the sustaining success of such institutions has been demonstrated by the success of SEWA bank in Gujarat. Low cost banking is not necessarily an unviable venture/ proposition.
- The IBA may explore the possibility of a survey about the coverage with respect to financial inclusion, keeping in view the geographical spread of the banks and extent of financial services available to the population so as to assess the constraints in extension of financial services to hitherto unbanked sections and for initiating appropriate policy measures.
- It may be useful for banks to consider franchising with other segments of financial sector such as cooperatives, RRBs, etc., so as to extend the scope of financial inclusion with minimal intermediation cost.

Simple to Use Cash Dispensing and Collecting Machines

Since large sections of low income groups' transactions are related to deposits and withdrawals, with a view to containing transaction costs, 'simple to use' cash dispensing and collecting machines akin to ATMs, with operating instructions and commands in vernacular would greatly facilitate financial inclusion of the semi-urban and rural populace. In this regard, it is worthwhile to emulate the example of the 'e-Choupal' project brought forth through private sector initiative.

Holistic Approach

It is becoming increasingly apparent that addressing financial exclusion will require a holistic approach on the part of the banks in creating awareness about financial products, education, and advice on money management, debt counselling, savings and affordable credit. The banks would have to evolve specific strategies to expand the outreach of their services in order to promote financial inclusion. One of the ways through which this can be achieved in a cost-effective manner is by forging linkages with microfinance institutions and local communities.

Banks should give wide publicity to the facility of 'no frills' account. Technology can be a very valuable tool in providing access to banking products in remote areas.

Banks need to redesign their business strategies to incorporate specific plans to promote financial inclusion of the low income group, treating it both as a business opportunity as well as a corporate social responsibility. They have to make use of all available resources including technology and expertise available with them as well as the MFIs and NGOs. It may appear in the first instance that taking banking to the sections constituting 'the bottom of the pyramid' may not be profitable, but it should always be remembered that even the relatively low margins on high volumes can be a very profitable proposition. Financial inclusion can emerge as commercially profitable business.

Emerging Challenges

On the retail side, financial services are yet to reach the majority of Indians. The single most frequently used source of loans for the median Indian household is still the moneylender. On the wholesale side, the financial sector is not able to meet the scale or sophistication of the needs of large corporate India and does not penetrate deeply enough to meet the needs of small and medium sized enterprises.

Financial Sector Role and Responsibility

The financial sector has an important role and responsibility, and has built capabilities such that, with appropriate policy changes, it can grow tremendously, both domestically and internationally. It can generate millions of well-paying jobs, and more importantly, have an enormous multiplier effect on inclusion and economic growth. Given the right environment, financial sector reforms can add between a percentage point or two to the economic growth rate. Financial sector reform is both a moral and an economic imperative. There is a need to enhance inclusion, growth, and stability by allowing players more freedom, even while strengthening the financial and regulatory infrastructure. We need a new paradigm shift in the financial sector to recognise that efficiency, innovation, and value for money is as important for the poor as it is for our new Indian multinationals, and these will come from deregulation, new entry, and competition. The role of the government is not to take on the tasks that should legitimately be delegated to the private sector, but to create an enabling environment by building sound financial infrastructure. If, for example, the enormous transfers to the poor through various government programmes can be channelised into savings accounts that the poor open, not only will leakage be reduced, but the poor will also be able to build savings histories with their bank which can then open the door to credit. Moreover, the financial experience of dealing with the account and the bank will help to build a greater business capacity which is a critical need in making better use of credit.

The committee on financial inclusion has recommended a national goal of ensuring that in three years 90 per cent of households, if they so desire, have access to a deposit account and to the payments system, and that government transfers under various schemes be implemented through this system. While the proposed Nationwide Electronic Financial Inclusion System (NEFIS) could utilise much of the existing infrastructure, some elements, especially the last mile, will have to be built out, and should be encouraged on an expedited basis.

Broader Economic Growth

Eventually, though, it is opportunities in the real sector, created by broader growth, which will give the poor the ability to use credit effectively. Instead of forcing credit to households that could thereby become heavily indebted; the focus should be on making them creditworthy so that when opportunities arise, they are able to fully utilise them with the ability to access finance or through the benign enabling environment of financial access.

Emphasis on Education, Health, and Other Basic Public Facilities

Along with sectoral policies aimed at improving livelihood support and increasing employment, a strategy of inclusiveness also calls for new emphasis on education, health, and other basic public facilities. Inadequate access to these essential services directly limits the welfare of large sections of our population, and also denies them the opportunity to fully share the benefits of growth. Indeed, inadequate attention to human resource development limits the growth process itself. A barrier to financial inclusion is that the rural economy has a huge volume of surplus labour as disguised, under and open unemployment.

Table 8.3 Unemployment Rates' Alternate Measures (Percentage of labour force).

Year	Usual Principal Status	Usual Principal and Subsidiary	Current Weekly Status CWS	Current Daily Status (CDS)
		RURAL		
1977–78	3.26	1.54	3.74	7.70
1983	1.91	1.13	3.88	7.94
1987–88	3.07	1.98	4.19	5.25
1993–94	1.80	1.20	3.00	5.63
1999–2000	1.96	1.43	3.91	7.21
		URBAN		
1977–78	8.77	7.01	7.86	10.34
1983	6.04	5.02	6.81	09.52
1987–88	6.56	5.32	7.12	09.36
1993–94	5.21	4.52	5.83	07.43
1999–2000	5.23	4.63	5.89	07.65
		ALL-INDIA		
1977–78	4.23	2.47	4.48	8.18
1983	1.90	4.51	8.28	–
1987–88	3.77	2.62	4.80	6.09
1993–94	2.56	1.90	3.63	6.03
1999–2000	2.81	2.23	4.41	7.32

Source: NSSO Survey, 43rd round, 50th round, and 55th round.

Unemployment and Underemployment

Agriculture creates a large number of job opportunities in the unorganised sector, but it also leads to seasonal and stochastic poverty. Casual wage labour is high in this segment. In the rural areas, in the last decade, the unemployment rate has increased from 5.6 per cent to 7.2 per cent. Unemployment and under employment are the proximate barriers to financial inclusion, creating a steadily marginalised and nomadic population which needs to be mainstreamed. Similar is the case of landless and marginal farmers.

The 11th Plan

The 11th Plan provides opportunity to restructure policies to achieve a new vision of inclusion based on faster, more broad-based and inclusive growth. It is designed to reduce poverty and focus on bridging the various divides that continue to fragment our society. The 11th Plan must aim at putting the economy on a sustainable growth trajectory with a growth rate of approximately 10 per cent by the end of the Plan period. It will create productive employment at a faster pace than before, and target robust agriculture growth at 4 per cent per year. It must seek to reduce disparities across regions and communities by ensuring access to basic physical infrastructure as well as health and education services to all. It must recognise gender as a cross-cutting theme across all sectors and commit to respect and promote the rights of the common person. The first steps in this direction were initiated in the middle of the 10th Plan based on the National Common Minimum Programme adopted by the government. These steps must be further strengthened and consolidated into a strategy for the 11th Plan.

Rapid Growth

Rapid growth is an essential part of our strategy for two reasons. First, it is only in a rapidly growing economy that we can expect to sufficiently raise the incomes of the mass of our population to bring about a general improvement in living conditions and secure inclusive growth. Second, rapid growth is necessary to generate the resources needed to provide basic services to all. Work done within the Planning Commission and elsewhere suggests that the economy can accelerate from 8 per cent per year to an average of around 9 per cent over the 11th Plan period provided appropriate policies are put in place. With population growing at 1.5 per cent per year, 9 per cent growth in GDP would double the real per capita income in 10 years. This must be combined with policies that will ensure that this per capita income growth is broad based-benefiting all sections of the population, especially those who have thus far remained deprived.

Access to Basic Facilities

A key element of the strategy for inclusive growth must be an all out effort to provide the mass of our people, the access to basic facilities such as health, education, clean drinking water, etc. While in the short run these essential public services impact directly on welfare, in the longer run they determine economic opportunities for the future. It is important to recognise that access to the basic services is not necessarily assured simply by a rise in per capita income. Governments at different levels have to ensure the provision of these services and this must be an essential part of our strategy for inclusive growth. At the same time it is important to recognise that better health and education are the necessary preconditions for sustained long-term growth. Even if we succeed in achieving broad-based and inclusive growth, there are many groups that may still remain marginalised. These include primitive tribal groups, adolescent girls, the elderly and the disabled who lack family support, children below the age of three and others who do not have strong lobbies to ensure that their rights are guaranteed. The 11th Plan must pay special attention to the needs of these groups.

Micro, Small and Medium Enterprises

The private sector, including farming, micro, small and medium enterprises (MSMEs), and the corporate sector, has a critical role to play in achieving the objective of faster and more inclusive growth. This sector accounts for 76 per cent of the total investment in the economy and an even larger share in employment and output. MSMEs, in particular, have a vital role in expanding production in a regionally balanced manner and generating widely dispersed off-farm employment. Our policies must aim at creating an environment in which entrepreneurship can flourish at all levels, not just at the top. To stimulate private investment, policy induced constraints and excessive transaction costs need to be removed. To increase the number of successful entrepreneurs a competitive environment must be created which encourages new entrants and provides enough finance for efficient enterprises to expand. Competition also requires policies to curb restrictive practices.

Increase in the Allocation of Public Resources for Plan Programmes in Critical Areas

While encouraging private sector growth, the 11th Plan must also ensure a substantial increase in the allocation of public resources for Plan programmes in critical areas. This will support the growth strategy and ensure inclusiveness. These resources will be easier to mobilise if the economy grows rapidly. A new stimulus to public sector investment is particularly important in agriculture and infrastructure and both the centre and the states have to take steps to mobilise resources to make this possible. The growth component of this strategy is, therefore, important for two reasons:

- It will contribute directly by raising income levels and employment.
- It will help finance programmes that will ensure more broad-based and inclusive growth. All this is feasible but it is by no means an easy task. Converting potential into reality is a formidable endeavour and will not be achieved if we simply continue on a business-as-usual basis.

Evaluation of Policies

There is a need for both the centre and the states to be self critical and evaluate programmes and policies to see what works and what does not. Programmes designed to achieve specific objectives often fail to do so even though substantial expenditure is incurred on them. It is therefore necessary to focus on outcome rather than outlays, including a disaggregated level to examine their impact on different groups and genders. The practice of gender budgeting already begun by the central government, should extend to the states, so that performance is judged on the basis of gender disaggregated data.

Investment in Human Resource Development and Skill Formation

The presence of a skilled young population in an environment where investment is expanding and the industrial world is ageing could be a major advantage. It is important to realise however, that we can only reap this demographic dividend if we invest on human resource development and skill formation in a massive way and create productive employment for our relatively young working population.

Agricultural Crisis: Regaining Agricultural Dynamism

One of the major challenges of the 11th Plan will be to reverse the deceleration in agricultural growth from 3.2 per cent observed between 1980 and 1996/97 to a trend average of around 2.0 per cent subsequently. This deceleration is the root cause of the problem of rural distress that has surfaced in many parts of the country and reached crisis levels in some. Low farm income due to inadequate productivity growth has often combined with low prices of output and with lack of credit at reasonable rates, to push many farmers into crippling debt. Even otherwise, uncertainties seem to have increased (regarding prices, quality of inputs, and also weather and pests) which, coupled with unavailability of proper extension and risk insurance have led farmers to despair. This has also led to widespread distress migration, a rise in the number of female headed households in rural areas and a general increase in women's work burden and vulnerability. In 2004–05, women accounted for 34 per cent of principal and 89 per cent of subsidiary workers in agriculture, higher than in any previous round of the National Sample Survey. The crisis of agriculture is not a purely distributional one that arises out of the special problems of small and marginal farmers and landless labour. In fact, agricultural deceleration is affecting farms of all sizes. To reverse this trend, corrective policies must not only focus on the small and marginal farmers who continue to deserve special attention, but on middle and large farmers too who suffer from productivity stagnation arising from a variety of constraints. It is vital to increase agricultural income as this sector still employs nearly 60 per cent of our labour force. A measure of self-sufficiency is also critical for ensuring food security. A second green revolution is urgently needed to raise the growth rate of agricultural GDP to around 4 per cent. This is not an easy task since actual growth of agricultural sector, including forestry and fishing, is likely to be below 2 per cent during the 10th Plan period. The challenge therefore is to at least double the rate of agricultural growth and to do so, recognise demographic realities – particularly the increasing role of women.

Doubling the growth of agricultural GDP to 4 per cent per annum will improve rural employment conditions by raising real wages and reducing underemployment. However, even if this is attained, an overall growth of 9 per cent will further increase income disparity between agricultural and non-agricultural households unless around 10 million workers currently in agriculture find remunerative non-agricultural employment. To make this possible, and absorb all new entrants into the labour force, non-agricultural employment would need to increase at over 6 per cent per annum during 11th Plan. This poses a major challenge not only in terms of generating non-agricultural employment but also in matching its required location and type. Care has to be taken to manage the resulting livelihood changes and to ensure that employment is generated at all levels of skill in non-agricultural sector. The inadequacy of widely dispersed and sustainable off-farm productive employment opportunities is a basic cause of most divides and disparities. Growth without jobs can neither be inclusive nor can it bridge divides. All avenues for increasing employment opportunities, including those that can be provided by micro and small enterprises need to be explored. If we fail to-do so, the demographic dividend can turn into demographic nightmare. Thus employment creation and raising employment opportunity is another major challenge for the 11th Plan.

Providing Essential Public Services to the Poor

A key element of 11th Plan strategy should be to provide essential education and health services to those large parts of our population who are still excluded from such facilities. Education is the critical factor that empowers participation in the growth process, but our performance has been less than satisfactory, both overall and in bridging gender and other divides. Overall literacy is still less than 70 per cent and rural female literacy less than 50 per cent with corresponding rates or even lower among the marginalised groups and minorities. While the Sarva Shiksha Abhiyan has expanded primary school enrolment, it is far from providing quality education. Looking ahead, we cannot be satisfied with only universal primary education; we must also move towards universal secondary education as quickly as possible. In the domain of health, there continues to be large gaps in the most basic services such as mother and child care, clean drinking water and access to basic sanitation facilities. The poor do not have even minimum access. While both education and curative health services are available for those who can afford to pay, quality service is beyond the reach of the common people. Other privately provided services are of highly variable quality. In this situation, access to essential services can only be through public financing. In most cases this means public provision or partnership with non-profit and civil society organisations. Major institutional challenge is that even where service providers exist, the quality of delivery is poor and those responsible for delivering the services cannot be held accountable. Unless such accountability is established and cutting edge service providers trained, it will be difficult to ensure significant improvement in delivery.

Environmental Sustainability and Human Well-being

We have already seen that neglect of environmental considerations, for example, profligate use of water or deforestation have devastating effects. The threat of climate change poses a real challenge to future generations. Our development strategy, therefore, has to be sensitive to these concerns and should ensure that threats and trade-offs are appropriately evaluated.

Improving Rehabilitation and Resettlement Practices

Our practices regarding rehabilitation of those displaced from their land because of development projects, conflicts, or calamities are very deficient. These have caused many people to feel vulnerable because of forced exclusion and marginalisation. In particular, the costs of displacement borne by our tribal population have been unduly high. Compensation has been tardy and inadequate, leading to unrest and insurgency in many regions. This discontent is likely to grow exponentially if the benefits from enforced land acquisition are seen accruing to private interests, or even to the state at the cost of those displaced. To provide displaced people, especially women with their due rights, it is necessary to frame a transparent set of policy rules that address compensation, proper resettlement, and rehabilitation and also give project-affected persons a permanent stake in project benefits. Moreover, these rules need to be given a legal format in terms of the rights of the displaced.

Improving Governance

Good governance and transparency should be ensured in the implementation of public programme and also in government's interaction with the ordinary citizens. Much more is needed to be done by both the centre and the states to lessen the discretionary power of government, ensure greater transparency and accountability, and create awareness among citizens. The Right to Information (RTI) Act empowers people to demand improved governance, and government must be ready to respond to this demand.

Addressing the Issue of Growing Disparities

Even as we address the specific challenges listed above, we must deal with the perception that development has failed to bridge the divides that afflict our country and may even have sharpened some of them. Some of these perceptions may be exaggerated, but nonetheless they exist. The 11th plan must seek to bridge these divides as an overarching priority. Foremost among these, is the divide between the rich and the poor. Poverty is declining, but only at a pace which is no longer acceptable given the minimalist level at which the poverty line is fixed. There is also a divide between those who have access to essential services such as health, education, features which are essential for growth and development of banking. Nevertheless, the overall financial system needs to be strengthened and developed through improved regulatory mechanisms in line with international best practices and by liberalising to encourage competition. The approach that has been followed has included an increased role for private sector banks and foreign financial institutions in the domestic market, and a carefully calibrated opening of the economy to international capital markets. This has generally succeeded in ensuring systemic stability while allowing financial development simultaneously.

International Experience

International experience has shown that interest rate ceilings on lending have been largely infructuous. Attempts to impose interest rate caps have resulted either in distortion of pricing by providers or withdrawal of lenders, thereby hurting rather than aiding improvement of access to finance. Given the experiences of a variety of service providers on the ground there would be real concern if, particularly for the poor, poorly capitalised entities are permitted to warehouse risk on their balance sheet. The points of failure could be multiple:

(i) Use of savings for on-lending into the same geography exposes client savings to systemic risk in the region. This approach does not leverage benefits of national diversification to provide security and liquidity to client savings. This concern is applicable to a wide class of service providers: (a) non-bank finance companies; (b) co-operative banks; (c) regional rural banks and (d) self-help groups that collect savings and use them for on-lending directly or as collateral in some form. For example, people in a region might be saving in order to build protection against rainfall failures. In a model in which deposits from these individuals are re-deployed as loans in the same geography, rainfall failure might imply loan riskiness and therefore, inability of savers to use deposits when they need it the most. As a consequence of the above, narrowly operating entities typically have to offer higher rates of interest to attract depositors. This in turn forces them to charge higher rates on loans. This gives rise to the concern that the loan portfolio over time will suffer from the problem of adverse selection - those who are willing to borrow at higher rates may be 'riskier' thereby affecting security of depositors in the same entity. An entity that accepts deposits in addition to a lending function must be able to manage the inherent asset-liability management issues and liquidity risks. This entails ability to invest in automation and information systems that can support these functions which is typically not the case with small entities. Additionally, lack of access to instruments such as credit derivatives impairs the ability of these entities to manage credit risk through strategies other than diversification in origination. This in turn is challenging for entities that by design operate in narrow regions.

Governments Choosing to Intervene Directly Rather Than at a Systemic Level

Governments investing in creating systemic infrastructure are seen to facilitate other providers to work in these markets. This systemic infrastructure could take the form of national identification numbers, credit registries, payment systems, electronic commodity and auction markets and weather measurement stations that are in the nature of public goods and stimulate market activity. This is superior to more 'interventionist approaches' such as government being a provider of subsidised financial services. The potential of the unreached – the future lies with those companies who see the poor as their customers. C.K. Prahlad was quick to divine the magic of the rural markets. The last few decades have seen considerable increase in the purchasing power of rural communities. The green revolution increased the usage of industrial and manufactured products. Rural marketing initiatives are driving manufactured or processed inputs or services to rural producers or consumers. The rural markets have roughly 742 million people using durables of 5,000 crores, agri-inputs of 45,000 crores, fast moving consumer goods of 65,000 crores, two and four wheelers of 8,000 crores. The estimated size of the market makes it attractive. In 2005–06, LIC sold 55 per cent policies in rural India and 41 million Kisan Credit Cards were issued. Though so far only 42 million households use banking services and only 6.6 million households have formal savings investments, the size of the market is huge and growing. If the rural market is to drive the economy, income needs to grow substantially. Rural credit paradigm, so far synonymous with the tripod of cooperatives, Regional Rural Banks, Public Sector Banks, directed credit and repressed financial markets, has not led to unleashing of economic growth and prosperity in the rural areas. The alternative is the financial systems approach which welcomes disintermediation, and the need for banking section to advocate cost covering interest rates and a self sustaining economic model.

Household As the Key Determinant of Outreach Success

At the core of the rural community is the rural household. Unless the household as a unit is able to generate surplus income; there cannot be widespread and all-encompassing prosperity in the rural areas. The real challenge then lies in the ability to ensure that every adult member of the household is able to generate surplus income through gainful activity. Rural growth and unemployment are the ingredients of jobless growth.

Provisional results of the 5th Economic Census 2005 reflect that though there has been growth and pick up in enterprises and employment, the unemployment rate has increased over the period. A plausible solution lies in priming the household cycle of savings and credit through effective intermediation. When activity is savings-driven it is low yielding activity, but when credit comes first it prompts high yielding activity.

The Challenges of Job Creation in India

Economic Growth Has Not Been Sufficiently Inclusive

The Indian economy is influenced by the complex interplay of three significant factors, namely, globalisation, technical change and competition. While there are several benefits emanating from these, they also present challenges in labour markets which cannot be swept under the carpet but needs to be acknowledged and addressed. The key challenge is how to translate productivity growth into increase in employment and real wages. Real GDP growth accelerated to 9.4 per cent in 2006–07 from 9.0 per cent in 2005–06 boosted by double digit growth in the services and industries sector. Real GDP growth thus averaged 7.6 per cent during the tenth plan period (2002–03 to 2006–07) higher than in any plan so far and much higher than the 5.6 per cent economic growth of the last development decade of the 1980s and 1990s. In the 1980s and 1990s the acceleration in GDP growth was 5.4 per cent per annum between 1983 and 1993–1994 and 6.5 per cent between 1993–94 and 1999–2000. This did not yield an employment dividend or lead to commensurable pick up in employment rates. The annual growth in employment decelerated from 2.06 per cent to 1.60 per cent in the corresponding periods. Though we have achieved high output and high productivity growth rates, corresponding rates of employment are lower. With at least 48 million Indians conservatively estimated to be unemployed and some 50.5 million new workers in the labour force, we face the formidable challenge of creating large numbers of productive and better paying jobs to absorb the unemployed and underutilised labour force. While economic growth is critical for generating jobs and improving standards of living the synapses of economic growth, job creation and earnings are complex. Data also shows that economic growth has not been particularly inclusive. The unemployment rate rose from 2.78 per cent in1999–2000 to 3.06 per cent in 2004–05. First, the low growth and stagnancy of incomes of those at the bottom of the pyramid is not encouraging. Second, inequality has increased between rural and urban areas. Third, gender inequality in employment growth has also sharpened. As per the NSSO data there is greater unemployment among women both in the rural and urban areas. In urban areas the unemployment rate of males fell to 4.4 per cent by 2004–05 from 4.8 per cent in 1999–2000 in rural areas. It remained unchanged at 2.1 per cent for females. The unemployment rates rose from 1.5 per cent (1999–2000) to 3.1 per cent (2004–05) in rural areas and from 7.1 per cent to 9.1 per cent in urban areas. The employment is either on the rise or remains persistent in the informal sector where production is typically carried out with minimal and traditional methods of production resulting in low productivity and low earning. Agricultural employment which is overwhelmingly informal, still retains its share of total employment. 90 per cent of total agricultural employment in India continues to be in the informal sector. Despite GDP growth of 5 percent per capita, in the years between 1993–1999 the share of the informal sector in total non agricultural employment increased from 80.5 per cent to 83.2 per cent. This shows that economic growth and growth in the expansion of employment in the formal sector are out of kilter; economic growth has not led to expansion of employment in the formal sector. In India the rural sector remains the key to improving labour market outcomes. Most of the workers are employed in the rural sector which is characterised by seasonal employment, a high degree of underemployment and low productivity.

There are a number of factors at play: the increasing inequality between rural and urban areas can be attributed in part to the neglect of productivity-enhancing public investments in rural areas where majority of workers are based. Increased public investments in rural infrastructure and provision of agriculture extension services are vital for raising productivity in agriculture. Significantly, increased productivity on the farm bring benefits to the non-farm rural economy. First, rural roads and rural electrification will directly facilitate the expansion of the non-farm sector. Second, this will lead to an increase in the credit absorption capabilities. Thirdly, increased incomes from improved farm productivity will raise demand for the output of the non farm sector. Jobs in the formal sector are also needed. Limited investment in the face of a rapidly expanding labour force has led to slow growth in formal sector jobs.

A diversification of production activities in new areas, restructuring of existing activities and increased coordination between public and private entities is needed to make this happen. The formal sector has to expand not only in terms of its contribution to aggregate value-added but should be labour intensive as well. One example of an industry which has great potential to expand is the food processing industry, which is labour intensive and has strong linkages with the agriculture sector. We process only 2 per cent of fruit and vegetables as compared to Thailand and Malaysia which process 30 per cent and 80 per cent respectively as we lack cold chains and cultivate only traditional varieties of fruit and vegetables unsuitable for processing and is weak in infrastructure, storage, transportation, processing, packaging, quality controls, etc. All these areas need to be urgently addressed. A major expansion and revamping of state agricultural extension systems involving state agricultural universities and Krishi Vigyan Kendras needs to be done using the Public Private Partnership Model (PPP) wherever possible. Encouraging the development of modern markets through Agricultural Produce Marketing Act, amendments and notifying the rules thereunder to implement reforms in agriculture marketing and restrictions of marketing beyond state bounds is important. Agricultural development strategies have to be reoriented to rejuvenate agriculture to meet employment growth. The centre and states urgently need to take steps to achieve the 4 per cent growth target for agriculture envisaged in the 11th Plan Policy document and to ensure utilisation of the Rs 25,000 crore commitment of the Central Government for public investment in the agriculture sector in the next four years. Policies for generating productive employment will require a big push in the rural sector while also promoting jobs in the formal sector. The policies will alleviate some of the downsides which globalisation with the adoption of capital intensive technologies brings in its wake. In the ultimate analysis, unless governments – both at the centre and the states —make job creation a fundamental part of their economic agenda backed by time bound, feasible, and credible policies, India will continue to grow but may continue to harbour more poor people by 2020. If we want inclusive growth and growth with equity we have to take a call on employment generation now.

Central to India's economic policies over the last sixty years has been the driving impetus of battling the scourge of poverty. India's strategy was of achieving self sufficiency in the production of food grains. This was the strategy of the green revolution of the '70s high yielding varieties of seeds, plenty of fertilisers and extension workers engaged in farmer education. There was a tripod of measures unleashed to buttress this strategy— the public distribution system was introduced to make food grains readily accessible to the poor, employment guarantee schemes as the food for work program and the integrated rural development programme formed the third leg of this tripod. The three-pronged attack on poverty has not changed is basic strategy even today. The IRDP metamorphosed to the Swarn Jayanti Gram Swarozgar Yojana and the employment guarantee programme has been re-introduced. Poverty has come down but 26 per cent of the people still live below the poverty line. In recent years, steps have been taken to strengthen the public distribution system with its distinction of APL and pink card BPL (Above and Below Poverty Line Users). The Green Revolution of the mid-sixties introduced an environment of Malthusian pessimism, which enabled the country to meet the objective of national food security as it ensured sufficient food production to meet the market demand. The increase in the production of food grains coupled with remunerative support prices offered by the government led to unprecedented food stocks of 65 million tonnes by the end of June 2002. The subsequent draw down of food stocks and stagnation of production with decline in productivity and deleterious impact on the overall food situation have again brought the debates on the centrality of agriculture and the need for food security into very sharp focus.

The Green Revolution had its successes and the country became self sufficient in food production. The successes are evident; the failures well documented, excessive injection of fertilisers ruined the quality of the soil and there are some areas, notably in the wheat bowl of the Punjab where the excessive use of fertilisers has increased the salinity of the soil and has made it fit only for growing rice. The increased reliance on fertilisers also spawned an intricate system of subsidies where it appeared that subsidising the fertiliser and electricity industries were subsidised and not the farmers. Agricultural subsidies began to choke any real initiatives in agriculture. Enhanced and sustained stable growth of the agriculture sector is central to the combat of poverty; agriculture sector contributes to on-farm and off-farm employment opportunities and to price stability. Inflation rears its ugly head when prices of basic foodstuff increase and it is a tax on the poor who suffer the most from it. The National Development Council in its 53rd meeting has adopted a timely resolution to reorient agricultural development strategies and called upon the state and central government to evolve strategies to rejuvenate agriculture. The factors responsible for temporal and spatial variations in poverty need to be considered in a holistic perspective. For rural poverty the neglect of agriculture is uppermost. A number of variables are employed to explain variations in rural poverty, agricultural output, inflation rate/relative food prices are important for explaining variations in urban poverty. The importance of these factors has varied from period to period. Green Revolution led to agricultural growth which was responsible for the decline of poverty in the 1970s and in the 1980s; rural non farm employment was responsible for the growth of real wages and reduction of poverty. Macro policies assign importance to agricultural policies. For reducing rural poverty agricultural growth is important. The pre-reform regime has been characterised as biased towards agriculture, due to heavy protection to industrial goods, an overvalued exchange rate and rigid controls on export. Though the economic reforms, as a consequence of structural adjustment in the wake of the economic reforms, concentrated on industrial delicensing and dismantling of the License Permit Raj and liberalisation, it did improve the terms of trade in favour of agriculture. The increasingly favourable terms of trade for agriculture were supposed to attract private investment into agriculture, thereby leading to growth in output and demand for rural labour. In a simple Neo Classical framework, since agriculture is more labour intensive, a rise in the relative price of its output, i.e. food, leads to an increase in real wages and investment thereby leading to a virtuous cycle of growth. There are however necessary correlations between private investment and public investment i.e., investment by the state in agricultural infrastructure. This continues to be an area of weakness and the agricultural subsidies have been repeatedly studied and shown to be wasteful and less than useful. There seems to be a trade-off between subsidies and investments in agriculture. Higher investment in agriculture and rural infrastructure is a necessary condition for increasing agricultural growth. The government's role is important not only for raising public investment but also for inducing private investment. To ensure meaningful impact on poverty removal, the SGSY and the employment programmes need to be closely monitored at the grassroots level; the design of programmes is not so much at fault as the flaws in delivery of programmes.

Having discussed the rural–urban divide in banking and the potential in rural banking, the question that remains to be addressed is – how can banks meet the challenges of banking in the hinterland?

(i) To begin with, fuller utilisation of existing capacity can itself give huge dividends. Given the existing number of nearly 48,000 rural and semi-urban branches, an increase of loan by rupees one crore per branch could imply additional profits of about Rs 480 crore to the banking system.

(ii) Currently each rural branch services only around 1,000 loan accounts. If we assume that a bank branch can serve at least 3,000 households, it would imply at the minimum tripling of the business at rural branches. This might require redeployment and some increase in staff, especially field staff, and would be more than worth the effort considering the increase in business and profitability that it would result in.

(iii) Banks would need to decide the kind of delivery channels required for meeting the banking and remittance needs of the rural population. Today the branch is not the only way of delivering banking services. All options such as mobile and satellite offices, rural ATMs, smart card and mobile phone based banking, use of intermediaries including SHGs and post offices need to be explored for penetrating into the rural markets. Several banks have tie-up arrangements with corporates engaged in contract farming. IT solutions can take banking to the remotest corner and cut costs apart from providing valuable databases for furthering business strategies. Whatever be the mode of penetration, it is clear that unless there are well thought out strategies for marketing, banking services in the hinterland, will be missing emerging opportunities. As mentioned earlier, 50 million households in rural areas have moved from low income to high income giving rise to equal number of potentially bankable households. To look at the scope for branch banking and provision of banking services through other delivery channels in rural areas, banks can make use of the research already available on the monthly per capita expenditure centre-wise and district-wise, corroborated by data on consumption patterns for FMCG and mobile phones as also other indicators of expenditure patterns.

(iv) Banks need to have appropriate strategies for rural banking. Rural clientele need savings, remittances, loan and insurance products. When banks think of agricultural credit they generally think of crop loans, especially, food crops. The needs of agriculture are, however, getting diversified and the required scale of finance is increasing. There is much more demand for allied activities such as dairy, fishing and livestock, cash crops, besides ancillary activities such as sorting, grading, processing, packaging and transporting to final destinations and markets. Other service sector activities that spin-off from the main activities are also growing. This is giving rise to additional credit demand from a variety of new enterprises, besides demand for retail and consumer credit. Are banks geared for the surging credit demand in the rural areas in all sector, particularly allied agriculture and services sector?

The strategies of banks will need to focus on the following:

Developing Products Aligned with Income of the Poor

Products need to be designed and packaged taking into account local culture, customs, language, literacy and social indicators. Also, rural households need to be provided credit in a composite way covering all their needs, including life cycle needs: the traditional crop loans, term loans and housing loans Consumption loans bouquet may not work. Regional offices of banks may need to be delegated with appropriate powers for product design, while ensuring consistency with Board policies. Banks need to look at the overall cash flow of rural households and fix general credit limits, which could be scaled up depending on new/additional activities taken up.

Creating Awareness and Brand Building

Banks need to consciously evolve strategies for financial education in the rural areas. Products developed for the region will need to be actively marketed in a responsible and effective manner, with top priority at all times being accorded to transparency, customer education and satisfaction.

Assigning the Right Staff for Marketing Products

In rural lending there is an imperative need for the marketing staff to be knowledgeable about agricultural practices and operations, besides being well-acquainted with the features of the products and their suitability to the targeted category of customer. In a sense, providing financial services will also involve providing extension services as a risk mitigant. Hence, banks will need proactive technical officers who can not only provide such services, but also train their field staff. Another very important requirement is relationship management in terms of face-to-face familiarity and continuity of contact. Surely, it is not without reason that the rural folks are comfortable with persons like the postmen and even the local moneylender, with whom they have occasions to regularly interact. Banks would do well to address this need for building up a relationship and rapport with the rural clientele.

Use of Information Technology (IT)

There are a variety of ways in which IT can be used by banks. Delivery of banking services through IT based solutions, such as mobile phones and smart cards, while keeping costs low, is one huge opportunity for increasing outreach afforded by modern technology that is rapidly developing. Other uses of IT are in credit risk management and pricing, which require maintaining a comprehensive computerised data base – this can be used for a variety of purposes, such as marketing, credit scoring, pricing, credit monitoring including rating migration and devising appropriate internal control systems, etc. There is clearly a need to have credit information companies across the entire country; the huge externalities associated with having comprehensive credit records can be derived for more efficient financial intermediation. With appropriate IT solutions in place and suitable field staff, banks can also provide market insurance and capital market products for increasing their non-funded business.

Developing and Using Risk Mitigants

The three important risks identified in agricultural lending are yield risk (or input output risk), calamity risk and price risk. Banks will need to aim at minimising these risks if they have to deliver affordable credit to agriculture. Extension work, including proper advice on use of fertiliser and pesticides, ensuring quality seeds and inputs are activities that minimise yield risk. Enterprises providing such services would need to be supported by banks and actively encouraged. Calamity risk minimisation involves insurance of crops and assets, including of livestock/cattle and fisheries. While restructuring of loans can provide more time for repayment, repeated rescheduling could lead to installments ballooning beyond the repayment capacity. Banks will have to evolve policies to address this issue while providing vulnerable groups opportunities to engage in activities that supplement the household income at times of natural calamities. Development of appropriately priced insurance products is obviously a challenge especially if such insurance has to be affordable and sustainable. Price risk in agriculture is inherent, having regard to the nature of agricultural operations where supply cannot respond to prices immediately. Hence, price support policies have been followed over the years. A more recent development is the future markets, which can provide opportunity to hedge risks. However, the players in these markets are mostly traders and speculators. There is a need to find ways in which commodity markets can be used to provide price support to farmers.

Microfinance

A separate strategy for microfinance may have to be introduced as this involves providing low income families with access to banking. Invariably, banks have found it advantageous to partner with community-based organisations and NGOs working in the area of microfinance. Promoting SHGs, nurturing them and transforming them from microfinance to micro enterprise is something many banks are already engaged in. Banks could explore the possibilities of working with the state governments by offering them efficient technology solutions, such as smart cards for distribution of budgeted allocations for NREGP, pension payments and various other social sector expenditures. A pilot project is under way in Andhra Pradesh (AP), where the AP government will tie-up with banks, who will offer smart cards to BPL families/pension recipients/NREGP workers for disbursements of wages, pensions and other benefits. These smart cards can be operated at village level through Voluntary Organisations (VOs)– federated SHGs registered as cooperatives – that are eligible to be used as business correspondents by banks. It is expected that as the SHG members get used to the smart cards, there will be return flow of funds as they use their bank accounts for savings. The cards could also be used as normal debit cards at merchant establishments.

Regional Rural Banks (RRBs) as Partners

One in every three rural/semi urban branch in the country is an RRB branch. Moreover, the staff members of RRBs belong to the region and have knowledge of local language and customs. These are significant strengths and need to be leveraged by sponsor banks who should view RRBs as their partners in rural banking. The initial costs for up-scaling technology and skills in the RRBs will be amply rewarded by the benefits that would accrue in due course.

Institutional Self-Sufficiency

Microfinance is working to ensure that the poorest families in the region receive positive benefits through credit linkages and access to loans. Institutional self-sufficiency is however essential for microfinance to be truly effective in meeting the needs of the poorest households on a sustainable basis. Financial inclusion is an imperative and an integral part of microfinance. Cost effective identification of the poor and the poorest women is essential to maximising the effectiveness and efficiency of providing microfinance services to them. The poorest have proved that they are bankable and illiterate women have shown their ability to grasp complex accounting and banking procedures. They are fuelling the microfinance revolution in India and helping to broaden its base. India today represents a window of opportunity for banks and the benefits of the program of financial inclusion are huge; without addressing issues of poverty and exclusion in India, it will be impossible to achieve the Millenium Development Goals. Financial inclusion is fast emerging as a global challenge and all efforts have to be made to address this issue.

Conclusion

There is a broad consensus on the major challenges faced in the process of financial inclusion. Distributive economic growth and ultimately growth with equity is what we are striving to attain. To accelerate growth, we need to ensure financial inclusion and to widen economic opportunities for the poor through higher investments and improved maintenance in key sectors (e.g., in agriculture, infrastructure) and a better policy environment. We also need to expand human capabilities, which means achieving goals of education through the Sarva Shiksha Abhiyan, education for all, and significant improvements in health, status and security through more effective provision of basic services at the local level. This also includes the need to ensure basic entitlements like food, safety, shelter for all people and to reduce risk and provide protection for the vulnerable, destitute and socially excluded. The ultimate aim of financial inclusion is to empower our poorest citizens, by including them in the process of decision-making at all levels. Financial inclusion thus forms an integral part of our overall strategy of poverty reduction which meshes with the strategy of inclusion.

Competition in urban areas is squeezing bank margins. Even though agriculture contributes only 20 per cent of GDP, the rural population constitutes 70 per cent of the total population and as reported accounts for 60 per cent of consumer durable market which brings us back to the oft reiterated and almost basic arguments. First, unless there is awareness and concern translating to pressure from the grassroots level and sensitivity to respond to the concerns raised at the higher echelons of policy makers and implementing agencies, rural development programmes, though brilliant in design will continue to falter in execution. Second, as the successes of the self-help group movement have more than amply demonstrated, a participatory strategy involving the stakeholders in the process of decision-making and transparent implementation has a higher success rate than a top down approach. Third and finally, as Andhra has demonstrated, only developmental states with commitment to a reformist strategy can succeed in delivering the complex policy mix required for sustainable poverty reduction. We have reached a stage when merely poverty programmes of the tripod are not enough, though they do provide a basic safety net; these have to be further buttressed with initiatives on literacy education and healthcare. There are three integral issues which have to be addressed. In agriculture, an attempt has to be made to remove all distortions that affect economic efficiency adversely; secondly it has to be appreciated that education and health enhance human capital and are good for economic growth. The High Performing Asian Economies (HPAE), the burgeoning Indian services sector and call sector economy and Amartya Sen who goes a step further to emphasise that capability and freedom enhancing social policies generate stable civil societies, have laid ample stress on these issues. The last and major point is that on all these major policies the state must take affirmative actions to convert remedial access to legally enforceable entitlements. The key elements of strategy are:

(i) Accelerating economic growth and development by increasing the effectiveness of government and the efficiency of financial inclusion. Second, increasing the effectiveness of pro poor interventions and finally, increasing the role of participatory institutions and state government in implementing reform and raising awareness of the benefits which will accrue financial inclusion at the grassroots level.

(ii) Given the enormous size and complexity of the task of financial inclusion in hand, the poverty reduction and financial inclusion strategy necessarily envisages a multi-pronged approach which is massive in scope but given the commitment and determination will prove to be the most vital and critical investment in financial inclusion and will yield positive externalities which will be well worth the effort.

(iii) There is a need for banks to redesign their business strategies to incorporate specific plans to promote the financial inclusion of low income groups. The business opportunity for banks lies in exploiting the penny economy of low margins and high volumes at the bottom of the pyramid. The rural market is expanding and has high potential.

(iv) In terms of fast moving consumer goods, agricultural inputs, consumer durables and two and four wheelers, LIC sells 55 per cent of its policies and BSNL 50 per cent of its mobile communications in rural and small towns. The estimated size of the rural market is Rs 1,08,000 crores. Considering this, there are business opportunities for banks in the rural areas.

(v) Considering the high volumes involved, banks have to look at technology-based solutions and low cost delivery mechanisms that will reduce transaction costs. Such models have to be sustainable.

(vi) Simple to use cash dispensing machines akin to ATMs with operating instructions and commands in the vernacular language greatly facilitate financial inclusion of the rural and semi-urban population. The use of intermediaries as NGOs, MFIs, civil society organisations will also undoubtedly aid this effort. The push for financial inclusion will make economic growth and prosperity a reality for all. The World Bank's India Development Policy Review 2006 titled 'Inclusive Growth and Service Delivery: Building on India's Success' focuses on two major challenges facing the country today:
(a) Improving the delivery of core public services
(b) Maintaining the momentum of growth dispersing its benefits.

Inclusive growth translates to growth with development, empowering the poor and marginalized, enhancing their capabilities, enabling them to avail and make the most of livelihood opportunities by investing in health education, nutrition, schooling facilities, self help efforts and promoting fair access to assets and markets as land labour credit and providing social protection for major household risks. Thinking of development as mere enhancement of GNP per capita excludes distributional inequalities. There are serious issues that financial exclusion costs to an individual i.e., no savings, no assets, no insurance, no access to money advice. The individual pays higher charges for basic financial transactions and credit. As there is no bank account, financial transactions as money transfer and cheque encashment become that much more expensive. There is a lack of security in holding and storing money thereby operating solely on a cash budget leaves individuals more vulnerable to loss or theft. This exacerbates deprivation as the amount used in raising resources impounds those resources leaving less for meeting all other essential needs. There is also a linkage between financial and social exclusion. Financial exclusion is more marked in developing countries but is an international phenomena. It is also accepted that it hampers and stymies the growth of a well-functioning financial system. Inclusion on the other hand has several positive externalities: it helps to empower economically and socially deprived people; it helps to create a safety net which serves as a hedge for the poor in case of economic shocks. In 2005, the United Nations celebrated the International Year of Microcredit and initiated a dialogue, a year-long global consultative process with participation of governments, international development organisations, a wide variety of financial institutions, the private sector, academia members of civil society from more than a hundred countries including the World Bank and the IMF. The Blue Book on Building Inclusive Financial Sectors for development was a result of this process. It sets forth a vision of inclusive finance, evaluates various factors limiting access to formal financial services and identifies critical challenges. It discusses the policy framework and the role of the public sector in inclusive finance. As Montek Singh Ahluwalia expresses it, 'Any strategy that does not pay attention to economic growth is going to be unsustainable but you cannot rely on growth alone. We have to ensure that the benefits of growth are widespread and need special measures for those who would normally not get included. We need an inclusive growth strategy. Without growth we cannot generate the resources needed for investment in social infrastructure, particularly primary health, primary education and physical infrastructure provided and maintained by the public sector.' Institutional reforms are required for more effective delivery and provision of public services. Raising agricultural productivity is critical and this requires technology investment infrastructure growth. The strategies are:

- Intensifying and increasing the output of existing activities
- Diversifiying to higher value added products and non farm linkages
- Financial deepening, as it is an important component of economic growth and has positive externalities as banking is a public good
- Financial inclusion to be considered imperative for banks to pursue as a sustainable approach

The vision set forth is of catalysing the processes of financial inclusion through a three pillar approach to create a self-sustaining model which succeeds in addressing grass roots level concerns. In this three-pronged approach the architectural framework envisages the involvement of the state government, the formal financial system and the civil society organisations as stakeholders.

The state government would provide the framework for inclusion and implement fiscal measures to develop basic infrastructure to enhance economic and social capital. The role of the state is critical in providing an inclusive framework through fiscal measures which increase investment in economic and social capital.

The formal financial system represented primarily by banks plays a critical role in reducing poverty by enabling the availment of savings facilities, livelihood opportunities, low cost credit efficient payment systems and necessary economic infrastructure. To this end the role of community based organisations (CBOs) and NGOs, which would catalyse local participation, encourage the formation of voluntary SHGs and development of linkages between the SHGs and banks, thereby enhancing the efficiency and transparency of services for financial inclusion, are essential. The concern with exclusion is one which is engaging the attention of policy makers in almost all nations, advanced or developing. They are grappling with the issue of ensuring financial inclusion so that the benefits of growth percolate to all. To address macroeconomic problem of this magnitude it becomes essential to be able to weigh the economy of all countries using the banking system. The most common yardstick available for estimating the extent of financial exclusion, the extent of the sector outside and beyond the pale of mainstream financial institutions is the degree of access to bank accounts and banking facilities both for households and adult individuals. 10–15 per cent of all households in USA, 8–10 per cent in UK, and 7–10 per cent in France lack a bank account. The severity of the problem in underdeveloped agrarian economies like India and China can be estimated. The extent of exclusion here varies from 30–70 per cent. In India it is estimated that over 50 per cent of banking business is conducted across eight major cities – Mumbai, New Delhi, Chennai, Kolkata, Bangalore, Hyderabad, Ahmedabad and Pune. The extent of financial exclusion is considerably skewed across states and regions while financial exclusion is as low as 27 per cent in the southern region. Andhra Pradesh boasts the lowest degree of exclusion at 25 per cent. 60 per cent of households in the eastern region are in the zone of exclusion with over 75 per cent of the households in the North East having no access to banking services. Financial exclusion imposes high costs on BPL borrowers, and the communities in which they live most are the poorest and the most backward, faced with a lack of low cost options, lack of transparency in the credit processes, pressure to take on more debt and as a last resort turn to the ubiquitous money lender. The borrower finds it unnecessary and hazardous to open a bank account, the banker desists from entering the penny economy concerned with the costs of administering small loans and weighing cautiously the profitability and risks. Both these concerns mutually reinforce exclusion. The 11th Plan document has focused on a series of measures to increase the inclusiveness of growth. These measures focus on agriculture, access to essential services, particularly education, health and rural infrastructure. Ulimately a lot will depend on the will and the ability of banks to leverage efforts to reach the financially excluded.

Analysis of Financial Exclusion

Extent of financial exclusion in a few states are as stated below:

- >75 per cent in Meghalaya, Arunachal Pradesh, Mizoram, Manipur, Assam, Uttaranchal and Jharkhand
- 50–75 per cent in Bihar, Chhattisgarh, Orissa, Himachal Pradesh, Jammu and Kashmir, Uttar Pradesh, Nagaland, Tripura and Sikkim
- 25–50 per cent in Karnataka, Kerala, Madhya Pradesh, Maharashtra, Punjab, Tamil Nadu and West Bengal
- <25 per cent in Andhra Pradesh.

An Overall Picture of Exclusion

Of a total population (tp) of Scheduled Castes, 15,592.650.235 are included and 49.77 per cent are excluded; of a tp of Scheduled Tribes, 11,924.1, 36, 32 per cent are included and 63.68 per cent excluded; of other backward castes of a tp of 37,043 the percentage included is 51.42 per cent and 48.58 per cent excluded, among others 24,688.4, 49.42 per cent are included and 50.58 per cent are excluded. Of a tp of 89248.1, 48.64 per cent are included and 51.36 per cent are excluded.

Initiatives for Financial Inclusion

- SHG–Bank Linkage programme: 2.2 million SHGs with loans outstandings of Rs 11,397.50 million, the average size of the SHG is 15 members and 90 per cent are women.
- MFI–Bank Linkage.
- Women Entrepreneurs Development Programmes (micro enterprises) with NGO assistance.
- Credit Marketing.
- Rural Entrepreneurship programme with the help of banks and NGOs of which 25 per cent are women.
- Area Development Programmes in clusters, skills upgradation and capacity building.
- Formation of 18,000 farmer's clubs with the help of banks for technological transfer and banking promotion schemes.

- Joint Liability Groups of Farmers (850 JLGs with Rs 124 million finance and comprising 4–10 farmers).
- Kisan Credit Cards for quick credit to farmers (59. 1 million cards)
- Swarozgar Credit Cards for the poor in inorganised sectors both rural and urban.
- Gramin Tatkal Card project for loans up to Rs 50,000 without collateral for families.
- Business correspondents and facilitators identified from January 2006 onwards to enhance rural outreach.
- Swarn Jayanti Gram Swarozgar Yojana (SJGSY) for poverty alleviation, restructuring various credit programmes like Integrated Rural Development Program (IRDP), Training Rural Youth for Self Employment (TRYSEM), Supply of Improved Tools to Rural Artisans (SITRA) and Development of Women and Children in Rural Areas (DWACRA).
- Cluster development Program for credit intensification with shared infrastructure, markets, services, common opportunities and growth (101 already started).

Financial exclusion means lost or neglected business opportunities. In the Indian context, financial exclusion leads to stifling of the growth of the agricultural sector and the small/unorganised sector cutting across the secondary and tertiary sectors which together contribute to 40 per cent of the GDP and comprise 80 per cent of the population. Excluding those at the bottom of the pyramid has deleterious and severe economic consequences. The poor also need bank accounts and savings facilities, payment and remittance facilities and financial counseling. In the absence of collateral and lack of assets, credit under the SHG model is extended to them on the JLG model. They also need insurance and credit cards which offer revolving credit facilities in exchange for minimal repayments in sum. They need both savings and affordable credit. India cannot afford the costs of financial exclusion; this is a barrier to achieving a high stable and sustainable rate of economic growth.

Extending Banking Benefits to Villages by Leveraging Technology

Internet kiosks set up by some banks in villages, provide one stop suite of financial products and services. As banking correspondents, they provide all kinds of banking and insurance, on savings, on consumer financing, agricultural financing, tractors pumps, small loans, with and without mortgages, jewel loans, group loans, insurance, life insurance, health insurance and rain insurance services. The key issue is how to mainstream rural credit from institutional sources so as to extend outreach. Lending to small borrowers dispersed over vast geographic areas involves high transaction costs. Leveraging technology significantly brings down costs and optimises benefits. Rural India has 700 million people in 600,000 plus villages, about 1000 persons per village have incomes of Rs 20 per day with per capita GDP of Rs 10,000 per year. Banking can be a vehicle of mainstreaming through financial inclusion. To scale up the effort throughout India, local entrepreneurs best drive the information and communication technology revolution. In the villages of Andhra today these rural hubs and kiosks have been set up at low costs. These kiosks provide facilities such as telephone, internet, multimedia, personal computers with web cameras, printer and power back up for personal computers with Indian language software, video conferencing, software training and maintenance and six months' unlimited internet. It provides multiple services: video conferencing, enables tele-medicine, vet care, e-learning initiatives and even e-agriculture. N-logue, Drishtee and e-choupal are all successful experiments in rural services provision which are owned and driven by local entrepreneurs. Information kiosks and mobile vans have been leveraged to provide information on various products and services. They can be run by the business correspondents or installed in public call offices (PCOs). All these should translate to proactive action.

Though we need to expand the frontiers of commercial microfinance the ugly truth is that despite the carefully constructed financial infrastructure of rural branches of commercial banks, regional rural banks and cooperative banks, rural cooperatives do not reach the entire population. There are still gray areas which lack basic banking facilities such as insurance, payment services and safe convenient reliable deposit services. The poorest households still rely largely on social safety nets, informal markets and self-finance for their requirements. In sum, market penetration is very low and this situation is clearly unsupportable for financial inclusion. As Kofi Annan, ex-Secretary General of the UN expressed it, the greatest challenge before us is to address the constraints that exclude people from full participation in the financial sector. Financial exclusion is the lack of access by certain consumers to appropriate low cost fair and safe financial products and services from mainstream providers. There is always scope for tailoring these to the needs of constituents and cutting costs making their delivery more efficient. Financial exclusion is of greater concern in the rural areas and where it applies to lower income consumers and or those facing financial hardships. Poverty and financial exclusion are inextricably interlinked. There is a large overlap between poverty and permanent financial exclusion. Both poverty and financial exclusion result in a reduction of choices which affect social and political interaction and empowerment and lead to reduction of these and also constrain choices. Financial exclusion thus goes hand in hand with financial discrimination, financial illiteracy and financial exploitation. There are also gradations of financial exclusion. The hardcore and assetless poor who operate their financial assets completely outside the regulated financial system may have a basic bank account but have poor financial habits and get little advice. Then there are those who are financially included but are constrained to use the products on offer which are very often inappropriate to meet the needs and requirements of the poor. These products have fees, penalties and attributes which do not address the emergent needs of poor borrowers and the repayment schedules are also inflexible. They are expensive and high cost alternatives which are an inefficient use of money. They thus become the victims of inappropriate products. Thus, the major financial exclusion occurs through lack of access to:

(i) Transaction accounts
(ii) Time deposits
(iii) Financial advice
(iv) Appropriate small credit suited to income streams
(v) Insurance
(vi) Loans for consumption, smoothening and for lifecycle needs
(vii) Mortgage loans
(viii) Loans for small enterprises

In this scenario, the financially excluded are the poor, the socially underprivileged, disabled, elderly people, children, women, uneducated, ethnic minorities and unemployed.

Extent of financial inclusion on approximate figures would roughly be as under:

(i) Check in accounts: 70 per cent
(ii) Insurance: 10 per cent
(iii) Financial assets: 2 per cent
(iv) Assets insurance: 2.53 per cent

(v) Health insurance: 0.20 per cent
(vi) Credit card: 3 per cent
(vii) Debit card: 5.66 per cent
(viii) Small overdrafts: 3.65 per cent
(ix) Entrepreneurial credit: 2.06 per cent

As regards SHG of coverage MFI outreach, out of 400 million poor people only 125 million are covered and of these 113 million are women. Out of 89.35 million small and marginal farmers only 34.70 million are covered, that is only 46.30 per cent households are covered. Thus in this paradigm the most needed services for the financially excluded remain:

(i) Access to small loans and overdraft facilities
(ii) Check in accounts
(iii) Small savings products
(iv) Health insurance
(v) Life insurance
(vi) Insurance against the failure of activity (rainfall insurance etc)
(vii) Financial assets
(viii) General purpose credit cards
(ix) Entrepreneurship credit

Now, let us take a look at the barriers which serve as the main drivers of financial exclusion. Most frequently these are low incomes, nil or low savings, lack of assets, unemployment, underemployment, use of inappropriate products, financial illiteracy and poor financial habits. Issues which are often not taken into cognizance and ignored but which are still significant as tangible barriers are disability issues, feeling of being excluded, indigenous issues of caste and ethnicity, geographic remoteness, physical distances like mountains, rivers, deserts and unfriendly terrain. Sometimes there is a constraint of time, at others it is the digital divide and lack of PC/internet access, availability of alternate products and suppliers coverage, cost of small value transactions, infrastructure, suitable products, flexibility, weak delivery model, community enterprise and financial management support. Preconditions for financial inclusion thus become technology and the ability to leverage it successfully are efficient delivery mechanisms, community development support and product innovation. Regulatory and policy interventions and the involvement of all concerned is the need for following a broad participatory approach, especially involvement at the grass roots level up i.e. village, block, district level. A new report from the global microfinance body CGAP (Washington, 30 April 2008) predicts that, with the right market conditions, mobile banking could reach large numbers of poor people who are outside the formal financial system and calls for the development of interoperable payment platforms, practical and risk-based approaches to regulation, as well as shared networks of cash-handling agents. There is also a need for product development that overcomes the lack of human interaction and reliability concerns that may hinder customer adoption today. 'Market forces are driving down costs. In the Philippines, we see that a transaction on a cell phone or at an ATM costs one-fifth that of a traditional visit to a bank branch,' said Gautam Ivatury, manager of CGAP's Technology Program and co-author of the report, 'Yet globally, we estimate that fewer than one in ten mobile phone banking customers are poor, new to banking, or doing anything more than payments and transfers.' Payments and funds transfers dominate mobile financial services for many reasons, the report finds. Mobile operators in particular prefer to market payments services as this is more aligned with traditional revenue models. These services are also less likely to cause operators to run afoul of banking regulation. 'When it comes to reaching poor people who live outside the formal financial sector, the reality of mobile phone banking doesn't match the potential, much less the hype, at least not yet,' said Ignacio Mas, CGAP advisor and co-author of the report. 'We see opportunities for service providers who move quickly to create new products, especially if they can establish shared networks of cash-handling agents to cover that 'last mile' of service delivery.'

Challenges to the growth of branchless banking include a reluctance on the part of banks to get involved, as well as outdated or inadequate regulations. This is true despite the benefits of branchless banking: convenience, better security, and lower costs for customers. In cases where market conditions are not driving broader banking services such as credit and savings, there may be a role to play for policy makers and those who advocate for increased financial, economic welfare, and distributive efficiency.

Challenges of Financial Inclusion

Thus, the basic challenges of financial inclusion are of coverage, access to diversified financial products and services and delivery model for day to day transactions. The use of Information Technology holds great promise for the future. These need to be translated to grassroots level initiatives on the ground for the challenge of financial inclusion to be efficiently and effectively addressed. The ongoing debate on the role of the state has challenged the ability of strong, centralised structures of government. To reduce poverty and unemployment the consensus of opinion has shifted firmly to giving more power to both the market and local jurisdictions.

References

Jhunjhunwala, Ashok. Initiatives at IIT Chennai IDRBT Conference on Financial Inclusion, 2006.

Chakrabarty, K.C. Chairman Indian Bank IDRBT Conference on Financial Inclusion, Hyderabad. 2005.

Inclusive Growth Role of Financial Education, Special address by Smt Shyamala Gopinath at BANCON 2006, 4 November, 2006 Hyderabad.

Appendix

Table 1. Outstanding Debt per Indebted Households.

		(Rupees)	
End-June	Rural	Urban	Total
Nominal terms			
1961	6.47	@	647@
1971	1,180	@	1,180@
1981	3,411	5,996	3,972
1991	8,166	18,805	10,607
2002	28,443	65,983	36,006
At 1999–2000 prices			
1961	12,829	@	12,829@
1971	12,356	@	12,356@
1981	14,904	26,300	17,359
1991	15,105	34,785	19,621
2002	25,711	59,645	32,548

@: Surveys of 1961 and 1971 collected information on rural households only
Source: AIDIS survey; various rounds.

Table 2. Indebtedness of Households – Asset Holding-wise*.

		(Per cent)			
Asset Holding	End-June 1991		Asset Holding	End-June 1991	
('000)	Rural	Urban	(Rs. '000)	Rural	Urban
Less than 5	11.8	9.6	Less than 15	15.0	10.7
5–10	19.9	13.8	15–30	19.0	14.8
10–20	20.3	18.1	30.60	25.2	14.3
20–30	24.1	17.2	60–100	26.5	18.3
30–50	24.5	19.6	100–150	28.9	19.7
50–70	23.9	20.1	150–200	28.7	20.0
70–100	24.0	22.6	200–300	28.7	19.9
100–150	26.9	24.7	300–450	28.7	18.7
150–250	25.6	25.8	450–800	31.0	22.5
More than 250	29.7	25.2	More than 800	32.9	21.4
All	23.4	19.3	All	26.5	17.8

* Indicates the number of indebted households as percentage of total households under each asset holding class (AHC)
Source: NSSO, 48th and 59th round surveys.

Table 3. Number of Indebted Households – Institutional versus Non-institutional Sources.

(End-June)

Credit agency	Rural					Urban			Total		
	1961	1971	1981	1991	2002	1981	1991	2002	1981	1991	2002
Million											
I. Institutional agencies	7.5	7.6	8.9	18.2	19.8	2.3 –	4.9	5.2	11.2 –	23.1	25.0
		(0.2)	(1.5)	(7.4)	(0.8)		(7.9)	(0.4)		(7.5)	(0.7)
Of which:											
(i) Government	4.7	2.6	1.0	2.0	1.2	0.5	1.0	0.6	1.4	2.9	1.7
(ii) Co-operative societies	6.9 –	5.9	6.1	7.8	10.2	1.1 –	2.0	2.0	7.1 –	9.8	12.2
		(–1.5)	(0.3)	(2.6)	(2.5)		(6.9)	(–0.2)		(3.3)	(2.0)
(iii) Commercial banks	0.3 –	0.3	2.9	8.7	8.4	0.7 –	1.5	1.8	3.6 –	10.3	10.2
		(2.1)	(24.0)	(11.6)	(–0.3)		(8.2)	(1.3)		(11.0)	(–0.1)
II. All Non-institutional agencies	35.6 –	24.2	9.3	11.4	22.9	2.7 –	3.9	5.2	12.0 –	15.3	28.1
		(–3.8)	(–9.1)	(2.1)	(6.5)		(3.7)	(3.7)		(2.5)	(5.7)
Of which:											
(i) Landlords	0.6	3.6	1.1	1.3	0.6	0.1	0.1	0.1	1.2	1.4	0.6
(ii) Agricultural moneylenders	22.0	8.2	2.4	2.7	4.9	0.1	0.2	0.1	2.5	2.8	5.0
(iii) Professional moneylenders	7.6	5.0	1.9	3.6	10.2	0.8	1.4	2.7	2.7	5.0	12.9
III. All agencies	43.1 –	31.8	18.2	27.2	39.2	5.0 –	8.1	9.9	23.2 –	35.3	49.1
		(–3.0)	(–5.5)	(4.1)	(3.4)		(4.8)	(1.9)		(4.3)	(3.0)
Per cent to Total Indebted Households											
I. Institutional agencies	17.3	24.0	48.8	66.7	50.6	46.0	61.1	52.2	48.2	65.4	50.9

(Continued)

Table 3. (Continued)

Of which:											
(i) Government	8.6	8.3	5.4	7.3	3.0	9.0	11.9	5.6	6.2	8.3	3.5
(ii) Co-operative societies	15.9	18.5	33.4	28.6	26.0	20.9	25.4	20.2	30.7	27.9	24.9
(iii) Commercial banks	0.6	1.1	16.0	32.1	21.5	14.0	19.2	18.0	15.5	29.1	20.8
II. All Non-institutional agencies	82.7	76.0	51.2	42.9	58.5	54.0	48.7	52.8	51.8	43.4	57.3
Of which:											
(i) Landlords	1.4	11.2	6.2	4.7	1.5	1.4	1.0	0.6	5.1	3.9	1.3
(ii) Agricultural moneylenders	51.0	25.8	13.2	9.8	12.5	2.2	2.1	1.1	10.8	8.1	10.2
(iii) Professional moneylenders	17.7	15.7	10.5	13.2	26.0	16.4	17.6	27.5	11.8	14.2	26.3
III. All agencies	100.0	100.0	100.0	100.0	100.0	100.0	100.0	100.0	100.0	100.0	100.0

-: Not available

Note: 1. Figures in parentheses are compound annual growth rates.

2. Sub-components may not add to total due to borrowings from multiple agencies.

Source: All India Debt and Investment Survey (AIDIS); various rounds.

Table 4. Outstanding Households Debt – Institutional versus Non-institutional Sources.

(End-June)

Credit agency	Rural						Urban			Total		
	1951	1961	1971	1981	1991	2002	1981	1991	2002	1981	1991	2002
Amount in Rs crore												
I. Institutional agencies	- -	413 -	1,094	3,794	14,215	63,648	1,813	10,662	49,060	5,606	24,878	1,12,708
			(10.2)	(13.2)	(14.1)	(0.8)	-	(19.4)	(14.9)	-	(16.1)	(14.7)
Of which:												
(i) Government	-	147	250	247	1,355	2,564	443	1,691	4,965	689	3,046	7,529
(ii) Co-operative societies	-	255 -	753	1,773	4,798	30,431	528 -	2,620	13.392	2,302	7,417	43,823
			(11.4)	(8.9)	(10.5)	(18.3)		(17.4)	(16.0)	-	(12.4)	(17.5)
(iii) Commercial banks	-	12 -	82	1,736	7,485	27,310	679 -	3,290	19,402	2,415	10,775	46,712
			(21.6)	(35.7)	(15.7)	(12.5)		(17.1)	(17.5)	-	(16.1)	(14.3)
II. All Non-institutional agencies	- -	2,376	2,658	2,399	7,996	47,820	1,210	4,570	16,266	3,610	12,566	64,086
		-	(1.1)	(–1.0)	(12.8)	(17.7)	-	(14.2)	(12.2)	-	(13.3)	(16.0)
Of which:												
(i) Landlords	-	25	324	247	888	1,115	30	91	131	276	980	1,245
(ii) Agricultural moneylenders	-	1,281	867	531	1,577	11,147	109	152	588	640	1,729	11,735
(iii) Professional moneylenders	-	416	517	512	2,332	21,848	269	1,401	8,623	781	3,734	30,471
III. All agencies	-	2,789	3,752	6,193	22,211	1,11,468	3,023	15,232	65,327	9,216	37,443	1,76,795
		-	(3.0)	(5.1)	(13,6)	(15.8)	-	(17.6)	(14.2)	-	(15.0)	(15.2)

(Continued)

Table 4. (Continued)

Per cent to Total Outstanding Debt												
I. Institutional agencies	7.2	14.8	29.2	61.3	64.0	57.1	60.0	70.0	75.1	60.8	66.4	63.8
Of which:												
(i) Government	3.7	5.3	6.7	4.0	6.1	2.3	14.6	11.1	7.6	7.5	8.1	4.3
(ii) Co operative societies	3.5	9.1	20.1	28.6	21.6	27.3	17.5	17.2	20.5	25.0	19.8	24.8
(iii) Commercial banks	*	0.4	2.2	28.0	33.7	24.5	22.5	21.6	29.7	26.2	28.8	26.4
II. All Non-institutional agencies	92.8	85.2	70.8	38.7	36.0	42.9	40.0	30.0	24.9	39.2	33.6	36.2
Of which:												
(i) Landlords	3.5	0.9	8.6	4.0	4.0	1.0	1.0	0.6	0.2	3.0	2.6	0.7
(ii) Agricultural moneylenders	25.2	45.9	23.1	8.6	7.1	10.0	3.6	1.0	0.9	6.9	4.6	6.6
(iii) Professional moneylenders	46.4	14.9	13.8	8.3	10.5	19.6	8.9	9.2	13.2	8.5	10.0	17.2
III. All agencies	100.0	100.0	100.0	100.0	100.0	100.0	100.0	100.0	100.0	100.0	100.0	

Not available

Note: 1. Figures in parentheses are compound annual growth rates.

2. Sub-components may not add to total due to borrowings from multiple agencies.

Source: All India Rural Credit Survey; 1951–52 and various rounds of AIDIS.

Table 5. Distribution of Indebted Households to Institutional and Non-Institutional Credit Agencies*.

(Per cent)

Asset Holding ('000)	End-June 1991 Institutional	Non-Institutional	All	Asset Holding ('000)	End-June 1991 Institutional	Non-Institutional	All
Rural households							
Less than 5	44.9	62.7	107.6	Less than 15	24.0	80.0	104.0
5–10	49.2	51.8	101.0	15–30	32.6	73.2	105.8
10–20	52.7	53.2	105.9	30–60	34.5	70.2	104.8
20–30	64.3	39.4	103.7	60–100	41.1	66.8	107.9
30–50	62.4	44.9	107.3	100–150	47.1	61.9	109.0
50–70	66.1	42.3	108.4	150–200	50.9	59.6	110.5
70–100	70.0	40.0	110.0	200–300	56.4	54.7	111.1
100–150	72.1	41.6	113.8	300–450	65.2	46.0	111.1
150–250	78.9	34.4	113.3	450–800	71.0	41.9	112.9
More than 250	85.9	26.6	112.5	More than 800	81.2	31.3	112.5
All	66.7	41.9	108.5	All	50.6	58.5	109.1
Urban households							
Less than 5	30.2	75.0	105.2	Less than 15	13.1	88.8	101.9
5–10	35.5	73.2	108.7	15–30	16.2	86.5	102.7
10–20	48.6	59.1	107.7	30–60	30.4	74.3	104.7
20–30	47.1	53.5	100.6	60–100	39.3	65.0	104.4

(Continued)

Table 5. (Continued)

30–50	57.1	54.6	111.7	100–150	42.1	61.9	104.1
50–70	59.7	52.2	111.9	150–200	44.5	60.0	104.5
70–100	54.9	51.8	106.6	200–300	55.8	50.8	106.5
100–150	76.9	40.9	117.8	300–450	64.7	43.9	108.6
150–250	67.8	43.0	110.9	450–800	75.1	32.0	107.1
More than 250	84.1	27.4	111.5	More than 800	86.4	19.6	106.1
All	61.1	48.7	109.8	All	52.2	52.8	105.1

* Percentage distribution of indebted households between institutional and non-institutional sources under each AHC.

Note: Total exceeds 100 as some households borrowed from both sources.

Source: NSSO, 48th and 59th round surveys.

Table 6. Annual Average Growth Rates in Agriculture and in Bank Credit.

(Per cent)

Period*	Agriculture and Allied Activities #	Index of Agricultural Production	Non-food Bank Credit	Bank Credit to Agriculture
1981–82 to 1991–92	3.0	3.5	16.4	16.1
1991–92 to 2002–03	2.3	0.6	15.4	13.2

* Represents period between successive rounds of NSSO surveys.
# Based on GDP data released by the CSO.
Source: Handbook of Statistics on the Indian Economy, 2006–07; Reserve Bank of India.

Table 7. Population Per Bank Branch.

(Thousand)

End-March	Rural	Urban	Total
1969*	82	33	63
1981	20	17	19
1991	14	16	14
2001	16	15	16
2007	17	13	16

* As at end-June.
Source: Basic Statistical Returns of SCBs in India.

Table 8. Credit Accounts with Scheduled Commercial Banks.

	(End-March)						
Year		1971*	1981	1991	2001	2006	2007
Rural	No. of accounts	–	16.4	49.9	36.6	50.5	53.1
	(million)	–	3.1	7.9	4.9	6.3	6.5
	Accounts per	–	5.2	12.7	7.5	9.3	9.6
	100 persons						
	Accounts per						
	100 adults						
Urban	No. of accounts	–	4.4	12.1	15.8	34.9	41.3
	(million)	–	2.7	5.5	5.5	11.3	13.1
	Accounts per	–	4.5	8.9	8.4	16.3	19.5
	100 persons						
	Accounts per						
	100 adults						
Total	No. of accounts	4.3	20.7	61.9	52.4	85.4	94.4
	(million)	0.8	3.0	7.3	5.1	7.7	8.3
	Accounts per	1.3	5.0	11.7	7.9	11.6	12.4
	100 persons						
	Accounts per						
	100 adults						

* As at end-June.
Source: Basic Statistical Returns of SCBs in India.

Table 9. Credit Accounts with Scheduled Commercial Banks – Region-wise.

(Per 100 persons)									
Region/ End-March	Rural			Urban			Total		
	1991	2001	2007	1991	2001	2007	1991	2001	2007
Northern	6.6	4.7	5.6	5.9	7.4	10.0	6.4	5.6	7.1
North East	4.4	2.6	4.1	4.4	3.7	5.5	4.4	2.8	4.3
Eastern	7.2	3.5	4.5	4.3	4.6	6.2	6.6	3.7	4.8
Central	5.8	3.6	4.3	4.4	3.4	5.0	5.5	3.6	4.4
Western	6.2	4.1	4.8	4.8	4.8	18.9	5.7	4.4	10.5
Southern	13.6	9.6	14.4	7.6	7.2	21.6	11.8	8.8	16.8
All-India	7.9	4.9	6.5	5.5	5.5	13.1	7.3	5.1	8.3

Source: Basic Statistical Returns of SCBs in India.

Table 10. SHG – Bank Linkage Programme.

Year	Cumulative Number of SHGs Financed	Bank loan (Rs. crore) (cumulative
1992–99	33	57
1999–00	115	193
2000–01	264	481
2001–02	461	1,026
2002–03	717	2,049
2003–04	1,079	3,904
2004–05	1,618	6,898
2005–06	2,239	11,398
2006–07	2,925	18,047
2006–07*	2,895*	12,366*

* Represents outstanding number and amount. The comparable figures for earlier years are not available.

Source: Progress of SHG-Bank Linkage in India 2005-06; NABARD.

Table 11. Regional Pattern of SHGs Linked to Banks.

(Per cent to total)

Region/End-March	2001	2002	2003	2004	2005	2006
Northern	3.4	4.2	4.9	4.9	5.3	5.9
North East	0.2	0.3	0.6	1.1	2.1	2.8
Eastern	8.4	9.9	12.7	14.7	16.4	17.6
Central	10.9	10.4	11.4	11.8	12.2	12.0
Western	5.9	6.4	5.9	5.1	5.9	7.4
Southern	71.1	68.8	64.6	62.5	58.0	54.3
All-India	100.0	100.0	100.0	100.0	100.0	100.0

Source: Progress of SHG-Bank Linkage in India 2005-06; NABARD.

Table 12. Institutional Credit Flow to the Agriculture Sector in India.

(Rupees crore)

Year	Cooperatives	RRBs	Commercial Banks	Total
1991–92	5,797 (45.9)	596 (78.2)	4,806 (2.8)	11,199 (24.7)
2001–02	23,604 (13.5)	4,854 (15.0)	33,587 (20.8)	62,045 (17.4)
2002–03	23,716 (0.5)	6,070 (25.1)	39.774 (18.4)	69,560 (12.1)
2003–04	26,959 (13.7)	7,581 (24.9)	52,441 (31.8)	86,981 (25.0)
2004–05	31,424 (16.6)	12,404 (63.6)	81,481 (55.4)	125,309 (44.1)
2005–06	39,404 (25.4)	15,223 (22.7)	125,859 (54.5)	180.486 (44.0)
2006–07	42,480 (7.8)	20,435 (34.2)	140,382 (11.5)	203,297 (12.6)
2007–08	43,684 (2.8)	24,814 (21.4)	156,850 (11.7)	225,348 (10.8)
Memo: Compound Annual Growth Rates				
1991–92 to 2001–02	13.6	21.0	19.3	16.8
2002–03 to 2007–08	13.0	32.5	31.6	26.5

Note: Figures in parentheses are percentage change over previous year.
Source: Reserve Bank of India and NABARD.

Table 13. Number of Credit Accounts with Institutions.

(Million)			
Institutions/End-March	1993	2002	2007
Scheduled Commercial Banks	46.4	43.3	76.6
Regional Rural Banks	13.0	12.6	15.0
Primary Agricultural Credit Societies	50.5	55.5	47.9
Urban Cooperative Banks	4.7	4.4	7.1
Self-Help Groups	0.0	7.4	40.5
Total	114.6	123.3	187.1
Total accounts per 100 persons	13	12	17
Total accounts per 100 adults	20	18	25

Note:

1. Data on UCBs for 1993 and 2002 are estimated assuming the same growth as observed in the case of SCBs.
2. Accounts with SHGs are estimated assuming on an average 16 accounts per SHG in 1993 and 2002 and 14 in 2007 (obtained) on request from NABARD). The average size of SHG has declined in recent years due to formation of several new SHGs with smaller size.
3. Number of SHGs is adjusted against the credit accounts with SCBs to avoid double counting.

Table 14. Savings Accounts with Scheduled Commercial Banks.

(End-March)							
Year		1971*	1981	1991	2001	2006	2007
Rural	No. of accounts (million)	–	56.9	153.8	169.8	194.4	213.8
	Accounts per 100 persons	–	10.9	24.5	22.9	24.2	26.2
	Accounts per 100 adults	–	17.9	39.2	35.0	35.8	38.8
Urban	No. of accounts (million)	–	40.9	99.2	110.2	149.1	159.7
	Accounts per 100 persons	–	25.7	45.6	38.5	48.1	50.7
	Accounts per 100 adults	–	42.3	73.1	58.9	71.4	75.2
Total	No. of accounts (million)	23.6	97.8	253.0	280.02	343.4	373.5
	Accounts per 100 persons	4.3	14.3	29.9	27.2	30.8	33.0
	Accounts per 100 adults	7.1	22.9	46.8	41.5	45.9	48.9

* As at end-June.
Source: Basic Statistical Returns of SCBs in India.

Table 15. Savings Accounts with Scheduled Commercial Banks.

(Per 100 persons)

Region/ End-March	Rural			Urban			Total		
	1991	2001	2007	1991	2001	2007	1991	2001	2007
Northern	30.1	27.3	29.9	62.6	50.3	64.1	40.0	35.0	41.5
North East	16.1	16.9	18.9	28.4	25.6	33.6	17.8	18.3	21.2
Eastern	17.7	16.2	18.4	40.0	37.4	44.4	21.8	20.2	23.3
Central	21.0	21.8	32.7	34.7	31.1	40.2	23.8	23.0	27.4
Western	24.7	21.9	26.4	53.8	42.0	53.6	35.5	3.1	37.5
Southern	34.6	31.9	38.7	42.7	35.9	53.8	37.0	33.2	43.8
All-India	24.5	22.9	26.2	45.6	38.5	50.8	29.9	27.2	33.0

Source: Basic Statistical Returns of SCBs in India.

Table 16. Number of No-Frills Accounts Opened in India.

(Number of Accounts)

Category	End-March 2006	End-March 2007	End-December 2007
Public Sector Banks	332,878	5,865,419	11,026,619
Private Sector Banks	155,388	856,495	1,560,518
Foreign Banks	231	2,753	30,260
Total	489,497	6,724,667	12,617,397

Table 17. Cost of Credit from various Agencies in India.

Lender Category	Interest Rate (Per cent per annum)
SGHs	18–24
MFIs	20–24
Informal credit providers	18–36
Banks (small borrowal accounts)	6.20

Source:

1. Report for the Technical Group to Review of Legislation on Money Lending.
2. Survey of Small Borrowal Accounts, 2004, RBI Bulletin, July 2006.

Table 18. Charges of Micro-Finance Institutions (March 2006).

State	Range of Cost to the Borrower (per cent)
Andhra Pradesh	17.0–32.5
Karnataka	12.0–40.0
Orissa	14.0–24.5
Rajasthan	16.0
Uttar Pradesh	13.0–26.0

Source: CAB, 2007. *Report on Costs and Margin of Micro Finance Institutions.* College of Agricultural Banking (CAB), Reserve Bank of India.

Table 19. Financial Inclusion Strategy in Select Countries.

Historically, Governments in many countries intervened on the supply side to address access to financial services in various ways. Religious and other civil society organisations have also sought to broaden access to formal financial services for the poor and low-income people. These measures include: (i) nationalising private banks; (ii) branch regulations; (iii) promoting specialised banks including national savings banks; (iv) directives on portfolio composition; (v) interest rate ceilings on credit to low-income households; (vi) voluntary charter or codes developed by banks themselves; (vii) enactment of legislations defining the right of access to formal banking services; (viii) setting up of empowered and dedicated agencies by Government; (ix) running specialised and sponsored schemes including those sponsored by Government and banks themselves using a blend of innovations, reforms in the existing structures of credit delivery and the existing infrastructure like post offices and passport accounts; (x) countering the operations of moneylenders, and (xi) community-based savings and credit societies and mutual savings banks, which in a way can be seen as precursors of the modern micro-finance movement.

For instance in Bangladesh, the Government while providing necessary space for NGOs to play the lead role in pushing the frontier of finance for the poor and by facilitating the establishment of the *Grameen Bank*, continued using the state-owned *Krishi Bank* (agriculture bank) and Building Resources Across Community (BRAC) extensively to provide access to credit and deposit services for low-income households. Most Asian countries, including Sri Lanka and Pakistan also resorted to nationalisation of private banks to expand banking services to the excluded and established new state-owned banks to serve low-income segments. The strategy, *inter alia*, includes micro-finance development plans, expansion of branch networks, promotion of new information and communication technology to reach rural people.

References:

1. Kempson E, Atkinson A. and Pilley, O. (2004). "Policy Level Response to Financial Exclusion in Developing Countries." University of Bristol.
2. World Bank (2008). *Finance for All – Policy and Pitfalls in Expanding Access.* The World Bank, Washington, D. C.

Table 20. Financial Inclusion Initiatives in Different Countries.

Country	Legislation/Instrument/ Policy Scheme	Objectives
United Kingdom	Social Exclusion Unit (SEU), 1997	To reduce social exclusion, of which financial inclusion in an integral part
	Policy Action teams (PATs)	To look in an integrated way at the problems of poor neighbourhoods
	Office of Fair trading	1. To enforce consumer protection law and competition law 2. To review proposed mergers and conduct market studies
	Financial Inclusion Task Force	1. Access to banking, access to affordable credit 2. Access to free face-to-face money advice
	Financial Inclusion Fund	1. Access to banking services 2. Access to affordable credit 3. Access to money advice
United States of America	The Community Reinvestment Act, 1977	1. Prohibits discrimination by banks against low and moderate income neighbourhoods 2. To make mortgage loans to lower-income households 3. Banks are rated every three years on their efforts in meeting community credit needs
	Matched Savings Scheme (MSS) 1997	1. Personal savings in Individual Development Accounts (IDAs) are matched by local and national funds 2. Matching money has to be spent on one of a range of prescribed uses such as education, business or home purchase.
France	Banking Act, 1984	1. Any person with French nationality has the right to open an account with any bank. 2. If refused, the aggrieved person can apply to the *Banque de France* to designate a bank that should open an account
	French Bankers' Association (Basic Banking Services Charter of 1992)	Committed to providing • Affordable account • Cash card • Free access to a cash machine • Distance payment facilities • Bank statement • Negotiable number of cheques
	Law on Exclusion, 1998	1. Reiterated the Banking Act of 1984 2. Extended right to transaction account to those banned due to bad credit history 3. Allowed bounced cheque, an extra month, for correction

(Continued)

Table 20. (Continued)

Country	Legislation/Instrument/ Policy Scheme	Objectives
Australia	Australian Bankers' Association (ABA) Code of Practice, 1995	1. Generic Account was introduced in 2002 2. Staff to give information about suitable accounts to low-income customers 3. Face-to-Face banking services even after branch closure through alternative means such as *franchising* 4. Three months written notice to customers before closing any branch
	Rural Transformation Centre Programme (RTCP)	1. To provide banking and other transaction services to communities without banking facilities 2. Using existing stores and post offices or stand-alone centres 3. Install Electronic Point of Sale (EPOS) equipment in post offices
Belgium	Charter on Basic Banking Services, 1996	1. Provide a basic bank account with no minimum balance and without overdraft facilities 2. Credit transfers, direct debits, and deposit and withdrawal facilities 3. If refused, customer must be informed the reasons, i.e. laundering, bad credit history, etc.
	Basic Banking Act, 2003	Sanctions if principles of Charter on Basic Banking Services, 1996 are not applied
Canada	Access to Basic Banking Services Regulations, 2003	1. Personal bank account to all Canadians regardless of employment or credit history and with minimum identification requirements 2. Banks/FIs to encash government cheques at no charge
	Financial Consumer Agency of Canada (FCAC), 2001	1. Supervising provisions on consumers under Canada's Bank Act 2. Access to Basic banking 3. Consumer protection measures and expanding consumer education 4. Rural banking, i.e. it requires bank to give four months notice of branch closures and six months notice if it is the only branch in a range of 10 km.

Bibliography

Aghion, P. and Howitt, P. (1998). *Endogenous Growth Theory*. MIT Press, Cambridge MA (2005). 'Appropriate growth policy: a unifying framework', Joseph Schumpeter Lecture delievered at the conference of the European Economic Association, 25 August.

All India Debt and Investment Survey, various issues.

Armendariz De Aghion, B. and J. Murdoch (2000). 'Microfinance Beyond Group Lending', *Economics of Transition*, Vol 8, No 2.

Baker, C. J. (1984). *The Tamilnad Countryside*, Oxford University Press.

Banerjee, A. (2001). Contracting Constraints, Credit Markets and Economic Development, Working Paper 02–17, Department of Economics, Massachusetts Institute of Technology.

Basu, P. and P. Srivastava (2005). 'Exploring Possibilities: Microfinance and Rural Credit Access for the Poor in India', Economic and Political Weekly, April 23.

Besley, T. (1995). 'Saving, Credit and Insurance' in Behrman J and T. N. Srinivasan (eds.), *Handbook of Development Economics*, Vol. III A, Amsterdam.

Bhaduri, A. (2006). 'Provisions of Rural Financial Services' in *Employment and Development: Essays from an Unorthodox Perspective*, Oxford University Press.

Binswanger, H. P., S. R. Khandker and M. R. Rosenzweig (1993). 'How Infrastructure and Financial Institutions Affect Agricultural Output and Investment in India', *Journal of Development Economics*, Vol 41, pp. 337–66.

Bose, S. (2005). 'Regional Rural Banks: The Past and Present Debate', Macrom Scan, URL: http://www. macroscan. com/fet/jul05/fet200705RRB-Debate. htm.

Burgess, R. and R. Pande (2002). 'Do Rural Banks Matter? Evidence from the Indian Social Banking Experiment' in Kochhar, K. and Charles F. Kramer (eds.) *India-Managing Globalisation and Growth*.

Catanach, I. J. (1970). *Rural Credit in Western India*, 1875–1930, Berkeley.

CGAP (2004). Interest Rate Ceilings and Microfinance: The Story So Far, *Occasional Paper*, Washington.

Chandavarkar, A. (1984). 'Money and Credit. 1858–1947' in D. Kumar (ed). *Cambridge Economic History of India*, Vol II, 1757–1970.

Chandrashekhar, C. P. amd S. K. Ray (2005). 'Financial Sector Reform and the Transformation of Banking' in V. K. Ramachandran and M. S. Swaminathan (eds.), *Agrarian Studies: Essays on Agrarian Relations in Less-Developed Countries*, Zed Books.

Chavan, P. (2005). 'How "Inclusive" Are Banks under Financial Liberalisation?' *Economic and Political Weekly*, October 22.

Chavan, P. and R. Ramakumar (2005). 'Interest Rates on Micro-Credit' in V. K. Ramachandran and M. Swaminathan (eds).

Ciravegna, D. (2005). The Role of Microcredit in Modern Economy: The Case of Italy, URL: www. flacso. or. cr/fileadmin/documentos/FLACSO/auCiravegna2. DOC

Dandekar, V. M. amd F. K. Wadia (1989). 'Development of Institutional Finance for Agriculture in India', *Journal of Indian School of Political Economy*, 1, 2.

Darling, M. L. (1925). *The Punjab Peasant in Prosperity and Debt*, Oxford University Press.

Diamond, D. (1984). 'Financial Intermediation and Delegated Monitoring', *Review of Economics Studies*, Vol 51, pp. 393–414

Dichter, T. (2004). Remarks to the Microfinance Club of New York.

Drechsler, W. (2005). 'The Rise and Demise of the New Public Management' Post-Autistic Economics Review, URL: http://www. paecon. net/PAEReview/issue33, September.

Dreze, J. (1990). 'Poverty in India and the IRDP Delusion,' *Economic and Political Weekly*, Vol XXV, No 39, September 29.

EPW Research Foundation (2007). 'Need for Calibrated Policy in Interest Rates and Credit', *Economic and Political Weekly*, February 24.

Fernandez, A. P. (2007). 'Sanghamithra – An MFI with a Difference: Are SHGs Only Financial Intermediaries?' *Economic and Political Weekly*, Vol SLII, No 13.

Fisher, T. and M. S. Sriram (2002). *Beyond Micro-Credit: Putting Development Back into Micro-Finance*, Vistaar, New Delhi.

Ghate, P. (2006). Microfinance in India: A State of the Sector Report, 2006, CARE and Ford Foundation, New Delhi.

—(2007). 'Consumer Protection in Indian Microfinance: Lessons from Andhra Pradesh and the Microfinance Bill', *Economic and Political Weekly*, Vol XLII, No 13.

Goetz, A. M. and R. S. Gupta (1996). 'Who Takes the Credit? Gender, Power, and Control over Loan Use in Rural Credit Programmes in Bangladesh', World Development, Vol 24, No 1.

Government of India (2005). Report of the Task Force on Revival of Cooperative Credit Institutions, Ministry of Finance.

—(2006). From Hariyali to Neeranchal: Report of the Technical Committee on Watershed Programmes in India, Ministry of Rural Development.

—(2007). Report of the Working Group on Rainfed Areas for the 11th Five Year Plan, Planning and Commission.

Haque, T. and S. Verma (1988). 'Regional and Class Disparities in the Flow of Agricultural Credit in India', *Indian Journals of Agricultural Economics*, Vol 43, No 3.

Harper, M. E. Esipisu, A. K. Mohanty and D. S. Rao (1998). *The New Middlewomen – Profitable Banking Through On-Lending Groups*, Oxford and IBH.

Hermes, N. and R. Lensink (2007). 'Impact of Microfinance: A Critical Survey', *Economic and Political Weekly*, Vol XLII, No 6, February 10.

Kabeer, N. (2005). 'Is Microfinance a "Magic Bullet" for Women's Empowerment?', *Economic and Political Weekly*, October 29.

Kalecki, M. (1954). Theory of Economic Dynamics.

Kannabiran, V. (2005). 'Marketing Self-Help, Managing Poverty', *Economic and Political Weekly*, August 20.

Keynes, J. M. (1927). A Treatise on Money, Vol II.

—(1935). The General Theory of Employment, Interest and Money.

—(1971). Indian Currency and Finance, Collected Writing, Vol. I.

Khandker, S. R. (2005). 'Microfinance and Poverty: Evidence Using Panel Data from Bangladesh', *The World Bank Economic Review*, Vol 19, No 2.

Krishnaswamy, K. S., K. Krishnamurthy and P. D. Sharma (1987). Improving Domestic Resource Mobilisation through Financial Development: India, Asian Development Bank, Manila.

La Porta, R., F. L. de Silanes and A. Shleifer (2002). 'Government Ownership of Banks', *Journal of Finance*, February.

Mahajan, V. (2004). 'Deregulating Rural Credit', Seminar, September.

—(2005). 'From Microcredit to Livelihood Finance', *Economic and Political Weekly*, October 8.

Marr, A. (2004). 'A Challenge to the Orthodoxy Concerning Microfinance and Poverty Reduction', *Journal of Microfinance*, Vol 5, No 2.

Marx, K. (1976). Capital, Vol III, Penguin.

Mayoux, L. (2002). Women's Empowerment or Feminisation of Debt? Towards a New Agenda in African Micro-Finance, Department of International Development, London.

McIntosh, C., A. de Janvry and E. Sadoulet (2005). 'How Rising Competition among Microfinance Institutions Affects Incumbent Lenders', *Economic Journal*, Vol 115, No 506.

Meyer, R. L. and G. Nagarajan (2000). Rural Financial Markets in Asia: Policies, Paradigms and Performance, Asian Development Bank.

Misra, B. S. (2006). 'The Performance of Regional Rural Banks in India: Has Past Anything to Suggest for Future?', RBI Occasional Papers, Vol 27, Nos 1 and 2.

MPBEC Report (1930). Madras Provincial Banking Enquiry Committee Report, Vols. 5 Government of Madras, Madras.

Murray, I. and E. Lynch (2003). 'What Do Microfinance Customers Value?' URL: http://www.womensworldbanking.org

MYRADA (2002). Impact of Self Help Groups (Group Processes) On the Social/ Empowerment Status of Women Members I Southern India, NABARD.

NABARD (2000). Task Force on Supportive Policy and Regulatury Framework for Microfinance in India.

—(2002). Ten Years of SHG–Bank Linkage: 1992–2002.

—(2006). Annual Report.

Naidu, B., V. Narayanswami (1946). Report of the Economist for Enquiry into Rural Indebtedness, Government of Madras, Madras.

Nair, A. (2001). Sustainability of Microfinance Self Help Groups in India: Would Federating Help? In Narayan, Deepa and Elea Glinskaya (eds.) *Ending Poverty in South Asia*, The World Bank.

Narayana, D. (2000). Banking Sector Reforms and the Emerging Inequalities in Commercial Credit Deployment in India, Centre for Development Studies, Thiruvananthapuram.

Nickel, W. and S. Khan (1993). Rural Credit – Towards a Sustainable System for the 21st Century, Indira Gandhi Institute of Development Research, Bombay.

NSSO (2005a). Situation Assessment Survey of Farmers—Indebtedness of Farmer Households, NSS 59th Round (January–December 2003), National Sample Survey Organisation, Government of India, Report No 498 (59/33/1).

—(2005b). Household Indebtedness in India as on 30 June 2002, All India Debt and Investment Survey, NSS Fifty-Ninth Round, January–December 2003, National Sample Survey Organisation, Government of India, Report No 501 (59/18, 2/2).

Pitt, M. M. and S. R. Khandker (1998). 'The Impact of Grouped-based Credit Programmes on Poor Households in Bangladesh: Does the Gender of Participants Matter?' *Journal of Political Economy*, Vol 106, No 5.

Puhazhendi, V. and K. C. Kadatya (2002). SHG–Bank Linkage Programme for Rural Poor – An Impact Assessment, NABARD.

Puhazhendi, V. and K. J. S. Satyasai (2000). Microfinance for Rural People – An Impact Study, NABARD.

Raj, K. N. (1974). 'Monetary Management and Nationalisation of Banking in India' in A. Mitra (ed), *Economic Theory and Planning: Essays in Honour of A. K. Dasgupta*, Oxford University Press.

Rajasekhar, D. (2000). 'Microfinance Programme and Women's Empowerment: A Study of Two NGOs from Kerala', *Journal of Social and Economic Development*, Vol 3, No 1.

Rajasekhar, D. and V. Vyasalu (1993). 'Managerial Changes, Rural Credit and Economic Development: A Study in Orissa, India', Saving and Development, Vol XVII, No 2.

Ramachandran, V. K., and M. Swaminathan (eds.) (2005). *Financial Liberalisation and Rural Credit in India*, Tulika Books, New Delhi.

Rap, C. H. H. (1994). 'Policy Issues Relating to Irrigation and Rural Credit in India' in G. S. Bhalla (ed), *Economic Liberalisation and Indian Agriculture, Institute for Studies in Industrial Development*, New Delhi.

RCA Report (1929). Report of the Royal Commission on Agriculture, Government of India.

Reddy, Y. V. (2006). Rural Banking: Review and Prospects, Centre for Economic and Social Studies, Hyderabad.

Reserve Bank of India, Banking Services: Basic Statistical Returns, various issues.

Reserve Bank of India (1954). All-India Rural Credit Survey Report.

—(1989). A Review of Agricultural Credit System in India.

—(1991). Report of the Committee on the Financial System (chaired by M. Narasimham).

—(1995). Expert Committee on IRDP.

—(1999). Report on Micro Credit, Micro Credit Special Cell.

—(2002). Report on Currency and Finance, 2000–01.

—(2004). Report of the Advisory Committee on Flow of Credit to Agriculture and Related Activities.

—(2005). Report of the Internal Group to Examine Issues Relating to Rural Credit and Microfinance.

—(2006). Quarterly Statistics on Deposits and Credit of Scheduled Commercial Bank, March 2006.

—(2007). Quarterly Statistics on Deposits and Credit of Scheduled Commercial Banks, December 2006.

Sahu, G. B., and D. Rajasekhar (2005). 'Banking Sector Reform and Credit Flow to Indian Agriculture', *Economic and Political Weekly*, December 31.

Sarkar, J. and P. Agarwal (1996). 'Banking: The Challenges of Deregulation', India Development Report, IGIDR, Mumbai.

Sathyanathan, W. R. S. (1935). Report of the Special Officer for Inquiry into Agriculture and Indebtedness, Government of Madras, Madras.

Satish, S., and K. K. Swaminathan (1988). Lending Costs and Margins: Agricultural Credit Review Report, Reserve Bank of India.

Schumpeter, J. (1942). Capitalism, Socialism and Democracy, Harper.

Scully, N. (2004). Microcredit MNo Panacea for Poor Women, Global Development Research Centre, Washington. URL: http://www. gdrc. org/ icm/wind/micro. html

Sen, K., and R. R. Vaidya (1997). *The Process of Financial Liberalisation in India*, Oxford University Press.

Shah, M., D. Banerji, P. S. Vijay Shankar and P. Ambasta (1998). *India's Drylands: Tribal Societies and Development through Environmental Regeneration*, Oxford University Press, New Delhi.

Shetty, S. L. (2005). 'Regional, Sectoral and Functional Distribution of Bank Credit' in V. K. Ramachandran and M. Swaminathan (eds).

Simanowitz, S. (2002). 'Microfinance for the Poorest: A Review of Issues and Ideas for Improving the Impact of Microfinance on Poverty', URL: http://www. microfinancegateway. org.

SPS (2006). Towards Tribal Empowerment and Development through Women's Self-Help Groups, Samaj Pragati Sahayog, Bagli.

Srivastava, P. (2005). 'Microfinance in India: Odysseus or Interloper', *Economic and Political Weekly*, August 13.

Stiglitz, J. (1993). 'The Role of the State in Financial Markets', *World Bank Economic Review*.

Stiglitz, J., and A. Weiss (1981). 'Credit Rationing in Markets with Imperfect Information', *American Economic Review*, Vol 71, No 3.

Swaminathan, M. (2007). 'The Micro-credit Alternative?', *Economic and Political Weekly*, Vol XLII, No 13.

Tankha, A. (2002). Self-help Groups as Financial Intermediaries in India: Cost of Promotion, Sustainability and Impact. A study prepared for ICCO and Cordaid, The Netherlands.

Tobin, J. (1970). 'On Limiting the Domain of Inequality', *Journal of Law and Economics*, Vol. 13.

Varman, M. P. (2005). 'Impact of Self-Help Groups on Formal Banking Habits', *Economic and Political Weekly*, April 23.

Vasimalai, M. P., and K. Narender (2007). 'Microfinance for Poverty Reduction: Kalanjiam Way', *Economic and Political Weekly*, Vol XLII, No 13.

Zinman, Jonathan (2002). The Efficacy and Efficiency of Credit Market Interventions: Evidence from the Community Reinvestment Act, Harvard University Joint Center for Housing Studies Working Paper No. CRAO 2-2.

Index